RED ROCKS COMMUNITY COLLEGE

U18960 042 234

JC 571 .G28

Gans, Herber

Middle American
 individualism

DATE DUE

Middle
American
Individualism

Middle American Individualism

The Future of Liberal Democracy

HERBERT J. GANS

RED ROCKS
COMMUNITY COLLEGE

THE FREE PRESS
A Division of Macmillan, Inc.
NEW YORK

Collier Macmillan Publishers
LONDON

60197
JC
571
G28
1988

#17585911

23.01

Copyright © 1988 by Herbert J. Gans

All rights reserved. No part of this book may be reproduced
or transmitted in any form or by any means, electronic or
mechanical, including photocopying, recording, or by any
information storage and retrieval system, without permission
in writing from the Publisher.

The Free Press
A Division of Macmillan, Inc.
866 Third Avenue, New York, N.Y. 10022

Collier Macmillan Canada, Inc.

Printed in the United States of America

printing number
1   2   3   4   5   6   7   8   9   10

Library of Congress Cataloging–in–Publication Data

Gans, Herbert J.
    Middle American individualism: the future of liberal democracy/
Herbert J. Gans.
        p.   cm.
    Bibliography: p.
    Includes index.
    ISBN 0–02–911251–6
    1. Individualism.   2. Political participation—United States.
    3. Representative government and representation—United States.
    4. Democracy.   I. Title.
JC571.G28   1988   88–284
320.5'12—dc19   CIP

This Book is Dedicated to the Memory of
Earl S. Johnson (1895–1986),
Late Professor Emeritus of Social Science,
University of Chicago

RED ROCKS
COMMUNITY COLLEGE

Contents

Preface

This is a book about some fundamentals of American life and more specifically about one of the country's basic values: individualism. However, I do not say much about the laissez-faire doctrines extolled in Op-Ed-page oil company ads, the narcissistic indulgence said to have surfaced recently together with an alleged me generation of yuppies, or even the much analyzed self-quest associated with Ralph Waldo Emerson.

Instead, the book deals with an equally old but much less often publicized individualism, that pursued by the blue, white, pink, and new-collar workers and their families whom I call middle Americans.* They are the people of moderate and middle income who have an average amount of schooling, but of course they are middle or average only in statistical tables. Numerically and culturally they are the majority in the U.S., and it is their American Dream to which every presidential candidate pays respect.

My main purpose in this book is to understand middle Americans, but I also seek to defend their individualism by showing how little it has in common with the individualism of corporate and entrepreneurial capitalists. Yet middle Americans are not loyal to liberalism either, for they reject its anti-individualistic

---

* They must be distinguished from Middle Americans with a capital M, a 1970s term for the conservative members of the white ethnic working class.

tendencies and its faith in collective action and solution. They support the welfare state, however, as long as it keeps their welfare in mind.

The book can be read as a defense of middle Americans too, for while they are hardly devoid of faults, they are not right-wing racists, greedy materialists, or uncultured "Joe Sixpacks." Even so, I am not writing to support the status quo, for I also identify the economic and especially the political problems that middle Americans help to cause. The book ends, therefore, with a number of suggestions for improving American democracy, as well as for a welfare state sufficiently egalitarian to offer economic security to all Americans.

Ironically enough, this book had its origin in a very different topic, for it began as a long paper I wrote in 1974 entitled "What Is Society?" That paper in turn was inspired by my study of two national television and two magazine news organizations that I had begun in the mid 1960s. While I was observing journalists as they chose and reported the news, I also looked at studies about and letters from the news audience. I was impressed not only with how rarely and how little that audience actually needs national news but also with how far removed it is from the national agencies and institutions about which the journalists report. For all practical purposes, Washington, New York, and the other centers of American society are, for many people much of the time, on other planets.

After I finished the study of journalists, published in 1978 as *Deciding What's News*, I returned to the subject of my paper, but in trying to figure out whether and how a national society can be said to exist in America, I found myself writing about what I now call middle American individualism. The outline of this book began to emerge in 1982, and I worked on it when I was free from other duties.

Middle American individualism is first and foremost a mixture of cultural and moral values for dealing with everyday life and of goals for guiding self-development and familial improvement. However, it also includes political values which help middle Americans cope with the economic and other obstacles in the way of their goals.

All these values are reflected in a general dissatisfaction with the country's formal institutions, Big Government and Big Business especially, but others as well. Although middle Americans use those organizations they need, they try to stay away from any they can avoid. Instead of getting involved with organizations, people continue to structure their lives around the family and a variety of informal groups in a pattern that I call microsocial, which has changed remarkably little over time.

Among the organizations people avoid most of the time are political ones, with obvious effects on political participation. The problem of political avoidance is larger than declining rates of voting, however, and can be traced to one of the principal reasons for the existence of middle American individualism: the need for self-reliance among people of comparatively lowly economic and social status. Middle Americans lack power over their employers, politicians, as well as over the country's significant economic and political organizations, for while they are numerous, they lack the resources to exert the power of their numbers. However, they are unwilling and unable to organize, in part because they are a highly diverse collection of people who do not, incidentally, even think of themselves as middle Americans. Moreover, they are doubtful that they could change society even if they wanted to do so. By their calculations, relying on their own efforts gets them what they want or close to it, and besides, political action is morally and psychologically unsatisfying, their hearts being in their microsocial lives.

In thinking about the future of democracy, I quickly became dubious that it could be strengthened by yet more appeals for the restoration of "community," or by the equally vain hope that people will somehow shed their political "apathy" and replace the incumbent rascals in Washington and elsewhere with dedicated altruists. Instead, I assumed that one possible solution was institutional change by which people could have political avoidance *and* democracy. In order to make democracy more properly representative, I decided that if citizens are unable or unwilling to come to political institutions to participate, these institutions must come to them, functioning as additional representatives and transmitting their wishes, complaints, and ideas for the country to elected and appointed officials. A more representative democracy should be politically more egalitarian, but political power is always in part a reflection of economic power. This is why such a democracy must also be liberal, using political means to reduce economic inequality as much as possible. The proposals and suggestions that follow from these assumptions aim to be feasible and practical even if they cannot be realized in the immediate future.

Policy and political recommendations notwithstanding, the book is yet another attempt on my part to understand America itself, an attempt that began when I arrived here in 1940 as a teenage refugee from Nazi Germany. Perhaps not so coincidentally, this book deals once more with somewhat the same Americans I wrote about in *The Urban Villagers* and *The Levittowners*, who are also members of the news audience in *Deciding What's News*.

This time, however, the picture I try to paint is of the country in general, and with a particular perspective—from the economic and political and social middle in which middle Americans live. I write about their individualism from the same angle, but I have not been elected, appointed, or even self-appointed to be a spokesman for middle Americans. Indeed, many of my conclusions and proposals may be unacceptable to them, for I still write from my own upper-middle-class liberal perspective as well. (Nonetheless, I do not refrain from questioning some of the conventional wisdom of liberals, as well as that of conservatives, centrists, and the Left.)

Last but not least, my perspective is shaped by my major topic and concept. Individualism being mainly a set of values, I write more about what some Americans want and feel than about how they behave, values being only one of a number of causal influences on their actions. Insofar as values are hopes and dreams, this perspective results in a more positive and optimistic picture of America and Americans than, say, a study of how people perceive their problems. Middle Americans and the country have enough problems that they also come up in the study, but still, because of its angle, the book fits somewhat better with volumes that see the American glass as half full rather than with those seeing it as half empty.

Although most of my earlier books have been based on my having lived with the people I studied, this one and the ideas and conclusions in it are not. I have not carried out any new fieldwork or formally interviewed anyone. In fact, the book is not intended to report the results of my research, but to set forth an argument. That argument is supported by years of informal observation combined with data from polls and other studies which illustrate, although they cannot prove, my assertions.

Sometimes I have not refrained from including my best guesses when data were lacking, and because I am making an argument, I have often generalized broadly, putting the necessary qualifications into notes or even leaving them out altogether when I felt they were not absolutely essential.

Acknowledgments

This book is dedicated to Earl S. Johnson, the University of Chicago sociologist who was one of my first instructors when I began graduate work. A student of John Dewey as well as of Robert Park, a founder of modern American sociology, Earl was a charismatic teacher who believed in the unity of all the social sciences and taught us to be social scientists as well as sociologists. At a time when the social sciences already sought to be as scientific as the natural sciences, he argued for the inclusion of humanistic values and for social policies based on them. I had forgotten how much he influenced my work until a few years ago when I reviewed his last book, *The Humanistic Teachings of Earl S. Johnson*, published in 1983 when he was 88. Earl had a large circle of loving students but never received the recognition he deserved.

I am grateful to Ted Lowi, who commented on the previous draft of what is now Chapter 6, and to Peter Saunders, Peter Marris, and my wife Louise, who critiqued the entire manuscript. The latter two deserve thanks for demonstrating that I needed to write one further draft. I owe further thanks to Joyce Seltzer, my editor, and Hunt Cole, my copy editor, who helped particularly by editing for clarity. Every one of my readers challenged me with tough questions, not all of which I answered, so that none can be held responsible for the faults of the book. Gwen Dordick, Judith Sedaitis, and particularly Thomas Jorge, helped with research assistance. Wendy Boyd and Beverly Greenfield taught me to conquer a very simple word processor, but then I went back to my favorite manual typewriter. As a result, Betsy Wright wound up processing just about every word in the penultimate and final drafts, concurrently making the initial repairs on my grammar, punctuation, and some of my prose in both.

H.J.G.
August 1987

Middle
American
Individualism

One
Popular Individualism

America has often been seen—and has seen itself—as constantly in flux.[1] Still, as anyone who has ever read de Tocqueville's *Democracy in America* knows after just a few pages, there are many ways in which the United States has changed only slightly in over 150 years, and one of the stable elements is the continued pursuit of individualism by virtually all sectors of the population.[2]

At its most basic, individualism is the pursuit of personal freedom and of personal control over the social and natural environment. It is also an ideology—a set of beliefs, values, and goals—and probably the most widely shared ideology in the U.S. Even so it comes in many varieties. For example, the explicit, often analytic, individualism written about by philosophers, commentators, and political ideologues is not the same as the implicit, almost taken-for-granted ideology of the ordinary person. The individualism of lay Americans is vernacular or amateur rather than expert.[3] Since vernacular and amateur are still slightly pejorative terms in some quarters, I prefer to call that individualism *popular*, and I shall use popular individualism as a synonym for middle American individualism.

Individualism being among other things a series of goals, what people want as individuals has been affected by changes in the country. The personal freedom and the ways of seeking it of

1

the late-20th-century office worker must be different from those of the 19th-century family farmer. Today the rugged individualism sought by entrepreneurs, the personal opportunity to act in a stable, even regulated, market looked for by corporate individualists, and the individual opportunity to perform needed tasks as one thinks best which is wanted by workers in large organizations all have distinctive features. Needless to say, work-related individualisms vary from those pursued in the family or as a consumer.

The Desire for Personal Control

The middle American search for personal freedom means liberation from unwelcome cultural, social, political, and economic constraints, but also from lack of economic as well as emotional security. Middle Americans, like most other Americans, want to be able to avoid involuntary conformity, whether it is required by the family, neighbors, or the government. They also try to sidestep obligatory membership in institutions and organizations, sacred or secular. Whenever possible, they hope to be free to choose goods, services, and ideas, especially those relevant to the process of self-development, so that they can learn their own needs and wishes and begin to be able to achieve as many as reasonably possible. Nonetheless, for most, popular individualism still involves a prior step, obtaining personal control over the general environment so as to minimize threat and unwanted surprise, and in order to lay the groundwork for self-development.[4]

The feeling of being in control is especially important to people whose parents or grandparents lived lives so dominated by insecurity that control—and self-reliance—become the prerequisites for nearly everything else. Greater control spells more security, and with sufficient security people can start to loosen unwanted social ties and to make more of their own choices about their lives. Even convenience and comfort are pursued in part to add to the feeling of being in control, for achieving these ostensibly materialist goals also allows middle Americans a little firmer grounding for the hope that they will never fall, or fall back, to a subsistence-level existence. One of the most widely desired—and accessible—means of obtaining control has been home ownership. The nearly two-thirds of the population who are homeowners at least control their place to live and often a piece of ground as well, even if in most instances actual ownership is held by a bank.

Popular individualism means the ability to make choices in a variety of social settings. It is the right to be neighborly or to ignore the people next door. It is the ability to be distant from incompatible relatives and to be with compatible friends instead; to skip unwanted memberships in church or union; to vote for candidates not supported by parents or spouses or not to vote at all; and to reject unwelcome advice or demands for behavior change from the spouse, employer, or anyone else.

Although the advocates of entrepreneurial and corporate, i.e., capitalist, individualism may not like to hear it, popular individualism does not preach the virtues of risk-taking. Most middle Americans hold jobs rather than pursue careers, and many people can lose these jobs quickly in an economic crisis. According to the 1986 General Social Survey of the National Opinion Research Center (GSS hereafter), only 28 percent of the respondents said it would be very easy to find new jobs.[5] When the median American family income hovers around $29,500, as it did in 1986, and half of all families earn less, money remains scarce, disposable income is limited, and luxuries or expensive necessities still require savings or financing. No wonder, then, that people shun needless risks and would like government to protect them from unexpected problems. However, many capitalist individualists expect government to protect them from the risks of competition too.

In effect, the preoccupations of middle American individualism remain modest. More important, individualism is not even an entirely fitting term for them. Many values of popular individualism are familistic, with control, security, comfort, and convenience being sought for the family. Personal development itself is conceived either to include or not to alienate the family.

In addition, popular individualism eschews originality and distinctiveness and is not opposed to some kinds of conformity, especially if these are voluntary. While people may seek to "do their own thing," they do not mind if others do exactly the same thing. Few look kindly on the competitive striving to be unique, which they may condemn as showing off. What used to be called keeping up with the Joneses is disapproved as well, because it is deliberate imitation in the cause of upward mobility that also aims to diminish neighbors or colleagues. Deliberate imitation done in sincere admiration for the taste of others is quite different, however, for it is a compliment to those others.

Furthermore, the goal of popular individualism is hardly separation from other people. Instead, it is to live mainly, and participate actively, in a small part of society, the array of family, friends, and informal relations and groups which I refer to as *microsociety*. Popular individualism is, therefore, very much a social phenomenon. To be sure, in one sense all individualism is social, for the components from which we construct our identities and with which we differentiate ourselves from others are themselves social, or else we could not communicate with anyone. We can only survive as individuals because we are in and of society. Even the individualism of the highly educated, which appears to aim for distinctiveness, is social, for the many ways by which they seek "self-actualization" are always conducted with, and for, others. The radically individual method of orthodox or classical psychoanalysis, in which one person seeks his or her own identity in the company of a normally silent analyst, has just about disappeared in America.

Middle Americans' individualism diverges considerably from the goals sought by others above and below them in the socioeconomic class hierarchy. Capitalist individualism is mainly economic, and varies not only between entrepreneurs and corporate executives but also by the extent to which the goal is profit maximization, market control, or escape from government regulation. As individuals, the very rich and the merely affluent usually pursue kinds of self-development that the average-income middle American cannot yet afford. The purposive questioning of social norms and the pervasive detachment from groups and group influence which David Riesman and his coauthors called autonomy remain, I think, mainly attributes of upper-middle-class individualism—of the people who were actually the principal subjects of *The Lonely Crowd*. Uniqueness used to be a goal of upper-class individualism, sought by people of independent wealth who did not need to work and aimed instead to create a personal lifestyle for themselves. Now uniqueness is more often an occupationally relevant goal of entertainers, artists, politicians, intellectuals—and professors—who must distinguish themselves from competitors offering a roughly similar product or service, and who yearn to be so original that they will be assured of fame and fortune in their particular line of work.

The poor may aspire to popular individualism and to become middle American, but they cannot afford much individualism of any kind, for economic insecurity and frequent crises mean lack of control, and thus dependence—on other people, the government, or charity. Poverty also virtually dictates conformity to an involuntary culture. That culture bears little resemblance to the culture of poverty associated with the late Oscar Lewis, but being poor sharply limits people's choices to a small number of alternative means of surviving. Some poor people nonetheless find ways of pursuing the goals of popular individualism, and appear in the media as sterling examples of the deserving poor.

Identifying the Middle Americans[6]

Middle America is above all a position in the U.S. social structure. Like other positions, it creates particular opportunities and limits for the people occupying it and as a result encourages them to choose a number of similar values. For example, control and security are so central in popular individualism because of where middle Americans stand economically, politically, and otherwise in society.

Middle America can also be described by the nature of its population. It is not an actual sector of the population, however, but an umbrella concept to enable me to write about a large slice of that population, literally the cultural, economic, and demographic slice in the middle. More accurately, it is largely the middle of the white population, for while middle America cannot be defined solely by income, many blacks and other racial minorities cannot yet afford its individualistic goals. According to the U.S. Census, in 1985 the white median family income was $29,150 but that of blacks was only $16,800. This huge income gap probably indicates as adequately as any other statistic the still sizeable differences in job and other kinds of economic security and control over the general environment.

Middle Americans are thus today mainly white, but they are neither yuppies nor real-life equivalents of Archie and Edith Bunker. While they are better educated than their parents, few are urbane types who pride themselves on intellectual or artistic sophistication. Still home-centered but by no means homespun, they live mainly in suburbs, small towns, or the small-town neighborhoods to be found in most American cities. While many may be conservative with respect to some specific social or religious values, cultural traditionalists and fundamentalists are few. Unless they are economically pressed or socially threatened by real or imagined dangers, they are generally good-hearted, generous, and charitable. However, they feel and act generously mainly toward other individuals, especially victims, and their generosity does not always extend to groups or classes of people, particularly those of lower status and darker skin.

Middle Americans constitute the most important audience for popular culture and are the people whom the makers of network television series and expensive Hollywood films want to attract. The days when that or any other audience could be thought of as a single mass are long gone, however, and younger middle Americans are particularly skeptical of the old pieties and sexual taboos of network television. Since the VCR became a mass production item, middle Americans, like others, often desert network television and watch movies on their VCRs instead. These are not always the kind labelled "family entertainment," particularly after the children have been put to bed.

Middle Americans do not read many books, but then a very small proportion of Americans have always bought most of the books, including even the popular best sellers and romances. Conversely, the increases in spare time, spare-time interests, and hobbies among middle Americans are partly responsible for the dramatic rise in periodical titles from 6,960 in 1950 to 11,328 in 1986.[7] Middle Americans are apt to spend their vacations visiting relatives and nearby U.S. landmarks and parks except when the house needs repainting. Childless and older people, however, have begun to travel widely, especially when airlines offer bargains to popular tourist areas and pleasanter climates.

A helpful way of visualizing middle America is in terms of occupation, education, income, and social class. Most middle Americans hold the better factory and service jobs as well as the generally routine clerical, technical, sales, and related bureaucratic office positions, and the humbler technician, semiprofessional, and supervisory jobs. Actually, many of the men in factory and service jobs no longer wear blue collars, and women in these categories of work are sometimes distinguished as pink collar workers.[8] Whatever they wear on the job, however, neither the most poorly paid service workers and laborers nor the highly skilled technicians, professionals, managers, and executives are within this range of middle American jobs.

The nature of their specific jobs notwithstanding, for virtually all middle Americans work remains a necessary—though personally frequently rewarding—evil with which to finance the rest of their lives. The evil aspect of work is most likely the bureaucratic, autocratic, or otherwise unsatisfactory character of the workplace or the employing organization. The more important satisfactions people seek are in the family, among friends and neighbors, in clubs and leisure-time pursuits, and, for many but by no means all, in various efforts to try to help the children obtain more secure or better jobs. The ultimate goal for the children is their chance at a career, that set of ever-improving positions in a single occupation that usually guarantees job and income security as well as higher prestige.

Despite widespread attempts to increase the amount and quality of schooling since World War II, most Americans still have only a high school diploma. The median years of schooling in 1985 were 12.6, and the amount has risen just a half year since 1970. Young adults aged 25 to 29 are a little more likely to have attended college, although the median years of schooling in this age group are 12.8, and the figure has increased only four-fifths of a year since 1950.[9] In 1985 among the majority of Americans in the middle, roughly 12 percent had completed one to three years of high school, 38 percent were high school graduates, and 16 percent had gone to college for one to three years.[10] Sixteen percent had less education, 19 percent had more.

Setting the income boundaries of middle America is extremely difficult, because middle Americans are not an income group. Cultural and social characteristics do not correlate with income, and the same jobs differ in pay between industries and regions of the country. Also, family and household incomes now vary more because of multi-breadwinner and single parent families. I think of middle American *family* income, that is, the income of families, as ranging from $15,000 to $37,500 these days. In 1984, this range covered two-fifths of all families, i.e., those from the 31st to the 71st income percentiles.[11] At the bottom of this range, middle Americans obtain at best a moderate income, their earnings not that far removed from the 1986 poverty line of $11,000 for a family of four. On the other hand, some of those at the high end of the income range can pay for parts of an affluent standard of living except in the ever more numerous expensive areas of the country.

Job, school, and earnings categories can be summarized in the language of socioeconomic class, and by that criterion, middle America is a combination of working-class and lower-middle-class families. Middle Americans are thus ranked above the lower class of poorly paid service workers, laborers, and the jobless poor, but below the upper middle class of generally affluent professionals, managers, and executives, as well as the upper class of top executives and coupon clippers, most of whom are rich or very rich. Middle Americans are also below a set of occupations many sociologists now think of as a middle-middle stratum.[12] People in that stratum work in the better technical and supervisory as well as the less prestigious and salaried professional jobs, with college degrees obtained at the above-average public and private colleges but not the so-called "selective" schools of the Ivy League and its peers.

Middle American is not equivalent to middle class, for by income, occupational, and educational criteria at least, middle Americans are not quite middle class. Furthermore, the term middle class is now used so broadly as to be virtually meaningless. Journalists, for example, generally describe all but the very rich and poor as middle class and the working class as lower middle class.[13]

A generation or two ago the notion of a combined lower-middle- and working-class population as middle American would not have made much sense, because the U.S. was still sharply and clearly divided into a working class holding factory jobs and a lower middle class in office jobs.[14] Since then, changes in the economy have led to a vast increase in the number of office workers, even if many of them are doing factory-like labor at typewriters and word processors in the office. The number of factory jobs has remained fairly steady, but the proportion of old-style "production workers" has declined continuously since the end of World War II.[15]

Although the working conditions of factory workers are still poorer than those of office workers, and the former remain hourly wage labor while the latter are salaried, past earning differences have shrunk and so have differences in how the two strata spend their earnings. Working- and lower-middle-class people usually do not live in separate neighborhoods or speak and dress differently. The once sizable gulfs in education, ways of raising children, furnishing dwellings, and spending leisure time have also declined. As long as note is taken of the remaining differences such as job security and working conditions, the two populations can often be described jointly as middle Americans.

Nonetheless, middle America is only a category, a way to

classify one sector of the total population. It must be remembered that the people in this category are dissimilar in many respects. Their dissimilarities are easily lost sight of in a single category, but, for example, middle Americans at the lower income levels still need to worry obtaining sufficient security. Those with better incomes not only can afford higher levels of comfort and convenience but can think more often about such goals as self-development.

Factors other than income or economic security also play a role in creating differences among middle Americans. Aside from the powerful role of race, middle Americans and popular individualism are also affected by gender and age. Many women are more involved in motherhood than self-development, while others must still overcome income discrimination, as well as patriarchal and "macho" male values that are much stronger than in upper-middle-class America.

Age differences play a fundamental role in shaping the values of middle Americans simply because security, control, comfort, and convenience have different meanings and priorities at all stages in the life cycle. Although "baby boomers" are currently being treated as a distinctive and homogeneous population category, the postwar baby boom took place between 1946 and about 1965, and 20-year age differences are immense. One of the myths that justifies the baby boomer category is that children born in this period are the first generation to grow up with television, but television cannot shape people's employment chances, standards of living—or values. (Besides, television programming is not all that different from the radio programs and movies from which earlier generations derived their entertainment.)

Religious affiliation still makes for differences among middle Americans, especially the 30 to 40 percent who attend services weekly. Ethnicity is of minor importance to most descendants of Irish, Italian, Polish, and concurrent immigrations of the turn of the century, but it matters a great deal to the recent newcomers from Asia, Latin America, and Europe, not only in how they live but in what kinds of work they can obtain, especially when their skins are dark. Region matters too, especially outside the big cities, where regional economies and cultures survive. Last but not least, people who live in much the same ways and hold roughly the same opinions may still vote differently, perhaps because of where they live but also because of familial party allegiances or simply their personal conceptions of the party or candidate they admire. Sometimes, researchers find middle Americans who describe themselves as socialists and vote Republican and who can explain that there is no contradiction in this combination.[16] However, their political thinking does not follow conventional Left-Right positions.

In short, middle American individualism is not a seamless set of values and cultural patterns. Concurrently, middle American values may also be shared by the rest of America. This is immediately apparent from national polls, for the answers of middle Americans are often not very different from those of other Americans except when economic interests are directly at stake. (As a result, when reporting polls I will usually cite results for the entire sample of respondents, indicating variations by income, occupation, and education only when they are sizable.) In effect, American values are surprisingly similar.

Nonetheless, that similarity of American values must be interpreted carefully, for values are personal preferences and goals for individual and social life. They are not necessarily expressions of or clues to behavior, or even what people want or expect from government and the economy.

Although values rarely determine behavior, under the right conditions they can exert influence on it.[17] Some people know what they want and go after it. They can be successful if they have enough of the needed material and emotional resources, the power to control the relevant environment, and the "wisdom" not to fight economic and political forces clearly beyond their control. While individualist ideology, particularly the capitalist version, proposes that everyone can be successful, most people must operate with lesser expectations and turn values into preferences between choices. The choices available to them depend mainly on the opportunities and constraints they encounter. All else being equal, the rich have more opportunities and fewer constraints, while the poor are dominated by constraints and live virtually without choice. Middle Americans are in the middle. The balance of opportunities and constraints is determined not only by money or power, however, or else the rich would always have their way.

Generally speaking, individualistic values play a bigger role during periods of economic prosperity, when ordinary people can turn these values into choices, material and nonmaterial.

The values do not disappear in years of economic decline, but they are often put on hold, perhaps even suppressed until it makes sense to bring them back into play. Meanwhile, people use them to maintain hope. When good times return, so do their individualistic values. Insofar as values are goals, people then try to move toward achieving them, but they must always first live in the present, exploiting opportunities and overcoming constraints, including the goals of others. Some goals, sudden wealth or world peace, may never be accessible and thus persist as hopes. Middle American individualism is essentially a set of values and goals that can, under optimal conditions, guide choices among the opportunities middle Americans encounter.

Popular Individualism as Historical Process

Popular individualism must be nearly as old as human history. If ordinary people had left an archaeological record, evidence of its existence would probably be found in the first era in which people stopped living in total mutual interdependence and could at least conceive of going their own way in some respects. Presumably this conception emerged and died out many times in human history.

Contemporary individualism is associated with capitalism, among others by Marxist thinkers, but feudal serfs observed the individualistic whims of their masters and must have considered the possibility that in another world they too could live by their own values. Unlike capitalist individualism, popular individualism is not a predominantly economic ideology, and there is no reason to believe that ordinary people had to wait for the arrival of capitalism to consider the possibility that they could dream about or claim individual rights.

In any case, America's popular individualism is as old as America, for the intent to move to a distant continent free from the existence of a state or a state religion and the search for happiness through the pursuit of property were invented in Europe. Indeed, the individualism pursued and achieved by the Americans with whom de Tocqueville talked 150 years ago seems not to have been very different from today's, or else the ethnographic portions of his book could not continue to ring so true.

The Europeans who took the U.S. away from the Indians came here for a variety of reasons and, among the nonreligious immigrants, some came not only by choice but to make a fresh start. Individualistic thoughts must have occurred to them before they set off for the U.S. Thus, from the 17th to the 20th century a number of the new Americans may have entertained early versions of today's popular individualism. Of course, many were driven here by economic or political necessity, although even necessity led some in an individualistic direction. For example, economic refugees appear to have become individualistic by being pushed out of their communities by joblessness and thus forced to sever communal ties even before their emigration.[18]

Whatever their reasons for coming to the U.S. and their hopes for their new lives here, a large proportion of the newcomers reestablished the communities and cultures they had left. Many had no choice because of language problems, but other immigrants settled near relatives and people from the same town or rural area in Europe whenever possible.

Whether they were farming or working in factories, they needed to be together to supply each other with the security and control over their lives they could not get from a laissez-faire economy, the strangers all around them, and the wealthy natives who ran most communities as well as the country. Mutual dependence brought and kept the newcomers together, but it frequently did so for pragmatic reasons rather than because of cultural and communal traditions that had long ago been internalized. When interdependence loses its traditional quality and becomes pragmatic, however, and people achieve more economic security, meet strangers with new ideas and are open to other influences, the cement that holds communities and cultures together can begin to chip away quickly.

Sociologists use the term acculturation to describe the process in which the immigrants, and particularly their descendants, first alter and then drop most of the culture they bring with them from the old country.[19] In the civic language, this is called Americanization. The ways in which immigrants actually adopt the values of America's popular individualism are still mysterious, but somehow millions of people from a large and diverse set of countries and cultures in each of the numerous waves of immigration have learned, often quickly, to start becoming American in this sense. It would be chauvinistic and wrong to assume that popular individualism is uniquely American because a number of newcomers arrived in America with individualistic values and had only to learn the distinctively American ones.[20] Others discovered that the communal values they brought with them could not be realized or that the old-country cultural patterns did not work and had to be abandoned quickly.

Somewhat the same process of acculturation appears to take place among rural native Americans who come to the cities, for they too gradually give up the ways of life of their place of origin. Moreover, as among immigrants, their culture starts to go first, followed by the community, as the newcomers to the city or their descendants no longer need or want to depend on the people with whom they or their parents grew up, or on the institutions they brought with them.

By that time they also become more aware of some drawbacks of their community. They may weary of the deference that must be paid to communal leaders, or the material privileges that go to them and their relatives. They also tire of the jealousies, enmities, and battles that accompany communal dependency as both personalities and interests clash. When people no longer see any need or reason to live together in proximate fashion, those who can afford better housing and neighborhoods move out. Many relatives and friends may choose the same new neighborhoods; in the longer run, however, many of them disperse. In the meantime, identities also change. People who came here as neighbors from the same Sicilian village first become Sicilians and southern Italians, but eventually see themselves and are seen as Italian-Americans. Likewise, people from the same Alabama village turn, over time, into Southerners and, in the long run, WASPs.

Culture and community may be transformed drastically or disappear entirely, but familial relations change more slowly, even if parents or in-laws no longer live next door. Family members are in the final analysis the most easily relied-on source of emotional and financial support, and in that sense the most reliable source of security. As a result, some though not all the familial relationships of immigrants—and those of rural Americans—persist for a long time, and so do bits and pieces of familial culture and ritual. Third- and fourth-generation descendants of European immigrants retain some allegiance to ethnic foods when the rest of the culture is gone, and all over the world there are families who light candles on Friday nights even though they cannot say why, and thus do not know they are descendants of Jews who centuries ago had to hide their Jewishness in order to escape the Inquisition.

Neither the necessity for mutual dependence nor the acculturation that moves individuals away from it happen automatically. Earlier versions of popular individualism were also affected or at least interrupted frequently by dramatic events, notably the ups and downs of the business cycle, prolonged periods of affluence and depressions, major foreign wars and the Civil War. The various economic changes wrought by the post-Civil War industrialization of the country, the arrival of the large corporation, and the first merger movements at the end of the 19th century also played their parts, although not all Americans were directly affected by these processes. Small family farmers, for example, could not survive without maintaining interdependence, and until World War II many factory workers were so poor and so often out of work that they had to hang on for dear life to families, churches, ethnic organizations, unions, and whatever other supports they could look to in hard times.

Even so, the first seeds of today's middle American individualism can probably be found in the late 19th century, when sales, clerical, and other office jobs became available in large enough numbers to encourage the emergence of the modern lower middle class. More seeds began to sprout by the 1920s, when some factory workers began to earn more than subsistence pay and a working class that was not poor appeared on the scene. These tendencies may not have been very visible, if only because the people writing about the country still focused on the rich and the avant garde. Even now the 1920s continue to be identified with "the jazz age," "flaming youth," and the discontents of expatriate American writers in Paris.

The Post–World War II Era

To understand today's middle American individualism, it is most important to understand the 20-odd years of rising income for most Americans from the end of World War II to the 1970s. Since the Great Depression was expected to resume after the end of the war, the federal government intervened actively to stave off that possibility and, when the economy boomed, it set off the continuing upturn in real income among white middle Americans and others that is now thought of as the postwar affluence. During the subsequent decades that upturn spread to blacks, and in the 1960s it even initiated a very visible increase in the then tiny black upper middle class. In the 1970s the good times slowed down for many, especially blacks. For some other

Americans, those good times have since been ending precipitously as a result of factory closings and the computer's inroads on other jobs.

The long period of postwar economic growth enabled people to increase not only their own comfort and convenience but their economic security as well. As a result, middle Americans *felt* more secure and were able to move away again from cultural and communal dependence, in the process loosening a variety of ties in what appeared to be a permanent break with the past.

For many, that process began with the move to new neighborhoods, especially in the suburbs, which some people used not only to obtain the house they wanted but also to put some distance between themselves and involuntary familial ties. In the communities or subdivisions into which they moved, they learned to make friends with strangers on the basis of shared interests rather than shared upbringing or history. Often all they shared at the start was common residence or children of the same age; later they found or developed other mutual interests. People who moved into brand-new communities or subdivisions or moved in among older residents in an established area, also started new clubs, voluntary associations, and the like. Most people limited themselves to an informal social life, however, with other people who were homogeneous enough that they could be approached to participate in freely chosen companionship.

Although the postwar suburbanization slowed down in the late 1960s and early 1970s, it has never really stopped, and a new generation is repeating the same process at a somewhat slower pace, in smaller numbers, and, due to the rising price of housing, at a higher cost to the family budget. Most of the adolescents who complained about being bored in postwar suburbia and threatened to return to the cities have not done so. Instead they have put distance between themselves and their parents by moving to newer areas yet further out from the central cities, in part because the jobs have also been moving out. Others have headed for different parts of the country where better jobs and a different set of strangers awaited them. Some bored suburban adolescents *did* return to the cities, but the gentrification in which they have been participating is not only bigger in visibility than in size but is almost entirely an upper-middle-class movement. Few middle Americans can even afford to live in a gentrified house or a newly built central-city townhouse.

Today other instances of the move to new areas and the initiation of freely chosen companionship among homogeneous neighbors have taken place. One example may be found among older couples who move into retirement villages where they invent full-time versions of what young suburbanites only do part time. In some ways the old people have it a little easier, being segregated with their own age and class groups, but on the other hand their task is more difficult since, lacking jobs or children, they must develop a nearly full-time set of leisure and social activities. The retirement communities are imperfect in many respects, and virtually all fail to serve their occupants if they become seriously or chronically ill with advancing age. These communities have also been criticized as artificial because they diverge from multiage residential areas and fail to pay respects to high culture and upper-middle-class conceptions of community. Nonetheless, the communities are early experiments in which some old people try new ways of being—and also not being—old.

Another example is the so-called "singles." Fifteen to 20 years ago, young middle Americans usually lived at home until marriage, and in prosperous times most married early. Now, increasing numbers, though still numerical minorities, are living by themselves as roommates or as unmarried couples, in the process inventing a variety of new household relationships.[21] The singles are perhaps the most pioneering for despite the glamour the entertainment media often attach to their new status, it is accompanied by considerable loneliness. Consequently, people who may have different occupational interests and recreation preferences but are brought together by singlehood and the absence of family responsibility have to invent sociable relations. These must deal with loneliness as well as with the instability of singlehood, which may be a temporary status for some while for others it is permanent—and, for many of the latter, involuntary. In addition, single women must constantly confront men who are looking for sexual adventures disguised as social relationships. Singles have to deal with more complicated issues than people who move into suburbia or retirement villages. With greater distance and fewer guidelines from American traditions to draw on, they will be dropping and revising innovations in ways of living in larger proportions.

A related set of singles who must try out innovations are the female heads of single-parent households. Some are voluntarily but most are involuntarily single. Almost all are involuntarily downwardly mobile, however, and many are or have become poor enough that survival is more urgent than new ways of living.

Concurrent with the move to new communities and areas and various freely chosen companionships middle Americans have been loosening their ties to a variety of traditional institutions. Surveys of religion indicate, for example, that while the number of people who say their belief in a deity, hell, or one or more other symbols of religious faith remains high, only about a third to two-fifths of the people appear to attend church regularly, and they are distancing themselves from the demands of organized religion and to some extent from the institution itself.[22] Instead, people are developing more individualistic conceptions of their faith and of their deity, which in turn leads to the decline of denominational loyalties and the establishment of new churches and synagogues in which people share these individual conceptions or learn them from each other. People continue to use the church for social opportunities, and, especially for singles, churches are safer places in which to look for and meet compatible strangers than bars.

Loyalty to religious practices and beliefs declines when these are no longer thought necessary or when they conflict with more urgent secular concerns. American Judaism made this discovery long ago, but the Catholic church is only learning it now. The decision not to go to Mass every week or to break with the traditional worship at Easter or the Jewish New Year probably is a significant step in the acculturation away from obligatory religious demands. When Catholics discover that ending weekly Mass attendance does not feel like a sin to them or their friends and that they can still be religious, a new, more individualist relationship to the Catholic church has begun. When people discover that they need not always obey pastors, ministers, and rabbis and that these men, and now women, still treat them as congregants, they can loosen their ties to the church or synagogue.[23]

The ties to political parties were never strong in middle America, for parties started to decline in relevance after the New Deal provided the public services and welfare programs that were once offered by political machines, urban and rural. The decline in party loyalty observed in elections and polls has often been blamed on television news and commercials, which have replaced political parties as the major campaign vehicles. However, I remember interviewing young suburbanites in the late 1940s, long before the invention of television news, who felt that neither political party dealt with their needs and who therefore described themselves as independents. Partly because many more people are independents now and partly because television is such an expensive campaign tool, the national parties are in the process of becoming funding organizations to pay for television time, and therefore are likely to obtain allegiance mainly from candidates, campaign workers, and job seekers.

Local parties are affected but not totally dominated by national trends, and many local political machines continue to flourish, even if they bear little resemblance to the traditional Chicago variety. By now, however, they too cannot offer many reasons for voter loyalty. People who become homeowners generally develop a fairly standard set of political interests connected to the preservation of property and status values and the reduction of local taxes. As a result, many suburban and some urban parties, Democratic or Republican, are mainly homeowner lobbies and attract people for this reason. When they do not take on this function or when they pay insufficient attention to the preservation of property values, voters find yet another reason to give up their allegiance to the parties.

The revival of national single-issue lobbies which began in the 1970s is partly a result of the availability of computerized mailing lists, but, except among religious fundamentalists, it also reflects the shift from supporting party issues to supporting individually chosen ones. At the same time, voters can now establish direct if vicarious relations with individual candidates, notably for the presidency. That shift is enhanced by the availability of television and by yet newer technologies which allow politicians to appear to speak or write personal letters directly to voters, but new technology alone is not the explanation. F.D.R. used the "fireside chat" to reach people but his success was more than an effect of the availability of radio, for in the nearly 50 years since he spoke, few presidents have been able to reach people the same way, on radio or television.

A more dramatic instance of the loosening of organizational ties among middle Americans is the diminution of the power of labor unions. Although corporate managements have used the emergence of world competition and the availability of low-wage labor overseas to weaken the unions, their effort often reinforces a trend begun under different auspices.

One by-product of postwar economic security for the better-off workers in stable industries was their declining need for a union.[24] Also, many of these workers distrusted their unions, most of which were monopolies and thus could allow some union leaders to assume autocratic power. Publicity about alleged and actual corruption did not help.[25]

Subsequently, when once secure workers in steel and elsewhere became jobless, the unions were already too weak to fight management for the retention of jobs, although they have not received any help from government or the national union movement. Unions have long been organizations of the employed and have often disavowed their own jobless members. A serious and prolonged economic crisis may bring workers back to the unions, as has happened in the past. In the meantime, however, the unions' shortcomings as well as their blue collar image have helped discourage white collar workers and others in the new service industries from considering unionization. Evidently the chances of potential economic and other gains from union membership are offset by the fear that joining a union entails a loss of economic prestige. So far, many of today's middle American workers appear to prefer to go it on their individual own.

When all is said and done, probably the most far-reaching change in post-World War II America has been in the nuclear family, as one generation has loosened the social and cultural ties that connect it to another. While family members still seem to visit about as much as ever, parents' influence on the lives of their adult children has waned. The diversity between generations is not absolute, as those observers who once thought they had spotted a generation gap discovered, and under similar conditions young people react no differently than their elders. Still, until some time after World War II, middle Americans tended to resemble their parents. The best predictor of voting patterns was parental voting, and people's cultural preferences, such as house styles, furniture, foods and cuisines, were not drastically at variance from parental ones.

Equally important, throughout most of the postwar affluence, the occupational and social status of middle Americans was still largely shaped by that of their parents. Once adolescence was over, non-mobile young adults moved into the occupational and social worlds of their parents. Since factory and other blue collar jobs appeared to be secure and wages were going up, sons frequently worked in the same jobs or industries as their fathers. Daughters were expected to stay home once the children came—and to consult their mothers and mothers-in-law about how to raise the next generation. Upward occupational mobility took place of course, but it was viewed as a break with the parental generation and with non-mobile brothers, sisters and friends.[26]

The arrival of "automation" in the early 1960s and other indications that safe and well-paid factory jobs might begin to disappear persuaded more children from blue collar families to head for college.[27] Upward occupational mobility became a necessity, and in some families, it separated the generations, although not necessarily by design. However, the young people made new kinds of friends and met different kinds of potential mates at college. Although they attended public commuter colleges and lived at home, increasing numbers found it hard to return afterwards to the life-styles they had learned from their parents.

In fact, during the late 1960s and the 1970s it appeared to some that familial ties were unraveling and that the nuclear-family household might become anachronistic. This prediction was largely the result of increasing rates of divorce as well as the first visible signs of sexual and related liberations. Hindsight indicates, however, that the most visible liberation took place in the upper middle class. Even the new occupational opportunities for, and aspirations of, women and the pleasures of young adulthood in an affluent society have not been as significant as first thought, partly because the jobs open to middle American women are not the glamorous professional careers available to highly educated upper-middle-class young women. In any case, women's median age of marriage has climbed only slightly in the last two decades, from 20.3 in 1960 to 22.5 in 1983.[28]

Nonetheless, today's middle American nuclear family is different in many respects from earlier ones. One major difference is that two incomes are now necessary to maintain a middle American household, and even so, a higher proportion of the family budget is now spent on housing than before. In the 1920s, the sociologist Ernest Burgess proposed that the changes he saw in the country at that time were producing a companionship family in which husband and wife would be friends in addition to their other roles. He was only partly right, because the family is also increasingly a haven from impersonal and involuntary institutions, supplying emotional and other supports more intense than companionship. If this becomes a significant and permanent family function, the family may become a more central institution than even Sigmund Freud could have imagined. Meanwhile, the only safe prediction is that the nuclear family has always changed and that so far it has always survived.

Inside the family and out, the loosening of some ties, the altering of others, and the invention of new social forms are not instances of an evolutionary step but of a process of adapting—and muddling through—that operates in zigzag fashion and may include a return to past solutions. For example, when middle American and other women discovered that gender liberation could bring sexual exploitation with it, they began to redefine the rules for sexual relations, even before herpes and AIDS. Wherever unemployment increases, some sons and daughters may move back with their parents. In this case the move is dictated purely by economic necessity, for even if the conflicts between the generations have not worsened in the last 25 years, people are less prepared to live with them—a by-product of what was once called the revolution of rising expectations.

The changes in familial and other relations are therefore frequently accompanied by anger as well as by self-questioning and anguish. Sometimes outside support is needed, which explains a part of the increase in ministerial and secular counseling and reasonably inexpensive kinds of therapy and pseudo-therapy.[29] Some find help in religion. One result is the resurgence of orthodoxy in all American religions, although not all orthodoxy represents the inability to cope with individualism.

It is certainly too early even to guess whether middle American individualism will increase or decrease people's happiness or mental health. Nonetheless, the increasing pursuit of self-development has been accompanied by a steady outpouring of alarm about increasing alienation and social disintegration, as well as predictions of a new era of selfishness and greed and yet more social disintegration.

Most of these alarms are exaggerated or have nothing to do with popular individualism, a matter taken up in Chapter 5. The opportunity for self-development will surely add to people's sense of happiness, even if some have troubles, probably temporary, in learning to enjoy new opportunities for choice as well. An increase in mentally positive idiosyncracies should also be expected, even if some people treat them as signs of new mental illness. New neuroses may appear, even if the rate of neurosis does not change. A rise in psychosis would not be surprising, not so much among the practitioners of self-development as among others who lose already eroding familial or other support systems. For example, if extended families disperse and fewer relatives are available, people who depend on them could turn into lost souls.

Just as freedom evokes demands for control, so individuality produces demands for conformity. Unmet demands eventually begin to disappear, however. While middle American parents continue to urge their daughters to marry and have children, it is getting easier for the daughters to remain unmarried or, if married, to remain childless if they choose, than it was in the past. As a result, single women are under less pressure than before, and the stigma that used to attach to spinsterhood is gone. In fact so is that term, and even the euphemism "career woman" is less acceptable than it once was. If there is a general reduction of punitive conformity pressures, say of the kind once exerted on spinsters, as well as more opportunity for people to make personal choices that spell self-development, popular individualism will surely be a boon to mental health.

The affluent period that followed World War II did not invent self-development and the rest of popular individualism, but helped to spread them, nourish them and give them a more secure footing. Whatever economic security middle Americans may have achieved, however, they know that it may not be permanent. Most are too young to remember the Great Depression, but they remain wary of what the economy and the government could do to their lives.

Two

Some Economic and Political Values

How middle Americans maneuver in the economy and deal with the government agencies that affect their lives depends on where they live and work, as well as a variety of other national and local factors. What middle Americans have in common, at least to some extent, is a number of economic, political and other values. These are mostly hopes and dreams which people express in their attitudes, but in their actions only when the times are good and people can pursue their values.

One of the traditional paradoxes of the general set of American values is that many people, including middle Americans, would like more government services but also lower government expenditures. In a 1985 poll, 80 percent of the respondents said that they favored cuts in government spending, but then on the very next question 68 percent indicated that they also supported "government financing to create more jobs."[1] This is hardly a new pattern, for in 1936 in the depth of the Great Depression, a majority of people in one poll came out for public ownership of the basic utilities, while 70 percent in another poll favored cuts in public spending. Later that year, however, the voters reelected F.D.R. by a record landslide.[2]

The desire for more services and lower taxes could be explained simply as an instance of the desire to get something for nothing, but the paradox also reflects a built-in ambivalence about government and the private economy. That ambivalence is to some extent created by the division of labor and the variety of roles that exist in modern societies. In such societies, people and organizations can be divided into those that are mainly *users*, that is, customers and clients for goods and services, and *suppliers*, those that fund, produce, and distribute these goods and services. Indeed, capitalism seeks to facilitate the conditions under which suppliers can produce, distribute, and make money. Popular individualism, on the other hand, justifies the rights of people not only to be but to look at the world as users.

Users and suppliers are not necessarily adversaries, but people who use a product or service view it differently than those who supply it. Many clients of the public library want currently popular books, but librarians would prefer supplying more elevated reading matter. They would also like to forgo having to order several copies of current nonfiction and fiction best sellers, which are expensive and are often soon forgotten, and they must worry about maintaining a balanced collection, take care of the building, and stay within the budget. As the example implies, the users' interests are often not the same as the suppliers.

Almost by definition, most Americans are users. Although many people work for organizations of suppliers, they are unlikely to think like those organizations even if work rules and the need to keep the job may force obedience to supplier rules. Workers will generally identify with their jobs and colleagues, but few are likely to identify with their employer.

Needless to say, not everything and everyone can be classified into or explained by the user-supplier dichotomy. It does not, for example, nullify distinctions between labor and management, but suggests only that when people have prosaic jobs, their values reflect a greater interest in the use of their money than in the work they must do to earn it. The dichotomy is not mutually exclusive either, for people can play both roles. Corporate executives must think like suppliers on the job, but after hours they are users of entertainment.[3] Nor do users reject all supplier values. Most citizens defend press and academic freedom, but they do not give it the same priority as do journalists and professors.

Because middle Americans are usually employees and not owners, and workers rather than decision makers, they view government and the private economy from a user perspective. One outcome is that they want public services because they are "free," but they also want lower taxes because then they can spend more of their earnings in pursuit of that set of user values we call the American Dream. They know, of course, that public services are not free, but that is yet another reason for wanting taxes lowered. They can make individualistic choices among the goods and services they can buy in the private economy, but they lack such choice in the offerings of government. These considerations have endless implications for the private economy and the government.

Jobs, Wealth, and Taxes

The first value of users is to be able to finance the American Dream, and for middle—and most other—Americans that means having a job which provides economic security, some satisfaction, and the feeling of usefulness. Many people also want a chance for advancement, which automatically builds in both the opportunity of a rising income and the economic security that comes with a better job. In effect, people whose ancestors were considered a commodity called labor—and who have not entirely escaped that position themselves—seek to be treated as human beings and to obtain as much security for themselves as possible. This reaction comes through clearly in a series of GSS polls over the last 15 years in which people always gave first priority to work that gave them a feeling of importance and accomplishment, second priority to jobs with a chance for advancement, third to work for a high income, and fourth to jobs with no danger of being fired.[4]

In the past, the ancestors of today's middle Americans sought these values through proprietorship. Farm laborers and sharecroppers wanted to be family farmers; factory workers hoped to escape the assembly line and establish workshops, gasoline stations, or taverns.[5] White collar workers sought to educate their children for the independent, therefore businesslike, professions ranging from accountancy and dentistry to law and medicine.

"Petty" ownership remains popular today among new immigrants, offering linguistic and cultural independence to them as well as a modicum of economic security as long as they have immigrant customers, free family labor, or the un-American willingness to work 14 to 18 hours a day. The ever-increasing capital needs and other problems of many small businesses seem, however, to have persuaded middle Americans to forgo proprietorial and entrepreneurial aims. A study of the desire of blue collar workers to go into business found that in 1936, 70 percent expressed this wish, but in 1976 only 40 percent did so.[6] Since wages, salaries, fringe benefits, and working conditions have improved for most of the four decades since World War II, at least in the more secure parts of the economy, middle America has settled for salaried status, at least for the moment.

A concurrent but less urgent value of popular individualism is for wealth, in the hope of guaranteeing economic security and all that goes with it. Middle Americans are not, however, interested in amassing great wealth or being acquisitive as an end in itself. When researchers ask people whether they would continue to work if they received enough money to live comfortably, 70 percent regularly indicate they would go on working.[7] So do most of those who become wealthy by winning the lottery. The winners do not turn into entrepreneurs or capitalists, although they do quit dirty or otherwise unpleasant jobs.[8] Nor do people believe that wealth solves all problems, for in response to another regularly asked poll question, only about 30 percent agree that "next to health, money is the most important thing in life."[9]

Still, the achievement of wealth is not rejected, and perhaps Richard Nixon was accurate when he pointed out that the American Dream is to become rich unexpectedly. Since most people cannot sell their memoirs or oceanfront properties, they turn to other ways, which may explain the continuing proliferation of opportunities to gamble modestly for a sudden windfall in casinos, through public lotteries, sports betting, the numbers, and million-dollar sweepstakes. Moreover, should luck strike, people want to pass their new wealth on to their children, as George McGovern learned in 1972 when blue collar worker audiences rejected his call for higher inheritance taxes. In fact, a 1986 study showed that 73 percent of the people interviewed said they were opposed to any tax increases to limit inheritances, and 79 percent disagreed with the notion that "there should be an upper limit on the amount of money any person can make."[10] Evidently people whose only equity is a mortgaged home continue to wish that they too could become wealthy. Nonetheless, poll respondents have consistently rejected the idea that business is entitled to maximize its wealth, i.e., profits, at the expense of consumers, workers, or the community.[11]

A more insistent, sometimes strident theme of middle Americans' individualism is the already noted wish for lower taxes. Actually their feeling about taxes is ruled by two contradictory pulls, the demand for fair taxes and the wish for tax reduction. Most polls, past and present, show that people believe the federal income tax system to be unfair.[12] In 1985, 80 percent of those responding to a *Washington Post*–ABC News poll went so far as to promise that "I wouldn't complain about the amount I pay in taxes if I thought the rich were paying their fair share." (True, they were not required to put their promises in writing.) Furthermore, a 1986 Roper poll indicated that 61 percent of the respondents considered the federal income tax "unfair to most people."[13]

The federal income tax may also be disliked because it takes the largest sums and because it is deducted from paychecks, leaving people less money to spend on themselves and their families and reducing their individual purchasing power. Sales taxes, although most regressive and thus least fair, appear to be less unpopular than income taxes.[14] Not only must everyone pay them, but they are paid *after* people have spent money on themselves, and they can sometimes be reduced or canceled with individual effort—by saving or shopping by mail or driving to areas where the sales tax is lower. Conversely, taxpayers still consider the local property tax almost as unfair as the federal income tax, perhaps because they see it as reducing the amount of money they could have spent on improving the house.[15]

Taxes not only reduce people's purchasing power, but are frequently viewed as a form of "waste," again at nearly all income levels. They pay the salaries of government officials, who are perceived too often as doing nothing, or nothing to benefit the unhappy taxpayer. When people who value the services for which they pay taxes feel this way, they are probably also expressing their distaste for "bureaucracy," a catchall pejorative that reflects a pervasive antipathy to large formal organizations.

Some people deem taxes another kind of waste when they pay for "public goods," services that are available to them but that they themselves do not use. Many small-town school officials are familiar with old people who oppose school taxes, and with young parents who feel the same way until their children are of school age. Once public services lose some of their funds to budget cutting, they also decrease in quality and then fall prey to a vicious circle. Lower quality means less use among those who have any choice, who then withdraw their political support, leading to further budget cuts. Finally, the people who have no choice, notably the poor, become the dominant users, occasionally causing other users to go elsewhere. Public schools and public parks have become facilities for the poor in a number of communities, but over most of the country, mass transit is perhaps the best example of a public service which most middle Americans can do without. It lost a good deal of its national constituency even before World War II, when the affluent were already in the suburbs and the ancestors of today's middle Americans were heading for low-density urban neighborhoods. The car is almost always more convenient than the bus, the only form of mass transit economically viable in low-density areas, and, once purchased, is also cheaper to use for regular commuting and leisure-time activities.

The Pros and Cons of Public Services

The reluctance about public services is neither a nationwide phenomenon that affects every community nor one that applies to all services. In fact, middle Americans almost always favor *sustenance* services which supply people with job and other forms of economic security, health and educational programs that have occupational payoffs, and regulation programs that maintain the safety of jobs, drugs, and other products on which people rely, as well as public safety. The public services of lower priority include some that contribute to the quality of life, such as programs for parks and recreation or support for the arts.[16] It would appear that a number of people consider quality-of-life services to be luxuries.

Most people are, however, fairly generous when answering poll questions about public services expenditures, and are at best likely to call for lower increases for those they disapprove of. This also includes antipoverty programs.[17] On some polls, majorities may come out against "welfare" and sometimes against food stamps, but the same respondents still want the government to help the poor or the needy, the implication being that they do not want to help welfare cheaters and other undeserving poor people.

People may not want to appear heartless on polls, and as noted earlier, Americans frequently favor increased services and lower government expenditures at the same time. The Reagan administration probably took advantage of their ambivalence about the conflict between public services and private spending, for it was able to eliminate or cut back a variety of popular federal programs during the height of its assault on the welfare state, including consumer protection, job safety, and educational programs—until it made a strategic mistake and attacked Social Security. A large number of antipoverty programs were emasculated or killed outright during this period, suggesting the possibility that people support such programs more enthusiastically when speaking to pollsters than when talking to their elected representatives. Also, too many supporters of anti-poverty efforts never speak to their elected representatives.

Public services, even those supplying sustenance, can have a variety of social drawbacks because they are public. All other things being equal, people prefer cars to mass transit, backyards and private pools over public parks and playgrounds, their own doctors to clinics, and, of course, single-family houses over apartments. Poor people who cannot often afford anything except public services do not feel very differently once they have overcome poverty.

Public services are at a further disadvantage because they must—and should—obey the law by being accessible to all, thus displeasing people who want them to exclude others. Services supplied in facilities that depend on voluntary attendance are most affected, perhaps because at times one group in the community takes them over and thus discourages others. Public—but also commercial—facilities are turned into personal turfs by such groups, for example adolescents or members of one ethnic or racial group, thus discouraging others of access. Whites shun some public facilities because they are open to citizens of lower status and darker skin, or because they cannot be informally divided up by class, race, or ethnicity. Parks and beaches sometimes lend themselves to such segregation, but swimming pools do not. Public services that are delivered to people can maintain discrimination practices more easily, including illegal ones, which helps explain why garbage removal tends to be better in affluent than in poor neighborhoods.

Cultural factors can add to the reluctance to use public services. Some services are so uniform that they must ignore variations among users in their habits and preferences. Public parks and playgrounds do not supply the kinds of attractions offered by commercial amusement parks. Community centers do not offer the activities supplied by private clubs, and they are not restaurants or taverns.

Still, when public services are unique or when commercially supplied equivalents are not financially feasible, people's reluctance toward them disappears. Most communities with underused playgrounds find that the publicly funded sports stadia in which professional and other athletic teams play rarely suffer from lack of attendance. Most national parks, being unique, now turn people away.

Americans dislike monopoly, in part because it implies bigness and power, even if generations of antitrust proceedings have not exorcised it.[18] Attitudes toward public services are affected by this dislike, for such services are generally provided on a monopolistic, and often on a take-it-or-leave-it basis. When the monopoly takes the form of a football stadium, the taxpayers may not know or care that they are paying for it out of their taxes as well as with their tickets. When monopolistic services reject or ignore user preferences, however, and users have alternatives, many just go elsewhere. Municipal recreation departments exercise monopoly control over outdoor facilities, and if they supply traditional playgrounds that many children find boring, children head for the streets instead.[19]

Because of their monopoly power, public agencies have a good deal of leeway in dealing with—or ignoring—public unhappiness with services unless there is a real voter rebellion. Rich citizens may be able to complain effectively because they have prestige as well as political influence, encouraging public agencies to woo or hold them as patrons. They also have access to private substitutes. If the public park is unsatisfactory, they can move to the country club, which may persuade public officials to attend to their complaints in order to get them back as users of public facilities. Average citizens lack the influence needed for effective complaining and the prestige that makes them desired users. They find it makes sense to obtain and equip a private backyard.

For users, commercial service monopolies are clearly no better than public ones. In fact they can be worse, since monopolistic public services are accountable to politicians who have to run for reelection and who may react to citizen complaints at election time. Commercial monopolies may not have to answer to anyone.

However, commercial services and goods are rarely supplied by monopolies and thus must nearly always compete for the users' favor, giving those users who can afford the price some choice and thus at least some control. Although in most communities across the country small retailers still predominate, many of the manufacturers and distributors of brand merchandise and the chains that dominate the shopping malls are now huge firms which may be regional or national oligopolies, sharing the national market with only a handful of other giants. Nonetheless, the people who use these facilities are concerned mainly with goods they buy, and oligopolistic chains usually do not offer goods on an oligopolistic basis. The manufacture of breakfast cereals has long been dominated by two firms, but each of these supplies many cereals which compete against each other. As a result even people who hate oligopolies may not know or care that they are buying from them. Of course, makers of brand-name goods can engage in oligopolistic pricing, but even then they often also supply cheaper private and generic brands.

In theory, monopolies-*cum*-utilities regulated for the benefit of the users are preferable to oligopolies, but regulatory agencies often end up siding with the suppliers—and electric utilities are very unpopular with their customers in many places. Under some conditions, therefore, even duopolies, two firms in control of a market, may still be better than regulated monopolies, for as long as minimal competition survives, so does minimal choice for users. The amount and kind of choice may be insufficient, but it remains better than nothing. The Yale political scientist Robert E. Lane puts it well when he writes:

> While the equal treatment associated with public goods appeals to some senses of justice, in general people prefer to tailor the satisfaction of their wants to their own particular tastes, something they can do in the market but not easily in their dealings with government. If they have the money they can buy the kinds of cars they want, but they cannot order the kind of road system they want.[20]

In the ultimate analysis, however, almost all services, public and commercial, have drawbacks when they are compared to goods. Although polls suggest that people may be unhappy about specific goods, for example the quality of American cars, and with the prices of many goods, their prime discontent is with services, particularly those which are virtual necessities. People are most unhappy about the value they get for their money, some being dissatisfied about quality, others with price. Their unhappiness ranges far and wide, including hospital services, bank fees, college tuition, insurance, and repairs of most kinds.[21]

Even when prices are too high, goods are nevertheless almost always more desirable than services, precisely because they increase the opportunity for individual choice. To begin with, goods can be manufactured, and therefore diversified more cheaply and easily than services, so that even moderate-income people can afford some choice. Goods which enable people to supply their own services are even cheaper. The arrival of the family's first child immediately makes the home washing machine cheaper than a laundry service or commercial automatic laundry, although only if the family can afford the machine.

Also, goods can be taken home and used privately, freeing people from undesired contact with others. The VCR is a perfect illustration; people can now obtain movies they can watch in the privacy of their own home rather than in a public theater, by themselves or with friends. They also have more choice than local movie theaters, television networks, and pay-cable companies in the average American community can offer.

Even the affluent, who can afford exclusive private services, may sometimes find goods preferable. Health-conscious Americans who can afford them are now buying their own exercise machines, mainly because they are cheaper and more convenient than private gyms but also because, as one woman quoted in the *New York Times* put it, "When you're out of shape, the last thing you want is to be surrounded by a lot of Jane Fondas dancing around."[22] The gym, like the movie theater, may offer an opportunity for communal gathering, but community brings with it the possibility of invidious comparison with, and unwanted criticism from, strangers.

Products are, finally, viewed as superior to services because the latter involve users in an ongoing supplier relationship, which can become dependent or unequal if the supplier is endowed with more power, prestige, or expertise, or is not accountable. Middle Americans must acknowledge status and power inferiorities when they use the services of a public official armed with monopoly power or a supplier who is a professional. Even when doctors and other professionals do not collect a fee, they still demand deference. In other cases users may have to acknowledge dependency, which reduces their control even more than the payment of deference. Most buyers of most goods rarely become dependent on sellers because they can always go elsewhere for their goods.

Middle America's feelings about goods are perhaps best illustrated by the two most expensive ones almost all of them buy: the single-family house and the car. People who can afford to buy such a house do so; those who cannot afford it rent or buy something else and wait for the day that they can get the house. In only a handful of American cities do people who can buy a home prefer to rent or buy an apartment, and, except in Manhattan, they are an insignificant minority. The preference for the house never seems to change, whatever the state of the housing market. According to the 1985 installment of a regular Gallup poll, 84 percent of the respondents said they prefer to live in towns, rural areas, or in the suburbs of various-sized cities, all of which are communities built up with single-family houses.[23] In eight of the last ten years, nearly 90 percent of all home purchases have been of a single-family house.[24]

One reason for the popularity of the single-family house is that it maximizes privacy, control over the immediate environment, and as much distance as possible from the next owner. Housing industry "folk wisdom" has it that the average American would ideally like to live in a farmhouse on 3 to 4 acres, but near a fully equipped suburban shopping center. The more money people have, the more acreage and distance from neighbors they are likely to buy. Even when the house and the lot are small, the free-standing house is usually preferred over the row house or the townhouse, both of which replace distance between houses with a party wall. Ownership of the house adds a little more control as well as security. It is also cheaper than a rented apartment, but that is a political bargain because home ownership is subsidized by governments. The subsidies themselves reflect the widespread and intensely felt demand for the house, to which politicians seeking election have therefore responded generously.

The car goes along with the house, although in fact people buy it first. Sometimes they must buy it because there is no mass transit, but too often there is no mass transit because everyone who can afford cars has bought the necessary number. The car still offers people the freedom to pick up and go off somewhere—which is one reason people sometimes "love" their cars. Like the house, the car is a private space, but it offers its owner other opportunities—for example, control over time except in traffic jams and a sense of power at high speed. Few highway drivers observe the *de jure* speed limit, and many violate the higher *de facto* one actually enforced by the police. Instead of obeying the law, drivers buy the "fuzz buster," which warns them when the police are in the vicinity, and which has earned its inventor $175 million in its first 10 years.[25]

Like houses, cars have a number of disadvantages and inefficiencies, but their users do not see them or admit to them once they are pointed out. Nor do the politicians, who make sure that the resulting costs are paid for out of general funds.

Government as the Guardian of Economic Security

Conservatives like to think of all Americans as being anti-government; one of them even suggests that "the distinctive aspect of the American Creed is its antigovernment character."[26] In a literal sense the conservatives may be right. Although middle Americans have little interest in government or business as abstractions, they are exposed to far more anti-government than anti-business propaganda.

Big Business is at this writing more unpopular than Big Government, but people have kinder feelings toward small business, and according to a Roper poll, nearly a majority think it does not have enough influence in the country.[27] Americans do not seem to have the same feeling about small government, however. Indeed, people think they get more for their money from the federal government than from state or local government, their dislike of "Washington" notwithstanding.[28]

That they feel this way is not surprising. Most of their doubts about public services are concentrated on the quality-of-life programs mainly supplied by local governments; they nearly always want government to be protective of their economic security, and that protection is supplied mainly by Washington.

Although some observers have described middle Americans as ideological conservatives and programmatic liberals, that description may itself be overly ideological. Whether people call themselves conservatives or liberals varies with the times and with who is in the White House, but popular demand for certain kinds of governmental economic protection never abates. In 1960, during a period of full employment, 63 percent of the respondents to a Gallup poll agreed that "the government in Washington ought to see to it that everybody who wants to work has a job"; and in 1978, when 7 percent were officially jobless, three-fourths of the respondents to a *New York Times*–CBS News poll, including 70 percent of those describing themselves as conservatives, agreed once more.[29] In 1980, with the unemployment rate the same, 61 percent of poll respondents supported the statement that "the federal government should guarantee a job to every person who wants to work," and in 1985 when the jobless rate was 7.1 percent, 50 percent agreed with the more drastic notion that governmental responsibility included "financing of projects to create new jobs."[30]

Similarly large numbers are in favor of government support of health costs. In 1960, nearly two-thirds of those polled endorsed the idea that "the government ought to help people get doctors and hospital care at low cost," and by 1978, 81 percent agreed.[31] In 1985, 84 percent supported a similar but not identical statement.[32]

In addition, people want government to guard their pay and savings against inflation, provide help with educational costs, clean up the environment, and more generally make sure that they can both work and enjoy the fruits of their labor. The desired protective pattern can be seen when people are asked questions about government regulation. Just as they would like the government to cut spending *in general,* so they would like either less regulation or no increase—an attitude that appears to have changed little since the middle of the Depression.[33] When it comes to their own pay, people are similarly opposed to regulation, but the picture changes with respect to prices. At the height of the inflation of the late 1970s, Roper found about a third favoring a wage freeze but a majority favoring a price freeze.[34] In 1985, three-fourths of the respondents to a GSS question felt it was government's responsibility "to keep prices under control."[35]

When people encounter other undesirable conditions, their opposition to regulation in general ends. Judging by a 1976 Harris poll, the conditions they want the federal government to regulate most often are "product safety standards, product quality standards, pollution controls, corruption, equal employment opportunities for women . . . for minorities [and] allowable price increases."[36] According to other polls, they also want to be protected against false advertising, dangers on the job, and loss of pensions. They generally say that they support protective regulation even at the risk of higher prices and costs.

That majorities of poll respondents support a variety of protective programs does not necessarily persuade the federal government to supply them, even in an era in which every president now keeps his own pollster on hand in the White House. Politicians (and their pollsters) know that what people say they favor is not always equivalent to what they demand, and because the moderate and low-income people who favor such protection the most do not vote as often as more affluent citizens, they do not provide enough political support for these programs. Poll respondents are drawn from all income groups, which is why I propose in Chapter 6 that polls are one possible mechanism for making American democracy more representative.

However, the ambivalence of middle and other Americans about government protection and sustenance services because of their opposition to higher taxes must also be invoked sometimes to explain the dearth of political action. For one thing, Americans may forget their demand for sustenance and go along quietly when the business community lobbies for service cuts in order to reduce taxes. Even badly needed services or those very popular with large majorities among the citizenry may suffer when politicians feel that budget cutting and tax saving are yet more popular—and when ambivalent Americans are unable or unwilling to disagree vocally enough.

Idealism in Middle American Individualism

Individualism is often perceived as equivalent to selfishness and self-interest, but it also includes idealistic values. Surely the most important component of middle American idealism is the continued pursuit of the so-called "motherhood" values. These include, among others, the beliefs in generosity, fairness, honesty, personal responsibility, and hard work, which are generally described as Judeo-Christian but are endorsed as secular ideals by nonreligious Americans as well. Not everyone subscribes to all of these values and not all who subscribe practice them at all times, but despite the cynicism of some social critics, far more people follow them than is commonly thought.

The vaunted American generosity is genuine, and help is freely extended to neighbors and even strangers as long as they do not look threatening. A 1986 Gallup poll reported that 39 percent of its respondents said they were involved in "charitable or social service activities, such as helping the poor, the sick or the elderly."[37]

People are equally generous and helpful to innocent victims of natural and human disasters—and villainies. Human interest stories about such victims in the news media usually generate donations sent in by audience members. As befits individualists, however, the feelings and acts of generosity are extended mainly to individual victims, and as noted previously, people appear to see no conflict between aiding an individual and denying help to the group or class from which that individual comes.

For example, poor individuals who have suffered particularly from injustice, bureaucratic inertia, or administrative bias may receive customized help from public officials, not to mention campaigning politicians, as long as they can show that they are deserving. However, as a population the poor are not treated in this manner and are sometimes thought to be guilty of undeservingness without a chance to prove themselves innocent. Ronald Reagan has been only too typical in this respect, having often been eager to help individuals but equally eager to deprive poor people as a class of the quite meager benefits of the War on Poverty.

Fairness appears to have become a more significant ideal over the last half century, probably because it is particularly relevant to and necessary for a diverse society. Fairness has many meanings, but in some respects it has turned into a simile for equality. Most of the time, equality means equality of opportunity or treatment, and perhaps the most frequent middle American conception of equality is equal opportunity for people to work hard so as to achieve success, whether in escaping poverty or becoming rich. However, that conception is also resolutely individualistic, since people are prepared to remove unfair obstacles to opportunity that stand in the way of individuals but are less willing to help entire groups or classes held back by unfair obstacles.

Americans may be aware of the degree of income inequality

in the country, but they do not necessarily favor egalitarian remedies. In a 1985 study of attitudes toward equality, for example, 59 percent of the respondents indicated that people should be paid on the basis of "the kind of work they do" rather than individual need, and 81 percent chose work skill over family need.[38] A 1979 survey of manual and clerical workers showed that 93 percent of the former and 84 percent of the latter felt corporations obtained more income than they deserved, but only 58 percent favored limiting business profits. Large majorities also felt labor unions and professionals were receiving too high an income, but 40 percent even placed welfare clients in that category.[39]

According to one study, only 21 percent agreed that there should be an upper limit on personal income, but when the question concerned reduction of income inequality between rich and poor, there was somewhat more support for an egalitarian policy.[40] In the 1985 GSS, 39 percent of respondents agreed that it was the government's responsibility to reduce income differences between people of high and low income, while 41 percent disagreed.[41] In the 1986 GSS, 51 percent thought the government should reduce income differences between the poor and the rich, but people probably knew they were not being asked for a sacrifice, since the main reduction method suggested was "raising the taxes of wealthy families."[42] Many other studies have shown that while there is some sympathy for demanding higher taxes from the rich, economic equality itself is not widely favored. Fairness does not require equality of results or outcomes.[43]

Fairness also translates into tolerance, but once more there are limits. People are willing to pay for public services used only by others if they are not too expensive, and to respect religions with which they disagree and cultures they consider inferior as long as these do not celebrate practices or values condemned in middle America. Over half the respondents to a series of civil liberties questions asked by NORC over the last 15 years go along with having atheists, socialists, communists, racists, and advocates of military dictatorship speak in their communities, but they are opposed to advocates of such views teaching in a college, perhaps because there might be a captive audience of young people.[44]

Whites say they are ready to live near blacks and support residential and school integration but not bussing.[45] Indeed, 25 percent of whites responding to the 1986 GSS said black families were living on their block, and another 15 percent that they were living one to three blocks or within a quarter mile.[46] When blacks arrive in large numbers or when they are poor, white tolerance often ends, however. Affluent whites can resort to quiet legal or political action to keep blacks out, but middle Americans often feel that they must move, and those unable or unwilling to do so sometimes react with visible and occasionally violent disapproval. Ever since the Kerner Commission decided it could see a motivational pattern underlying such white behavior and invented the term racism, middle Americans have sometimes been called racist, but there is no reason to believe they are more racist in motive than other whites. They may at times give in to their fears about threats to their economic or social status, their property values or their safety, and talk or act in openly discriminatory fashion. However, they lack the ability of many affluent whites to live and work under conditions in which such fears are irrelevant. Sometimes the fears are imagined and sometimes the real villains are economic and political forces that set blacks against white middle Americans, but poor blacks are convenient scapegoats and so—albeit to a lesser extent—are white middle Americans.[47]

Middle American idealism is thought to be applicable not only to individuals but also to organizations and institutions. People hope that these entities will pursue the relevant values as if they were individuals, although few are surprised when this is not the case. As a consequence people distinguish between immoral organizations and moral individuals in them.[48] One result of this distinction is people's impulse to behave immorally toward organizations unless they are dealing with representatives they perceive as moral. Whenever possible, however, they search for moral individuals in organizations with which they must deal, usually through the use of personal contacts. Another consequence of the distinction is the typically American conception that the governments of opponent or enemy nations ar morally faulty but their individual citizens are not, and that people-to-people contacts which avoid governments can overcome foreign policy conflicts and even enmities.

Honesty is the principal value for which people "test" in their dealings with organizations, but when it comes to government and private enterprise they also want something more. Political leaders are expected to be representative, to represent the interests and values of the ordinary people who provide most of the votes that elect them. However, people also want their politicians to represent the country, and to do so honestly and competently as well as in an altruistic fashion. Elected officials should transcend their self-interest, working together with citizens in behalf of the public interest, an ideal that demands universal sharing and personal sacrifice in behalf of the country, or the general welfare— a term that emphasizes the welfare of those not able to exercise economic or political power. In effect, people want American democracy to be altruistic.[49]

A parallel goal applies to the economy. While business firms are not expected to act altruistically, they are supposed to be responsible—to seek reasonable profits but not to put profit ahead of their social responsibility to the country. In addition they are expected to produce safe goods and not exploit workers or cheat customers in the process.

The importance of the ideals of altruistic democracy and responsible capitalism may be one reason for the public's low degree of confidence in the leaders of Big Government and Big Business. Pollsters have been measuring the public's confidence in the country's major institutional leaders since the 1960s, and generally speaking, these days people tend to have confidence in the leaders of medicine, the church, and science but not very much in those of the major corporations or the executive branch of the federal government. In 1966, 55 percent of the GSS respondents indicated that they had a great deal of confidence in the leaders of major business firms, but then that proportion began to decline sharply, hitting bottom in 1975, when only 19 percent had a great deal of confidence in them. It rose to 23 percent in 1980 and stood at 25 percent in 1986.[50]

Confidence in governmental executives has always been somewhat lower than that in business executives. In 1966, 41 percent of NORC's respondents said they had a great deal of confidence in them, but that percentage dropped precipitously in the 1970s, falling to 14 percent in 1974 and 12 percent in 1980. The figure has, however, gone up again during the 1980s, doubling to 24 percent in 1986.[51] Indeed, from 1982 to 1986 confidence in governmental institutions increased somewhat more than in all nongovernmental ones, including Big Business.[52]

Pollsters have also asked questions that require respondents to evaluate the altruistic aspects of government, and the answers indicate that many poll respondents feel the government performs poorly. One such question about altruistic democracy asks people to say whether "the government is pretty much run by a few big interests looking out for themselves or for the benefit of all the people," and in the last 15 years most people have felt it was run by the big interests. When the question was initially asked in 1964, only 28 percent of the respondents believed that government was run by and for the big interests, but that proportion climbed rapidly soon after; it was 55 percent in 1970, 73 percent most of the decade, and 77 percent in 1980. It declined a little subsequently, however, and stood at 59 percent in 1984.[53]

Some of the other questions asked about altruism are answered in different proportions, but the answers follow the same general trend lines.[54] Whether people are asked about their confidence in national leaders or about the ability of government to achieve altruistic values, their responses follow similar ups and downs and most likely reflect their general feelings about what is happening in the country. No one has yet proved which events, if any, have a decisive influence on these poll response trends, but lack of confidence in the leadership and criticism of the government's democratic performance began to increase at the time of the ghetto disorders and the conflicts over the war in Vietnam—as well as the arrival of Richard Nixon in the White House. The critical attitudes rose further during Watergate, the OPEC oil price increase, and the stagflation of the 1970s, and the various crises in the latter part of the Carter administration. All the negative answers declined again during the first term of the Reagan administration, presumably because of the President's political successes.

Nonetheless, one regular factor behind people's answers, particularly to the confidence questions, appears to be a decline in the inflation rate and even more so in the unemployment rate.[55] In fact, Lipset and Schneider, who have done the most comprehensive study of these questions, go so far as to suggest that a 1 percent drop in the unemployment rate leads to a 3 percent rise in confidence in the government.[56] Perhaps people do not make distinctions between leaders and the institutions they lead. Consequently, in responding to the pollsters they may be saying that when the country and they are in economic difficulties, they lose confidence in most leaders and in the credibility of the economy, the government and the major institutions as well. While people wish private enterprise would be responsible and government altruistic, for them the main purpose of Big Business and Big Government and perhaps of all institutions is to safeguard their economic well-being. In the end people's idealism may be tempered by their continuing need for economic security.

Meanwhile the countrywide dedication to ideal political and economic leaders and institutions is restated ritually once a week by the very popular "60 Minutes," which reports in highly dramatic form violations of the ideals by political and economic villains. True, the program focuses mainly on graft, concentrates on petty villains, and ignores systemic governmental and corporate corruption. In addition, it only exposes villains and upholds the ideals; it does not generally look at the conditions that produce violations of the ideals. These conditions may be kinds of economic growth that encourage the selling and buying of zoning changes or the forms of scarcity that spawn black marketeers, but neither the viewers nor the producers of the program are interested in the temptations thrown up by economic or political conditions. Resolutely individualistic, "60 Minutes" tells stories about people who give in to such temptations.

Three

Organizational Avoidance

The values with which middle Americans judge government and business are connected to the structure of their own lives. These lives are organized around a family or household in which members have *intimate* (though not solely sexual) relationships. The family, as well as each of its members, is also involved in a number of *informal* groups or networks, usually consisting of nonintimate relatives, friends, and some neighbors, but also of schoolmates, work colleagues, club members, and others. Everyone has dealings with *formal* organizations, beginning for most adults with the workplace but ranging over a variety of local and perhaps even national organizations. Most of them are voluntary associations or bureaucracies, from churches to government agencies.

This structure of everyday life is common to virtually all Americans. Middle Americans may differ from upper-middle-class and upper-class America in that they are more likely to follow a pattern of *organizational avoidance*. They seek mainly intimate and informal relations and groups, and try to avoid all but the essential contacts with formal organizations, not only the national ones of the "larger society" but also local ones.

Some observers believe organizational avoidance to be a contemporary condition, seeing it as a "reprivatization" effect that occurred in the 1970s as an escape from collective action by disappointed protesters of the 1960s.[1] Since active protesters numbered at most 1 percent of the total population, however, they could not possibly have invented such a widespread practice. Actually, organizational avoidance is a normal and very much older by-product of American individualism, for Alexis de Tocqueville observed it 150 years ago. It was then already so taken for granted that he described it at the very beginning of his analysis of American individualism:

> Individualism is a mature and calm feeling, which disposes each member of the community to sever himself from the mass of his fellows and to draw apart with his family and friends, so that after he has thus formed a little circle of his own, he willingly leaves society at large to itself.[2]

Informal Groups and Formal Organizations

The family or household and its various intimate and other relations are obviously of the highest importance for virtually all people, for there they carry out their most private activities and express their most private feelings. In the family, people can "be themselves," undertaking the private component of their search for self-development. Single and divorced adults must look to other institutions for some of these pursuits.

Informal groups come in many varieties. They can consist of two friends who get together regularly, or a half dozen neighbors who meet for consciousness raising or athletics. They can mix family, friends, and neighbors, as in the peer groups of the same age and gender still found in working-class communities, or they can be work colleagues who relax in a coffee shop after work.[3] Whatever their size or makeup, however, all informal groups lack the explicit rules, bylaws, charters, tables of organization, and other structures found in formal organizations. Some informal groups come into being for a specific task and then disband—or grow into permanent and probably formal voluntary associations, for example, baby-sitting exchanges or reading clubs—but most are less explicitly purposive. They are called hanging groups and gangs among younger people; cliques, friendship circles, and even clubs among adults, although often they are not formal clubs. In fact they are so informal that they are not easily named. Many seem to be devoted mostly to "having fun," but they perform other, more "serious" functions at the same time. People often find spouses from among those of their companions with whom they can "have fun." Concurrently, informal groups are sites for discussing topical issues, from entertainment preferences to social and individual dilemmas and problems.[4]

Although friendship and other informal group relations are distinct from familial ones, they often overlap with familial activities. Some friends are so close to the family or to individuals in it that close friendship becomes a private and intimate relationship. Even more distant friends may participate in some family social activities, and families often know the people and relationships that dominate the informal lives of their members.

Formal organizations exist for nearly every kind of human activity, in tiny workplaces or large corporations, churches, schools, armies, and nuclear-freeze lobbies. Formal organizations normally have stated goals and purposes, even if other goals may be pursued with more energy; they strive to carry out pre-scheduled and more or less planned activities even if schedules and plans are often not followed.

Conversely, informal groups are generally spontaneous, but they nonetheless have regular routines and unspoken rules; otherwise they could not persist. Informal groups lack explicit membership rolls, but there are those who belong and those who do not, and entry is hardly open—which is why clique is a pejorative term. People invite, choose, and exclude, so that associates tend to be like-minded and fairly homogeneous in some traits and major interests. In the absence of formal rules, the major regulating devices are mutual trust, reciprocity, gossip and social pressure, and banishment if nothing else works. Formal organizations, on the other hand, either are open to everyone if they are public bodies, or recruit people for particular functions. In doing so, they frequently pay little attention to people's personal traits and therefore to people as distinctive individuals. Conversely, an informal group which fails to respect some individual peccadillos will not last long.

Formal organizations and informal groups differ particularly around modes of participation. Informal groups can exist only as long as people participate in them, and as a result, informal group participation often requires some degree of emotional involvement in or loyalty to the group. Formal organizations cannot exist without participation either, except on paper, but they want something quite different. They need people who can help achieve the organization's overt and covert purposes, and they are willing to pay them for doing so, which is how most of us earn our living. Formal organizations do not reject emotional involvement and may have to depend on it if they can only afford to pay with honor, status, or the promise of salvation. Still, achievement of organizational purposes remains uppermost, and usually growth and the maximization of influence or control, profit, and prestige are major purposes.

Unlike most informal groups, formal organizations have virtually permanent divisions of labor as well as authority, even if they pay only in promises of salvation; thus, some people are always in charge of the organizational purposes and of other people who are expected to carry them out. "Whistleblowers," employees who place higher priority on ethical norms or performance standards even if they interfere with organizational purposes, are usually stigmatized as disloyal and forced out. The mass media have helped make heroes out of whistleblowers, but they are still generally fired once the glare of media attention has been turned off, so much so that federal legislation to protect their jobs was passed in the mid-1980s.

Most formal organizations need people either as workers or as users of what they supply or both, whether the organizations are firms selling goods, hospitals providing health, or churches serving worshippers. Workers typically want organizations to treat them as responsible people and in a democratic fashion; users would like organizations to be responsive to their needs and wishes. The organizations do not necessarily give priority to either workers or users unless they are very scarce or must be coddled for other reasons. Otherwise, organizational needs tend to come first. Customers exist to be sold, and the serving of clients may be arranged to fit the needs of the organization or the convenience of the senior staff, as anyone who has ever been a hospital patient knows. Patients as well as college students come and go, but doctors and professors can be there for a lifetime. Where and when such suppliers are strongly favored over users, users with some choice go elsewhere, and as I suggested in Chapter 2, people sometimes prefer buying goods instead of using services because buying involves only a superficial contact with a supplier.

Partly because of their distinctive characteristics—and shortcomings—almost all formal organizations generate informal groups which exist inside them and are essential to their operation. One type may be thought of as organizational *motors,* because they help keep the formal organization running. These are typically found in workplaces, where they carry out needed actions or make required decisions not facilitated by the official purposes, rules, and structures. For example, Michael Burawoy has shown how workers in a machine shop invented their own production "game" that enabled them to guarantee the shop a profit, maximize their own earnings, and in the process obtain more emotional rewards of working.[5] Other types of factory floor motors "redesign" work orders and plans supplied by engineers distant from the production process so that the product can actually be manufactured.[6]

At the higher levels of formal organizations, the people in charge usually set up informal groups not to be found in tables of organization to do the final decision-making work. Some decision-making motors consist only of the most trusted advisers of the top-ranked individuals, excluding even people with the official responsibility for making decisions. Presidents of the U.S. typically have three to six close advisers chosen from the White House staff and at times the Cabinet, but they also listen to "kitchen cabinets" that include old friends and confidants. They not only help make decisions but also assist the president in coping with the power struggles endemic to the White House and its formal structure.

Even the lowliest body of elected officials is likely to establish an informal decision-making group to discuss and rehearse what it plans to do before it must present its decisions in a public meeting. The informal group, which may consist of the entire body or a steering committee, seeks to create the image of a cohesive decision-making body for the public meeting that cannot be swayed by citizen pressure or public protest.[7]

Another type of motor group develops when the law or social norms prevent the formal organization from doing what it exists to do. "Organized" crime has only vestigial formal organizations, and is actually run by informal groups that demand so intense a level of trust, secrecy, and cooperation that they are often called families. In some "families" the leaders are tied to each other further through marriages. Because political parties and governments are highly visible, informal political machines come into being to establish the fund-raising mechanisms and alliances that are prohibited or stigmatized by the norms of altruistic democracy. The traditional urban machines are nearly extinct today, but less picaresque versions can be found in virtually every American community of any size in which incumbents aim to get themselves reelected.

Perhaps the most dramatic illustration of the informal group motor comes from World War II studies that indicate that soldiers in combat fought less against the enemy or for their country than for an informal group of buddies that existed alongside the formal platoon.[8] Their friendships maximized the likelihood of their own survival, the unspoken agreement being that everyone would help everyone else, and they supplied an emotionally rewarding social relationship which helped soldiers do the grisly work of war. Similar motors exist in mines and other dangerous workplaces.

A further type of informal group can be called a *haven* because it literally supplies temporary shelter from a difficult or dangerous world.[9] Resembling families in this function, havens allow colleagues at work, for example, to meet and gripe about the rule violations and other outrages of their supervisors, executives, colleagues, and the organization itself. In this relationship, they not only defend each other and their values from the formal organization, but they become emotionally closer than formal workplace colleagues. An additional function of the haven is to supply relaxation and play to offset the routine and boredom of work, members meeting during coffee breaks, at lunch, in bathrooms and corridors, or at nearby taverns and coffee shops after work.

A particularly useful kind of haven can be found in factories and offices, among assembly-line workers and members of typing pools, for example, to help people cope with unreasonable demands from management. First spotted by industrial sociologists after the arrival of the time-and-motion engineer, these havens learned how to alter or sabotage the formal work rules of the organization to prevent speed-ups.[10] When they establish ways to discourage ratebusters—workers who produce more than, and show up, their colleagues—and regulate the amount and flow of production in other ways, they also take on some motor functions. Likewise, motor groups can become havens during or after work hours.

A somewhat different kind of informal group appears in voluntary associations, those typically American formal organizations people join to pursue political, civic, charitable, and related purposes. Neither a motor nor a haven, it is best described as exactly what it is, an informal sociable group which may use the facilities of the formal association for meeting in exchange for becoming members and helping the association with money or man—and womanpower when the officers or paid staff need some assistance. Sometimes the informal group is a preexisting one; sometimes it is formed when people meet each other in the voluntary association itself. In either case, the members may have only a superficial interest in the purposes and activities of the association, but the organization benefits from their periodic financial and other contributions and from their being on its membership roll, which increases its size. Not all voluntary associations invite such members, but virtually all associations combine work—or money raising—with some informal group sociability. Churches and synagogues use this approach as well, attracting additional worshippers by providing opportunities for informal groups to meet or to form in their social program.

A final type is not an informal group, but an informal relationship that develops when suppliers of goods and services, working for formal organizations, establish *quasi-friendly* connections with users. Policemen on the beat often make such connections with store owners, exchanging information or a cup of coffee on a cold day for a little more protection. Department store supervisors or supermarket managers may establish similar connections with some regular customers, trading special handling and a little personal service for good will, store loyalty, and a touch of friendliness. National corporations which establish branch factories and offices generally expect their local managers to develop these relations and to join formal community groups to build good will.

As these examples suggest, quasi-friendly relations are not necessarily spontaneous; they are generally purposive, providing reciprocal benefits for their participants. Such relations can, however, be turned into techniques for selling and manipulation. Flight attendants and other women workers are forced to develop a manufactured—and nerve-wracking—friendliness, while corporate branch managers may be asked by their national superiors to use the good will they have developed through quasi-friendly relations to advance the organization's local economic or political aims.[11] Investigators, whether they work for news organizations, police departments, or welfare agencies, sometimes use quasi-friendly techniques to trap unsuspecting people into giving up information they would normally withhold.

In small towns, a nonmanipulative and only partly purposive kind of quasi-friendly relation is virtually automatic and all-encompassing (unless people do not get along), because everyone knows almost everyone else. Even so, the same kind of informal relation comes into being in other places, wherever and whenever formal organizations are too unwieldy or inefficient. Cities are stereotyped as places where quasi-friendly relations cannot flourish, but they are particularly prevalent there because people need to dispel the insecurity and unpredictability associated with living amidst strangers. Such relations can at times turn into urban havens.

The point that informal groups often make formal organizations viable or bearable is hardly original. A good deal of early sociological research stressed this point, but it is sometimes forgotten. Today American society and our image of it are dominated by its formal organizations, particularly large national ones which issue a good deal of publicity about themselves. Nevertheless, informal groups may be more important now than in the past. As formal organizations grow in number and size, the need for motors and havens increases as well. The formal organizations that have taken over functions once performed by the family or that are supplying families with previously unknown goods and services have spawned their own informal groups, and these probably play a greater role in people's lives—and in society itself—than is commonly recognized. Putting it another way, the informal groups connected with home and family in earlier times have now been supplemented by informal groups operating in the interstices of formal organizations.

Informal groups must not, however, be romanticized. Nor should they be equated with the warm, closely knit, highly consensual groups associated with the idealized image of small-town America or the immigrant ethnic enclave. Informal groups are often exclusionary, and relations inside them can be competitive, manipulative, and conflict-ridden. Even havens are not havens 100 percent of the time. Informal groups do not avoid power struggles simply because they are informal, and if they control resources or power, struggles over these can be expected. In this respect, the cliques that run local voluntary associations are no different from those which make the decisions in huge corporations, even if the stakes are higher in the latter.

Acceptable, Unavoidable, and Avoidable Organizations

Educated professionals and managers, whether upper middle class or upper class, are directly or indirectly trained to operate in, as well as to run, formal organizations, but many middle Americans are not. They are "far less skilled at the antagonistic cooperation which characterizes a great deal of professional and upper middle class work."[12] Their dealings with formal organizations being mainly as employees and users, they are likely to see the underside of the administrative apparati, to suffer from the mistakes of higher-ups, and to be treated as people of low status. Accordingly, middle Americans divide formal organizations into three kinds: a handful of acceptable ones, those that are unavoidable but have to be endured, and those that are avoidable other than for brief contacts, in which case they can be ignored.

Among the prime acceptable organizations are retail firms in which people can maintain the minimal, even distant relationship involved in being customers. Many people seem to enjoy shopping, and particularly the successful hunt for bargains, which enables them to save a little of their still disposable income and at the seeming expense of a large company.

Another acceptable organization is the voluntary association, although comparatively few middle Americans belong to it. In fact, while Americans are known as "joiners," the label is not entirely fitting, since people typically join only one or two.[13] While 70 percent of the 1986 GSS sample reported memberships, 60 percent of the joiners belonged to one or two organizations, and the most frequently mentioned was a church group, which is not always voluntary.[14] Generally, association membership is very much an upper-middle-class activity. For example, according to a 1976 survey which separated union membership (also not always voluntary) from other memberships, only 10 percent of grade school graduates and 27 percent of high school graduates but 56 percent of college graduates and 73 percent of those who went to graduate school reported associational memberships, and occupational and income data showed the same skewed patterns.[15]

Membership studies do not indicate how many people are active or how many are mainly using the associations as bases for informal social or other pursuits. Some light on this topic is shed by a 1982 Gallup poll, according to which a quarter of all people who said they did volunteer work were actually involved in "informal activities done without organizational support."[16] In addition, middle Americans volunteer far less often than upper-middle-class people. In a 1981 study of volunteers, Roper found that 44 percent of college graduates but only 21 percent of high school graduates reported doing volunteer work regularly.[17] Class differences in participation have always been present, however, for virtually all kinds of organizational participation.

As suggested previously, the prime unavoidable organization for most people is the workplace. While people's feelings about their jobs and colleagues are often positive, the workplace and the working conditions in it can be a burden. A majority of Americans are still employed in workplaces with fewer than 20 workers, and some of these may be organized like informal or quasi-friendly groups. However, autocratically run small workplaces, including family-owned ones, and bureaucratically run larger ones encourage their workers to develop emotional distance and to defend themselves with suspicion and cynicism.

I have been struck over the years that people who work for large organizations often believe that their organizations are headed by ruthless leaders who do not shrink from cutting moral corners to achieve the organization's and their own aims—and that these leaders are probably no different in private life. Fictional media depictions of executives reflect popular beliefs and are therefore often drawn to the same specifications.

The polls about people's confidence in the country's business and government leaders discussed in Chapter 2 do not measure intensity of feelings, and thus cannot indicate how often lack of confidence is actually distrust. However, occasional polls, mostly about politicians, make it possible to guess that such distrust is widespread. For example, in a 1985 ABC News–*Washington Post* poll, 71 percent agreed that "most members of Congress will lie if they feel the truth will hurt them politically."[18] More telling is the fact that 25 years after President John Kennedy's assassination, large numbers of people still think he was the victim of a conspiracy. Even before the "contragate" investigations began in 1987, more than half the respondents in several national polls thought that President Reagan was lying about his own involvement in the affair.

Americans may dislike bureaucracy, but concurrently they dislike formal organizations for being unbureaucratic, for permitting activities they often summarize as "politics." These activities include nepotism, the rewarding of flattery and servility, financial and other kinds of corruption, and occasional outright—usually white collar—crime. Workplace havens exchange reports and outrage over the latest instances of unbureaucratic malfeasance by executives, supervisors, and ambitious coworkers.

People learn about these practices—and develop attitudes toward them—long before they are adults, in the formal organization that takes up many of their hours as children and adolescents: the school. In the early grades, students become familiar with the fact that some teachers have "pets" as well as other children against whom they discriminate on personal grounds. When students are older, they also learn about "politics" on the part of school staff members or students.

What young people—and adults—have learned at first hand or via the grapevine is backed up by the news media. "Sixty Minutes" and other forms of investigative journalism are popular because they usually present, with underplayed outrage, exposés of various kinds of "politics."[19]

Most people do not have to spend much time in any unavoidable organizations except the workplace, and most formal organizations are avoidable most of the time. Because so many American organizations are set up as voluntary associations, people can choose not to join unless they are subject to familial, peer, or other pressure. Others they can join but not attend. Over the years, less than 5 percent of union members come to regular meetings, although three-quarters of the members cast ballots in strike votes and union elections.[20] People can become members of organizations yet never do anything except send money and show up for social programs.

The avoidance of formal organizations extends into the realm of the sacred. Far more Americans believe in God than attend churches or synagogues, and those who dislike an overly bureaucratized church can find others that seek to function like informal, quasi-, and pseudo-familial groups, notably in the fundamentalist and pentecostal movements. Jews who want to avoid the synagogue altogether can worship at home, and they do. According to a 1975 survey of Boston Jewry, the five most frequently practiced religious rituals all took place at home.[21] The Passover seder, which can be celebrated with family and friends as part of a dinner and requires no synagogue attendance, has become the most popular form of Jewish worship, for 85 percent of the sample participated in the seder.[22]

"Dallas": The Formal Organization as Rich Family Gone Wrong

Popular fiction does not necessarily reflect public opinion, but the feelings middle America holds about various types of formal organizations are sometimes well represented in what people read and watch. The rugged individualist as problem solver is the central figure of the traditional western and particularly the detective story, in which the private eye or the rogue cop corrects the mistakes of the police department and other formal organizations. Since the start of the Cold War, the heroes and heroines of espionage novels have often done what the government could not do, and in the Superman comics, the James Bond novels, and their film versions, the hero has often stood in for a paralyzed president.

The moral and other themes about formal organizations are particularly well expressed in the best-known and very popular television family melodrama of the 1970s and 1980s, "Dallas," and in other representatives of the genre like "Dynasty," "Falcon Crest," and "Knots Landing."

"Dallas"—and "Dynasty"—are, at one level, exposés which report the decadence of familial life and individual character among business leaders. Although the principal figures in the dramas include good people, some of them weak, the major characters are robber baron capitalists who cut moral and other corners to gather unreasonable amounts of wealth and power and to defeat their competitors. They are strong, stubborn, and manipulative people running their corporations in arbitrary ways, evading the rules when their hunger for money or power impels them, and doing so with a ruthlessness that does not stop short of hurting family members. Employees in these organizations see their employers constantly violating moral standards, but they cannot object because they are powerless and subject to the whims of arbitrary and autocratic authority. The programs elucidate, with all the dramatic exaggeration for which popular fiction is known, why there is little confidence in business leaders. Perhaps they also reflect how factory and office employees among the viewers see some of their own bosses.[23]

"Dallas" and "Dynasty" reached the television screen in the late 1970s at a time when public confidence in national business leaders was lowest; they could thus be viewed as effects and indicators of people's fears and doubt about the country's economy. Still, the major themes of the programs are of venerable age, and both would probably have been just as successful if they had been invented in earlier decades. They are actually not very different from the novels of Arthur Hailey, Sheldon Leonard, Harold Robbins, and Irving Wallace, writers who have been producing best sellers about large businesses for many years, even if their villains are not quite as villainous as, say, J. R. Ewing.

"Dallas" and "Dynasty" touch yet another chord in middle American individualism because of their essentially familial conception of the contemporary economy. Although the major protagonists of both dramas are heads of international corporations, their companies are run as family businesses in which decisions are based on intrafamilial dynamics, especially competition among spouses, ex-spouses, siblings, parents, children, and assorted other relatives. The firms appear to be quite small, and except for receptionists, secretaries, and occasional hired experts, all other staff positions are held by family members. The corporations of "Dallas" and "Dynasty" lack production workers, clerks, middle managers, and any vestige of bureaucracy.

True, the programs are television melodramas, and television's small screen is most suited to small numbers. In addition, the programs are written for a home audience and are not intended to attract business viewers with either naturalistic or idealistic depictions. Still, the police station of "Hill Street Blues" and the medical wards of "St. Elsewhere" had much larger staffs than the Ewing Oil Company of "Dallas," or all the companies controlled by the battling ex-spouses of "Dynasty." In effect the

two programs can be viewed as dark fantasies about one kind
of modern capitalism in which the corporation is equivalent to
a rich family gone very wrong.[24]

Middle America's Distance from the Larger Society

The greatest number of avoidable organizations can be found
in what de Tocqueville called society-at-large. This is no coincidence, because middle America's concentration on life in the family and informal groups detaches and distances people from most
formal organizations which are not immediately and directly relevant to their lives and their most important purposes. Even though
people may know that Big Business, Big Government, and very
large formal organizations exert a long-term influence on their
lives, their concern and their knowledge about them remain limited as long as that influence remains indirect.

The ability of middle Americans—but not of them alone—to
ignore much of society-at-large is remarkable. Big Business does
not publicize the market research that indicates how little attention
people pay to the activities of major firms, but it is known that
people's memory of the products and firms they see continuously
in television commercials is poor, even when they enjoy the
commercials.[25]

Many studies have been done about the extent to which people
distance themselves from the activities of governmental and other
public organizations. Two almost concurrent polls illustrate the
pattern. A 1985 Gallup poll indicated that 95 percent of the respondents were then already familiar with AIDS—and this was long
before that illness became a regular page 1 news item—but according to a 1986 *New York Times*–CBS News poll, just 25 percent
knew the name of the secretary of state. The other 75 percent
of the population are not necessarily uninterested in public affairs,
however. Most can supply opinions about foreign policy, especially if the pollsters' questions remind them of the basic issues.
What they lack—or fail to remember—is specific information about
details, especially those details which are unnecessary for reaching
opinions.[26] (This is probably why few Americans seemed to be
concerned about Ronald Reagan's equivalent lacks as long as
his policies were effective and popular.) The belief that Americans
must know a series of historical and other facts in order to be

proper citizens is not new. As a result, every so often historians and cultural critics earn momentary national fame by complaining about the citizenry's ignorance of facts from which, among other things, these writers earn their livelihoods.

Lack of knowledge about foreign and national affairs or large-city politics can be explained in part by geographical remoteness. For most Americans, the federal government is far away simply because of the sheer size of the U.S. Californians frequently regard Washington as the capital of another country. Foreign affairs are affected even more by distance, since both Europe and the Far East are about 3,000 miles away from Americans who live on the East and West Coasts respectively, and much farther from Midwesterners. Even Mexico is close only for southwestern Americans.

Because of America's size, middle Americans usually deal with regional offices of the government, branch plants, offices, and franchises of national corporations, or, in the case of voluntary associations, local chapters. From their perspective "national" is frequently an unreal and at times incompetent initiators of policies that do not fit the local scene. Conflicts between central offices and branches are universal in formal organizations, and from the perspective of the former, the branches are parochial and incompetent. Both are busy correcting the "mistakes" of the other.

Geographical distance does not seem to be as crucial as social distance, however, for politicians and civic leaders in small towns complain about how many people are able to ignore the avoidable in front of their noses, knowing virtually nothing about their own communities. When I returned to Levittown, New Jersey, for a brief restudy of a community I had studied intensively 15 years earlier, several community leaders expressed surprise at the number of people who were unfamiliar with what was taking place at town hall even though they lived no more than a quarter mile away.

Statistics and other data indicating people's widespread shortage or superficiality of knowledge about current events are sometimes used to demonstrate their lack of intelligence, their apathy, or their lack of "future" orientation," said to make them incapable of considering issues to be resolved in the future. Some people undoubtedly are ignorant, or apathetic, or unable to think ahead, but many say they are bewildered by the complexity of the political world. As a result, large numbers (77 percent in 1985) agree with

another frequently used poll statement, that "politics and government seem so complicated that a person like me cannot really
know or understand what is going on."[27] What explains lack of
knowledge for some is most likely excuse for others, there being
no shortage of information that makes these subjects comprehensi-
ble. Lacking incentives to learn, a sizable number of people make
a fairly deliberate choice not to know too much and thus not to
reduce the social distance between themselves and the larger
society. Their families and informal groups are more important,
and until they have a reasonable degree of control over their
own lives, they are not very interested in society-at-large.

Consequently, social scientists, civic leaders, political activists,
and others like them who properly warn that seemingly faraway
national—or local—organizations actually have a major impact
on people's lives have always had difficulty getting their message
heard. Likewise, local officials trying to mobilize a community
to deal with a common threat often find the citizenry unwilling
and unable to see the threat until it is immediately upon them—
when the schools are actually overcrowded, or a local factory
officially announces its closing, or the nearby nuclear plant is
declared unsafe. If interviewed, people understand fully that potential threats can directly affect them some day, just as they
know that the secretary of the treasury or a national corporation
thousands of miles away can make decisions that will impose
economic hardship on them. Nonetheless, they have structured
their own ways of perceiving, and living, to keep these matters
distant until they become an immediate danger.

Instead, people "keep up" with avoidable organizations, and
with potential dangers in the larger society, through the news
media, although they do so while keeping their distance from
the news media as well. News audiences treat journalists as their
messengers from the world of formal organizations, but the messengers themselves are well aware of how uninvolved most of
their audience members remain in such organizations—and in
the news. Consequently the journalists try to make the news
relevant to people's own lives—an impossible task even when
they are supplying local news in a small city, since few events
other than the weather are relevant to everyone. The journalists
also turn the news into stories, hoping people will pay attention
to their dramatic components even when their substance is not
of personal interest to them.

Television journalists compete with the print news media by using their technology to make news stories "immediate," so people can see selected excerpts of "actual" events. Even so, television journalists have not managed to reduce significantly the distance people feel from the formal organizations reported about in the news. In 1987, the average audience for the three national half-hour evening news programs was around 26 million households (about 30 percent of all households), and the figure has been declining in the last decade, partly because viewers can get enough national news from local news programs. Frequency of viewing the network news has been going down too; in 1987, fewer than 4 percent of the households viewed 17 to 20 of the 20 programs shown over a four-week period, while about half the audience watched only one or two programs during that period.[28]

Compared to people in many other countries, many Americans, middle and others, do not seem to need daily information about the government and the other large organizations that appear in the national news. They are able, in effect, to live a good deal of their lives without a regular informational or other tie to them. The poor and the jobless, who have to depend on government for survival have greater need of such news, but they know that the news media do not often report the governmental information that they require. Corporate executives and others whose organizations depend on government contracts need news equally urgently, but they can subscribe to special newsletters.

The distance that people feel from governments is made manifest in a somewhat different way by polls that ask them to compare the condition of their personal lives with that of the country. One study that began in 1971 asks them to judge their optimism and pessimism about their own lives and then about "the situation of the country," and these judgments are placed on a 10-point rating scale. People's feelings about their own lives are always more optimistic, even when the economy is not doing well.[29] During most of the 1970s and 1980s, people's ratings for their lives averaged between 6.3 and 6.5, but their ratings for the country's situation ranged between 4.3 and 5.3 over these years.[30]

The contrast between people's personal and national assessments was even stronger in a 1972 University of Michigan study. About two-thirds of the national sample said they were delighted or pleased with their jobs and family life, but only 29 percent with life in the U.S. and 9 percent with "the way our national government is operating." A 1979 Gallup poll showed that over 60 percent said they were satisfied with their personal lives, while a third felt that way about how democracy was operating in the U.S.[31]

Although personal and country assessments go up and down with the state of the economy and other events following a pattern similar to other poll questions, the gap between the two assessments remains nearly constant. Evidently people see the country as sufficiently separate from their own lives so as not to depress their personal optimism.

The separation middle Americans and others make between their own condition and that of the country also reflects emotional distance, for otherwise people should feel personally more upset about their perception of the country's state. Last but hardly least, that distance is also moral. Middle Americans would like the morality of the family and of informal group relations to determine the actions of formal organizations and of their leaders, and they are disappointed when this is not the case. The low confidence in the leadership of so many national institutions is another expression of that disappointment.

This attitude spills over to the country as well; when pollsters ask people what is wrong with the country, they choose personal and interpersonal moral explanations. This is well illustrated by a periodic Roper poll in which respondents can react to 12 "possible causes of some of our problems in this country." The possible causes are volunteered by the pollsters, but in 1982 seven of the nine with which 40 percent or more of the sample agreed were based on personal or interpersonal shortcomings.[32] They are worth listing: "a letdown in moral values," "permissiveness in the courts," "selfishness," "people not thinking of others," "wrongdoing in government," "permissiveness of parents," and "too much emphasis on money and materialism."[33]

That people make a sharp distinction between their own lives and the state of the country does not indicate a wish to cut themselves off from the latter, for evidently they think and worry about it. Individualists that they are, they may be suggesting that they can take care of their own lives but that they are part of a country that cannot take care of itself, morally and in other ways. They may also be suggesting that they cannot take care of the country, and therefore view it with pessimism. Nonetheless, the fact that the answers to just about all of the pollsters' general questions about the country, its government, and its leaders rise and fall with the state of the economy indicates once again that people's economic security comes first and perhaps the prime function of the country, for them, is to look after that security.

Loving the Nation

The distance middle America feels from the country and the doubts it has about government and its leaders contrast sharply with the close and supportive feelings it appears to have for "the nation." In a November 1985 *New York Times* poll in which 49 percent of the people said that they trusted the federal government to do what is right only some of the time or almost never, 87 percent also said they were very proud to be Americans. Bellah and his coauthors of *Habits of the Heart* reported similarly that "we . . . found a widespread and strong identification with the United States as a national community. Yet, though the nation was viewed as good, 'government' and 'politics' often had negative connotations."[34]

People can feel close to and identify with the nation because it is neither Big Government nor "the country," both of which are associated with domestic politics. For them, the nation is a symbol. Although that nation may officially be represented by the makers of foreign policy, judging by the polls, people appear to treat it as an abstract and expressive symbol to be identified with rather than to be used for debating foreign policy.[35]

Consequently, the nation may be the kind of symbol people can fit to their own needs and wishes, and many seem to believe that it entails no special obligations. The 1983 *New York Times* Patriotism Study showed that only a third of the sample felt that any action was required to love one's country. In answer to another question, 60 percent of the actions people considered patriotic were actually compulsory: serving in the armed forces and obeying the law. Two-thirds of those who were asked what made them proud about the country referred to various kinds of freedom, and another 12 percent to the standard of living or the opportunity for upward mobility. Evidently, for many people national pride—and perhaps even patriotism—can mean the individual pursuit of various freedoms. In effect, one can love the nation because it justifies popular individualism.[36]

Furthermore, hostile acts against the nation such as the taking of hostages and terrorist attacks appear to evoke personal feelings of insult and humiliation. Governmental military actions to counter such acts, even if they are not successes, can make people feel better. Although Americans are usually opposed to sending American troops overseas to all but America's closest allies, small warlike ventures involving a handful of troops and no significant losses are acceptable (at least *ex post facto*), and there are a string of such ventures in the American past, many in Central and Latin America. Following the invasion of Grenada, President Reagan was credited with restoring people's self-respect, "making us feel good again."

When small military victories occur, the nation also becomes a team for which people can cheer, but international athletic victories that can be assigned political significance sometimes have the same effect. A wave of national joy followed the 1980 victory of the U.S. Olympic hockey team over the Soviet team, perhaps because of the recent and painful national defeat incurred by the Iranian hostage-taking. Many people seem to have been proud of the large number of medals the U.S. amassed in the 1984 Olympics, even though they must have known that a number of the American victories resulted from the absence of Soviet and other athletes.[37]

If the nation is a team, it needs a coach, and Ronald Reagan always enjoyed being called "The Gipper," after a 1920s Notre Dame football coach now viewed as a mythical leader.[38] Professional, collegiate, and high school coaches are often enthusiastic supporters of the American military establishment and its concept of patriotism, so that the difference between athletic and military heroes is further diffused or confused. Ronald Reagan expressed that diffusion on the campaign trail in 1986 when, discussing the alleged aggressive acts of the Nicaraguan government, he said:

> Even with all the tanks and gunships from the Soviet Union, . . . the Sandinistas would make it about as far as . . . Pecos before Roger Staubach came out of retirement, teamed up with some off-duty Texas Rangers and the front four of the Dallas Cowboys, and pushed the Sandinistas . . . right back to Havana where they belong.[39]

At other times the nation turns into a revered symbol—for example, around national holidays and the birthdays of national figures. Although these occasions are commingled with leisure-time activities and many have turned into retail sales events, they are also concurrent services of the civic religion.[40] Not many people may show up to worship at these services, but several polls indicate that a majority of the respondents were upset by the commercialization of the anniversaries of the Statue of Liberty and the U.S. Constitution.

Being a flexible symbol, the nation serves further needs and wishes. It is, for instance, probably more a men's than a women's symbol, at least when military victories are celebrated, for women have generally been less enthusiastic about the use of governmental force than men.[41] Accordingly, men may identify with the nation as a symbol of strength, supporting their desire for security from the Soviet Union as a military threat, a critic of American lifestyles, and an enemy of popular individualism. People may also use the nation as a symbolic weapon against internal enemies and fears. American politicians have, after all, often won reelection and prominence by attacking holders of unpopular opinions as threats to the national security. It is even possible that some Americans may feel close to the nation to compensate for their doubts about the government and their mistrust of its leaders.

Whether the nation is a sometime team or symbol of strength, in popular wars many—but by no means all—young men are prepared to fight for it and to risk their lives doing so. In some small countries the nation becomes nearly like a family in wartime, and casualties are mourned virtually as family members. America is too large and diverse to be more than a rhetorical family, but even here, the nation turns into a quasi-familial symbol during some wars.[42] The strength of nationalist emotion during wartime and the intensity of hate toward the enemy may be partly explained by familistic qualities projected onto the nation at war.

To what extent the nation remains a collective family in peacetime is hard to say, and it is probably mainly coincidence that the president of the U.S. and his wife are called the First Family. The British royal family has, however, used its marriages, childbirths, and similar events to create national ceremonies, perhaps to encourage its people to forget the country's economic and political difficulties.

Since the nation is a symbol with diverse meanings rather than an acting or policy-making agency, opinions about it are also variable. For example, when Americans become tourists overseas, they frequently become more patriotic, defending national practices and policies to their foreign hosts that they criticize when they are at home. People who are overseas for extended periods usually become homesick for more than family, friends, and community, and they may be missing the nation or certain features of the national culture.[43] Conversely, people's positive feelings about the nation may decrease if and when U.S. foreign policy proves costly or repugnant to them, as during an unpopular war like Vietnam, or if the loss of American jobs to overseas workers is blamed on the makers of foreign policy.

Opinions can be manipulated to some extent by elected—and royal—politicians. As a result, the same Americans who lack confidence in the policies and the leaders of Big Business and Big Government can feel enthusiastic about the nation. No doubt some of these feelings can be evoked by clever nationalistic advertising, but even the cleverest ads are generally effective only because they build on a foundation of feelings already held by those they are designed to affect.

Microsociety and Macrosociety

The overall structure of middle American social life can be summarized in a simple way. Because people's familial and informal group relations are often connected, these two can be thought of as their *microsocial* relations. These are set off from people's ties to formal organizations, which may be called their *macrosocial* relations. Microsocial relations are clearly at the center of middle American life, while macrosocial ones, however crucial the unavoidable ones may be, are largely at the periphery.

The sum total of a person's microsocial relations I call his or her microsociety; the macrosocial ones, his or her macrosociety. (Every person thus has a distinctive microsociety and macrosociety.) The two are marked by different purposes, activities, values, and rules, but middle Americans judge those of their microsocieties to be more desirable.

Literally, macro means large, but my dichotomy has little to do with size. Nor am I making the conventional distinction between private and public spheres of life, since microsociety refers both to informal groups connected to the privacy of home and family and those inside public formal organizations. Further, while macrosociety implies national institutions, it also includes those local organizations which middle Americans avoid as readily as national ones.

My distinction is also different from the famous pair *Gemeinschaft* and *Gesellschaft* developed by the 19th-century sociologist Ferdinand Toennies. Microsocial groups are not preindustrial or communal groups in which all relations are personal and close-knit and virtually all values are shared. Formal organizations come in a greater variety than rationalistic and rationalized business and bureaucratic structures, and besides they are shot through with informal groups and decidedly unbureaucratic "politics."[44]

Toennies—and his sociological colleagues writing in the same vein—were trying to understand and fight the spread of the industrial and corporate economy. To them it seemed as if their society was caught in an inevitable, almost evolutionary trend in which the business relations of the *Gesellschaft* were displacing the communal ones of the *Gemeinschaft*.[45] While Big Business, Big Government, and other formal organizations have grown larger over the last century and are still growing, informal groups are increasing in number as well, not only inside formal organizations but because people have more leisure and money to devote to microsocial life.[46]

Micro- and macrosociety are labels, but they help signify the extent to which people view and treat families, informal groups, and formal organizations as different social worlds.[47] The labels also highlight the social and other distances between micro and macrosocieties. Indeed, at times people treat formal organizations like strange, disliked, or feared cultures on the other side of a border or as alien territories they would prefer not to enter. The territorial analogy is relevant because one can visualize, analytically, a "gap" or "border" between informal and formal organizations that people do not like to cross. When they must cross the metaphorical border, they look for a friend inside the formal organization, and if they must spend any amount of time in the organization, they seek an informal group of people and the haven it can offer.

One possible unintended consequence of organizational avoidance is to increase the autonomy of formal organizations. If people avoid participating in these organizations, they can pay more attention to other formal organizations with which they must compete or divide the labor. Perhaps the fact that many Americans try to avoid formal organizations also frees these to go their own ways at times. However, if and when formal organizations must justify and legitimate their existence to their users, be these customers, constituents, or clients, the organizations must be *respon-*

sive to them. If middle Americans and others do not cross over the metaphorical border to participate minimally in formal organizations—or at least let them know what they want—the formal organization has to cross over that border to make contact with people in their microsocial world.

Ever since the invention of the mass media, they have been used to enter into people's microsocieties with microsocial or pseudo-microsocial messages. Politicians who run for election call attention to their familial roles, and big corporations sell themselves (and their products and services) as if they were informal groups. Middle America hardly controls the country's big organizations, but at times it requires those organizations to come calling and to behave as if they were "just microsocial folks."

Four

Political Participation and Representation

AMERICA being a voluntaristic democracy, people are not required to participate in any political activity, not even voting, so that all political institutions and organizations are automatically avoidable.

Still, political avoidance conflicts with the democratic ideal, which demands participation from the citizenry, applauds emotionally involved but disinterested activity, and calls for responsiveness of political organizations to the citizens in turn. The failure of citizens to participate in accordance with the theory is often ascribed to a moral disease called apathy.

Political organizations, from local governments to national parties, are disadvantaged by the fact that they are viewed as being avoidable. They would probably carry out their organizational purposes most efficiently if they could depend on paid staff, but when money is scarce they must depend on volunteers, who are not always reliable performers. Some volunteers will also want promises of jobs, contracts, or nominations for electoral office. Voters are equally unreliable, since they are not required to vote or to be loyal in their voting habits. Parties in power, being unable to pay voters, must induce governments to hire enough party members to obtain a loyal critical mass, even if jobholders cannot be required to vote loyally either. In any case, political party organizations still try to generate enough patronage jobs to obtain such a mass. In the meantime, no one turns down unreliable volunteers, fickle voters, or any other kind of citizen support and approval.

National political organizations, parties included, are disadvantaged by the country's size, for between elections, citizens can usually participate actively only by calling, wiring or writing to politicians. Only a few can meet with their elected representatives if and when these visit their constituencies on weekends, and equally few can get to Washington. Groups can and do go there occasionally to meet with or demonstrate against elected officials, but that requires a good deal of arranging and organizing. As a result, most citizen participation at the national level is now indirect, being carried out largely by lobbies, including public interest ones, and by professionals working for them. Only at the local level is direct participation still feasible, except in large cities.

Actually, many political organizations discourage direct face-to-face participation—other than the offering of approval—because citizens can behave unpredictably. Elected bodies are always eager for support, but they dislike protest and disagreement, as well as demands that are politically or financially too costly for the government. Although they cannot admit it, elected politicians can sometimes do without active citizen participation of any kind, because it adds further uncertainty to the often fragile processes of communication and negotiation that precede political decision-making.

However, citizens are normally not eager to participate actively in the first place because they dislike formal organizations, cannot take time from work, or are reluctant to cut into the time reserved for the family and leisure. Often, but not always, they can be "free riders," letting others do the participating because in many instances the benefits will accrue to all citizens including those who do not participate.[1]

Political organizations are aware of most people's reluctance to participate actively, and since they can normally control the conditions under which participation takes place, they can make it difficult for those few who are active by withholding information, making decisions in secret, or scheduling meetings and setting up procedures to wear them out.

Being discouraged, citizen participation can become discouraging. Leaders have to work hard to mobilize and organize others to show up at relevant meetings and exert significant pressure. Usually the leaders are unpaid amateurs leading other unpaid amateurs who must confront paid officials and professional lobbyists. Except in small towns, the politicians they must influence are themselves professionals, but even in small towns, experienced politicians are skilled in outmaneuvering amateur participators.

Citizen participation is therefore strenuous and, because the chances of success are usually small, frustrating.[2] Even when the citizens win, politicians are unlikely to admit that they bowed to "pressure." Amateurs faced with the difficulties, discouragements, and frustrations of participation get angry and drop out, reducing the power of those left behind. Increasingly, therefore, even local citizen participation is becoming professionalized, at least in larger communities, through the hiring of part-time professional participators such as lawyers, public relations persons, out-of-office politicians, and local lobbyists. This trend means yet another handicap for citizens without the necessary funds.

Additional reasons to discourage participation follow from anachronisms in the conception of citizen. Democratic theory is based on the hope that citizens will act in a disinterested fashion to pursue the public interest and the expectation that those not disinterested would be neutralized by the checks-and-balances system. In centuries past when economies were simpler, the number of roles people played and the interests they developed around these roles were fewer, adding to the possibility that citizens could act disinterestedly on many matters. Actually, however, people have always participated most actively when their own interests have been involved, remaining passive bystanders on other matters.

In today's world, people play many roles, which increases the number of interests they must juggle and reconcile. For example, as consumers alone people use hundreds of goods and services, and if they had to be politically active every time the price, quality, or supply of one of these goods or services was threatened, no time would be left for using them. In addition, the routine division of labor places people in conflicting roles. As parents they want good schools for their children; as taxpaying homeowners they prefer inexpensive ones. Middle Americans are often caught in this bind, for as old blue and white collar jobs disappear, they are particularly concerned that their children get enough education to prepare them for secure jobs, yet they are also hard pressed to pay the necessary taxes.

The resulting conflicts account for some of the logical and ideological inconsistencies in people's political thinking and in the polls. More important, voting studies have found that when people are under cross-pressures from different roles, they may refrain from voting. The temptation to become bystanders increases.

Although the strenuousness and other difficulties of political participation keep many people out of the political arena, their place in the arena is often taken by people with a single overriding interest strong enough to overcome the obstacles to participation and turn them into perpetual participators, often relentless ones. Or else they contribute money to organizations furthering their interests, which can then hire professionals to participate and lobby.

People with one overriding interest have helped bring about the recent increase in single-issue politics, around the environment, for and against abortions, in opposition to nuclear industry and nuclear weapons, as well as around gun control and secular humanism. Some single-issue groups work on an ideologically or otherwise connected set of issues; thus the opponents of secular humanism also support government deregulation and increased military expenditures, while the opponents of nuclear war are likely to favor a more comprehensive welfare state and the protection of civil liberties.

Nevertheless, the prime participators in the political arena are the same interests that have always dominated it: the suppliers—including the manufacturers, distributors, and sellers—of goods and services. They also have a single interest, the particular goods and services they supply, and thus have a greater day-to-day stake in government than either the users of those goods and services or the supporters and opponents of particular issues. The suppliers also have more time and money to defend their interests, and thus can hire professionals to plead for them, further discouraging political activity by amateur users.

In fact, there are so many reasons for amateurs to avoid political activities that it is surprising to find any citizen activity taking place at all. The question to ask is not why political apathy, but why political participation.

Varieties of Participation

How much citizens participate in politics is virtually impossible to measure because there are many forms of participation, and because some are politically very important even though they are not normally thought of as participation. Being an executive in a politically influential corporation, union, or religious organization, and participating in a court case that could alter a significant political institution, are just two examples.

Most citizens who participate do so in more conventional ways, and most of that participation takes place at or near home, or in and through informal groups. Thus, citizens can be involved yet avoid contact with formal political organizations.

The most prevalent form of informal participation is surveillance, Harold Lasswell's term to describe monitoring of the environment.[3] People carry on surveillance to learn about potential dangers to their interests and lives, drawing information from strategically placed members of their microsocial world, including friends inside relevant formal organizations. The principal source of data about dangers in the macrosocial environment is the news media. People keep up with the news primarily for surveillance reasons, and continue to want "bad" news because they want information about possible threats to their microsociety. According to one study of television news viewers, only 7 percent were interested in *political* surveillance, but then politics is neither perceived to be of great importance nor a potential source of danger to most people.[4]

Surveillance is not usually thought of as participation, but it should be because politicians know that it is taking place, that people doing it may vote, and that their vote could be affected by dangers they have learned about. Politicians must therefore try to avert all the dangers they can, and to make sure their successes in doing so are publicized in the news media. Still, surveillance is only data gathering, and as such it is less important than griping. How much people gripe about the performance of governmental, economic—and all the formal—organizations they must deal with is not known. Nor is it known which gripes, and whose, reach the ears of elected or appointed officials and thus could have political impact.

A variation of griping is the occasional, sudden, but widespread and at times even massive spurt of citizen reaction to a particular event. For example, several times during Watergate and at the time of the Iranian hostage-taking, comparatively large numbers of people wrote, called, or wired the White House and their senators and representatives to express their opinion, apparently completely spontaneously. Western Union is said to have received a half million wires following the "Saturday Night Massacre" when Watergate Special Prosecutor Archibald Cox was fired by the Nixon administration. This represented a tiny percentage of the adult population and even the voting population, but it constituted a huge increase over the number who normally write, call, or wire. Such magnitudes are rarely reached, and often the majority of communications are the result of organized campaigns. About 150,000 wires were sent in support of or opposition to Lt. Col. North during the congressional investigation of "contragate" in the summer of 1987, and others called or wrote.[5] Still, many of these communications were produced by organized campaigns, and politicians therefore discounted them accordingly. Indeed, subsequent polls reported comparatively little support for Col. North's activities and the Central American policies he favored.

Accurate data about the extent of more typical forms of citizen political participation are scarce, partly because people may be reluctant to admit that they do nothing at all. Even so, most people do nothing beyond voting. Twenty years ago, citizen participation in the U.S. was summarized as follows:

> Only about 4 to 5% are active in a party, campaign, and attend meetings. About 10% make monetary contributions, about 13% contact public officials, and about 15% display a button or sticker. Around 25 or 30% try to proselytize others to vote a certain way, and from 40 to 70% vote in any given election . . . there seems to be a hierarchy of political involvement, in that persons at a given level of involvement tend to perform many of the same acts, including those performed by persons at lower levels of involvement. . . .
>
> About one-third of the American adult population can be characterized as politically apathetic or passive; in most cases they are unaware, literally, of the political part of the world around them. Another 60% play largely spectator roles; they watch, they cheer, they vote, but they do not battle . . . the percentage of gladiators does not exceed 5 to 7%.[6]

In 1986, nearly the same figures were derived from a study that measured political sophistication rather than participation. The population was seen as consisting of three publics: There were an activist population of 5 percent and a totally apolitical aggregate of 20 percent. The remaining three-fourths were thought to constitute "the great middle stratum . . . marginally attentive to politics . . . [who] accept the duty to vote and . . . do so with fair regularity."[7] In the 1986 GSS, 4 percent of the respondents indicated they belonged to a political club or organization.[8]

Participation in single-interest or issue groups may be higher than that in other groups, however, although membership in such groups may involve nothing more than signing a form and sending it back to the organization. A 1981 Gallup poll reports 13 percent of the respondents saying they had joined an "interest group," while another 23 percent indicated they had given money to one. The most frequently mentioned organizations protected wildlife, were antiabortion or anti-gun control groups, or defended the rights of Vietnam veterans or blacks. The poll indicated once more the extent to which participation remains more of an upper- and upper-middle-class activity, for 21 percent of people with college or graduate degrees claimed to be members, as compared to 11 percent of high school graduates and 2 percent of people with grade school diplomas.[9]

Voting is still the most widely engaged-in form of participation, with about 53 percent of the voting-age population voting for president in the last three presidential elections, about 48 percent voting for U.S. senators and representatives during the years of those elections, and between 35 and 38 percent voting for the latter in the last three Congressional election years.[10] Over the last generation, these figures have been declining, 63 percent having cast a vote for president in 1952 and 58 percent for U.S. senators and representatives.[11] The lows were reached in the 1970s, but the number of voters has increased by only a couple of percentage points in the 1980s.

Furthermore, voting is far more prevalent among people of higher class position, with more income, more education, and better jobs. In 1984, when median family income was $26,433, 61 percent of family members earning $20,000 to 24,000, 67 percent of those earning $24,000 to 35,000, and in the top income bracket 76 percent of those earning $50,000 or more said they had voted— as compared to 37 percent of those earning under $5,000.[12] (These voting figures are based on what people told the U.S. Census, and election researchers have determined that such figures are 8 to 10 percent too high.[13]) Likewise, 44 percent of people with less than three years of high school voted in 1984, as compared to 59 percent with a high school diploma and 79 percent of those with four or more years of college.[14] Similarly, 44 percent of the jobless but 62 percent of the employed cast a ballot that year.[15] The percentages for Congressional election years and primaries generally indicate a yet lower participation rate by Americans with only a few years of school. For example, 67 percent of people with four or more years of college voted in 1982, nearly double the 36 percent with eight or fewer years of elementary school.[16]

Although voting for national elected officials is an activity dominated by better-off Americans, election researchers are not yet fully agreed on the reasons. Since over 80 percent of those registered to vote actually cast a ballot, the principal reason is nonregistration, but whether it results primarily from inability to register or from unwillingness, or from both, is not yet known. America has generally made it difficult for people to register, and the major reason for the very low registration and voting rates among the poor and poorly educated is the various obstacles put in their way, including the unwillingness of the major parties to have them in the electorate.[17] The poor are likely to make costly demands for jobs, higher unemployment and welfare benefits, housing subsidies, and the like.[18]

Undoubtedly some people do not register or vote because they feel that it is useless, and that politicians will not pay attention to them. Undoubtedly too, poor and moderate-income people who need to depend on the government for economic security and for varying proportions of their income are more skeptical about its attentiveness than high-income people, whose economic demands usually obtain a respectful hearing in Washington. Ironically, the greater the unwillingness of low- and moderate-income people to register and vote, the greater also the unwillingness of politicians to represent them. Often that unwillingness is already high because of their fear that more affluent constituents will then desert them.

The regulations that govern voter registration illustrate that in many, although a now declining number of, communities, registration involves direct contact with government officials or functionaries of other formal political organizations. Voting, however, is essentially a microsocial political act. People can and do talk about electoral politics in familial and informal groups, while casting the ballot requires no contact with formal political organizations or politicians, except for a few minutes in the voting booth. No wonder then that while the proportion of Americans who are registered to vote is lower than that of Western Europeans, the proportion voting as a percentage of those who are registered is about the same as in Western Europe.

Political Activity: Unusual Motives, Unusual People

The conventional activities associated with citizen participation in the democratic ideal, as well as such others as civil disobedience or taking the government to court, require that people participate in or confront formal political organizations. Such activity is likely to be carried out by people with unusual incentives or motives, or by unusual people.

The largest number of politically active people are not unusual, however; they are in politics as a career. Some are professional politicians; many are best described as employees in the participation industry—officials, bureaucrats, and experts who work for lobbies or citizen organizations or for the political and governmental agencies that exist to deal with them. In small towns and suburbs, retailers, insurance and real estate agents, and lawyers become involved in the civic side of politics, using the visibility and prestige of being active to compete for customers and clients. They may shun party politics, however, because it could alienate some customers. In low-income areas where anyone willing to risk going into politics is admired—but also distrusted—funeral directors have sometimes done so, and in the black community ministers are only now losing the virtual monopoly they once held on political activism.

Some of the active may be personally unusual individuals, insofar as they chose politics because they like the spotlight it can offer. Others have ideological or personal interests including the desire to be of public service, to improve society, or to lead others because they are good at it and enjoy doing it.[19] Some need so much power or are sufficiently unusual in other ways that Harold Lasswell could once write a book arguing that politics had intimate connections to psychopathology.[20] The vernacular analysis, that some people "catch a political bug," is less pejorative and probably more accurate.

A further set of atypical people are those with an extremely high level of energy, which is a too rarely recognized prerequisite for political activism and other kinds of leadership. Indeed, many and perhaps most organizational leaders are men and women with a great deal of extra energy, without which they could probably not survive the pace of the work, whether it is paid or unpaid.[21]

Behind the people who participate full time in politics are the temporaries, who become active periodically. Many do so for microsocial reasons, to help a relative or friend in an election campaign. Another type of temporary participant is active largely because of the prevalence of political avoidance. When private firms, government, and other avoidable organizations threaten family, personal, or community life, people sometimes spring into action at the last minute to try to ward off the danger. Upper- and upper-middle-class people do not often need to do so because they have been warned in plenty of time, can join lobbies, exert their own pressure on the "right people," or can obtain special legislation.

Middle Americans unaffiliated with an effective political organization must come together on an ad hoc basis, with the professional politicians waiting to see if the group is effective and respectable enough to justify their own participation. Such ad hoc organizations tend to spring up mostly in reaction to local threats, among them health dangers such as chemical plants and nuclear installations, commercial ventures that increase traffic or attract users of lower status, and new residents who might increase the crime rate or reduce home prices.

More often than not, these spontaneous ventures may begin as informal groups of friends or neighbors, and grow because they express the strong fear people feel toward an enemy or their bottled-up disapproval of government. The groups often come into being too late or are too inchoate to be effective, and thus peter out when people get frustrated. When the threat is too large and powerful to be dealt with by spontaneous informal protest, people can become frustrated before they even organize. Occasionally they erupt into violence instead.

Since the ad hoc groups are generally local and seek to hold back change, they are not thought of as social movements even if they are similar to them in many ways. Instead that term is mainly reserved for temporary political groups and organizations that try to overcome social injustice, emphasize social change, and reflect liberal or Left ideologies. Although they may be led by trained organizers, the people who supply the participatory man- and womanpower often remain only temporarily because social movement participation is unusually strenuous, even when people are not risking job loss or disapproval from family and friends.[22]

Probably most social movements make only a minor impact, but some turn out in retrospect to have been in the vanguard of political innovation or society-wide change, when the right kinds of leaders and members stay together under the right conditions. The civil rights movement, which took more than two decades to become the national movement that helped initiate society-wide change in the 1960s, is still the best American example. Most of America's post-World War II social movements have been led or dominated by professionals and union leaders, with much of the membership upper-middle-class young people, particularly college students. With some notable exceptions such as those involving union members, social movements have not yet attracted more than a token number of middle Americans. Movement activities—and leaders—remain at odds with the tenets of middle American individualism and political avoidance.

Virtually the same observation can be made about the local community organizations which sprang up first at the end of the 1960s, partly as a reaction to the frustrations and failures encountered by the national protest movements of that era. Some of these community organizations have become permanent and may win important local victories but others survive for only a short time. Even the nationwide federations of local groups remain on an unsteady footing because their main bases are local, while geographically and politically broader connections are hard to establish permanently. National ventures, such as participation in national electoral politics, require infrastructures that they cannot easily mount. Even monies for national meetings are difficult to come by, and so are membership numbers that will impress professional politicians.

In the mid-1980s, the largest national bodies were ACORN and Citizen Action, but their main strengths are their professional organizers. These are typically overworked and underpaid, and as a result, few stay more than a few years. Meanwhile, they make the plans and decisions, so that often the elected leaders are little more than figureheads. The memberships function largely as an infantry. In effect, these organizations have begun to resemble lobbies in structure. Their achievements are in many ways impressive, but they too have not persuaded many middle Americans to stop practicing political avoidance.[23]

A graphic illustration of the staying power of individualistic political avoidance can be found among the jobless steel, auto, and other factory workers of the Rustbelt, who are still middle American other than in income. Although they do not necessarily feel that their joblessness is their own fault, they retain other individualistic reactions. For example, they feel that going out to look for work for themselves is more effective than group political activity in their own behalf and that of their jobless colleagues.[24] Being particularly vulnerable to feelings of worthlessness and depression, the unemployed feel an unusually strong need to be self-reliant and thus have a further reason to go out personally to seek work.[25] The irony is that in communities of mass unemployment few jobs are to be found, thus increasing people's emotional vulnerability and eventual frustration.

If political activity had a reasonable chance to save or create jobs, then the most individualistic middle Americans might decide that such activity was itself a form of self-reliance. Some of the unemployed appear to sense that government has not been willing to do much to provide them with the kind of jobs and wages that they once enjoyed. Nevertheless, according to the *New York Times*–CBS News Election Day exit polls, 32 percent of the jobless voted for Ronald Reagan in 1984.[26] They seem to have ignored both his administration's responsibility for increasing joblessness, for example in the Rustbelt, and its failure to take deliberate action to create or save jobs. Perhaps they decided that Ronald Reagan's cheerful faith in the return of massive economic growth was as helpful as anything else government was likely to do, and at least made them feel better about the future for the time being.

In the 1980s much of the *ad hoc* political protest against the state of the economy has been undertaken by farmers, but they are business people rather than workers. Another kind of temporary political protest has been carried out by farmers and jobless workers who were losing their farms and homes to foreclosure.[27]

Defense of the home or farm may be a more effective spur to political activity than joblessness, perhaps because it is sometimes successful, the federal government and the banks having occasionally been persuaded to postpone foreclosure. The loss of a job is partly compensated by unemployment insurance; losing the farm or the home is not. One of the few alternatives to political activity is violence against the banker or the marshall, and both have taken place.

The people who lose their jobs and farms are unusual insofar as they can trace their losses to the direct impact of economic and governmental organizations on their own lives. More often the impingement is less direct and only a few see how they are being—or will soon be—directly affected. Political avoidance has become sufficiently institutionalized and internalized, fighting the government or a locally important corporation is difficult, and in many places people who protest too readily or militantly can still be accused of being communists. In the end, people are encouraged to remain bystanders. "The average person stays out of trouble and can live with the system as it is."[28]

While it is dangerous to extrapolate the present into the future, it is also hard to imagine that the current patterns of political participation and avoidance are likely to change. Because political avoidance is still considered a moral failing, civic sermons demanding that people modify their behavior still appear, and the sermonizers may be able to imagine that they can initiate such behavior modification. Unusual future events may lead to citizens' mass mobilizations and protests, but one would be foolish to count on them. Even the Great Depression failed to produce sizable protest organizations.

America has, however, always generated smaller social movements both to demand and to hold back change. Even when their leaders and/or members have not been drawn from the American mainstream, the movements have at times inspired that mainstream and at other times affected its—and the country's—behavior. For example, whether the radical antiwar movement of the 1960s and early 1970s played any causal role in ending the Vietnam war cannot be proved, but that it played none is impossible to prove too. Its very visible and vocal presence must have made a difference. The even smaller socialist movement did not bring about the New Deal, but it inspired many New Deal programs, and its presence led to some Roosevelt administration action to prevent the growth of other socialist or revolutionary movements.

Social movements are therefore an intrinsic part of the larger political process and in often subtle and serendipitous ways are surrogates for citizen political participation that must be respected. At the same time, the mere existence of a social movement should not be expected to produce mass protest or to create dramatic change.

Substitutes for Participation—Responsiveness and Representation

Although—and partly because—middle Americans try to avoid political and formal organizations in general, such organizations do not avoid *them*. Despite their image of great power, Big Government, and to a lesser extent, Big Business, are prepared to be *responsive* to people, satisfying and at times anticipating their demands and wishes above and beyond what the requirements of profitability or reelection are thought to be. Responsiveness may sometimes be used to prevent citizen participation, insofar as organizations seek to forestall such drastic and feared forms of participation as strikes, boycotts, and revolts. Conversely, organizations and politicians control or manage their responsiveness, ignoring or "stonewalling" demands and actions they are unable or unwilling to consider.

The basic reasons for responsiveness are simple. Most organizations which supply goods or services to users prefer to stay on their good side or maintain their credibility with them, whether the organizational business is selling consumer goods, supplying education, or curing disease. Users who can afford to make choices can be fickle, political party or brand name loyalties notwithstanding. As a result, political parties and incumbents can be voted out of office in one fell swoop, and giant corporations can suddenly find their most profitable products going unsold. Organizations with a guaranteed monopoly may be immune to these dangers, but they are subject to others, such as severe criticism or investigation. Consequently, even large suppliers remain more vulnerable and insecure than their size or power would suggest and are impelled to be or appear to be responsive.

From the perspective with which large formal organizations look out at the country, the microsocial life of middle (and other)

Americans is a mysterious culture that proceeds by rules that the people who run these organizations have difficulty understanding. For them, middle America is a sleeping giant, partly because of its immense size when looked at as a "mass," which is how national organizations frequently see it, and partly because of its ability to behave unpredictably.

The process by which unpredictable and damaging behavior develops resembles what the film industry calls "word of mouth," the judgment moviegoers express to friends and associates about a new film they have just seen.[29] Word of mouth is in fact microsocial consensus: what people decide to talk about in their families and informal groups and agree to believe, act on, and occasionally get excited about.

A remarkable illustration of damaging word of mouth—and its power to produce corporate responsiveness—was the rumor that Procter & Gamble, the giant soap maker, was run by Satanists and was contributing 10 percent of its profits to Satanic causes. After the failure of five years of extensive efforts to defend itself, Procter & Gamble finally had to remove its 100-year-old trademark illustration, the offending symbol, from its soap boxes.[30]

Not all formal organizations are vulnerable to word of mouth, and for many the major agents of victory or defeat are other formal organizations with which they must deal. Defense contractors, for example, need worry mainly about their competitors and the Pentagon. However, if a new weapon fails and the company also makes consumer goods, ordinary Americans may react in the stores. The Dow Company had some difficulties overcoming its reputation as the producer of the napalm used in Vietnam, and defense contractors that bill the Pentagon $500 for $5 hammers may get in trouble even if they make no consumer goods at all.

Given the fickleness of users, most formal organizations are prepared not only to be responsive, but to monitor their environments for this purpose. Just as ordinary people keep up with what formal organizations are doing, so these organizations carry on surveillance to keep up with what goes on among ordinary people.

Once upon a time, political organizations had precinct captains who conducted surveillance, while manufacturers and distributors expected their salespeople to do so as they made the rounds. Increasingly, however, formal organizations bureaucratize their surveillance mechanisms, for, slowly but surely, all of them seem to be turning to polls and other surveys. During election campaigns, presidential candidates and others who can afford the costs mount virtually continual polls to see if their campaigns are winning votes—and if not, they may use the poll data to alter their campaigns. Even after the winner has arrived at the White House, the polls continue, which is one reason a pollster is now part of the President's inner circle.

Polls and surveys being expensive, even when conducted over the telephone, political and commercial research organizations now also resort to "focus groups," small sets of strangers assembled by researchers for conversations about products, advertising campaigns, and political candidates or their campaigns. Focus group results have sometimes been found to be more useful than those of polls, perhaps because they are, in effect, research substitutes for informal groups and their microsocial word of mouth.

Even so, the fastest—and cheapest—surveillance tool is still the news media, for politicians and business executives view national journalists as stand-ins for the "mass public," assuming that the stories the news media report will either shape the opinions of that public or reflect its initial reaction to an issue or event. Government and business leaders are therefore apt to be responsive to what appears in the media. One of the more famous examples of media-induced responsiveness followed CBS News anchorman Walter Cronkite's on-air statement opposing the continuation of the war in Vietnam, for it crystallized Lyndon B. Johnson's decision not to seek reelection in 1968.

One purpose of surveillance is to assess the need for responsiveness, but whatever the need, formal organizations aim to manage their responsiveness so that they can ignore or deflect demands they cannot or will not satisfy. Political organizations big and small preprogram their public meetings carefully and rehearse what they plan to say so that the attending citizens will be supportive or at least quiet. Even responsiveness to unexpected citizen demands or protests must be rehearsed when at all possible, to minimize both political harm and embarrassing policy precedents.

However, the best way to manage responsiveness is to limit the need for it. Consequently, politicians try to manage important news, providing journalists with the kind of information that will produce supportive stories and therefore support from the citizenry. Television enables the politicians with enough funds and power to create newsworthy events, and the White House soon learned that by creating only one such dramatic event a day, news executives could virtually be forced to show their viewers the presidential activities the White House wanted the country to see.[31] Even presidential news conferences, in which the president must respond spontaneously to unknown questions, can be managed to some extent, first by rehearsing the president with all the questions that could possibly be asked, and second by having him only call on journalists with reputations for predictable and relatively uncritical questions.

The Reagan White House took news management one step further by trying to manage the public reaction to presidential decisions and speeches as well. This was done by sending out what columnist William Safire call "spin-meisters," government officials who interpreted presidential actions or speeches in preplanned ways in order to influence the "spin" the journalists would put on the stories, in hopes of shaping the journalists' and the public's interpretations of the actions or speeches.

There are, however, limits to the management of responsiveness, for politicians cannot restrict journalists from obtaining information from other sources and listening to a variety of spins on presidential actions. In addition, journalists can make a news story out of the fact that politicians are using spin-meisters, thus discrediting both the practice and the politicians. The inherent limitations of response management devices force politicians to invent new ones constantly, and if none work, panicky politicians may resort to an old but temporarily foolproof one, the cover-up of information.

Formal organizations do, however, respond in unmanaged ways as well, or at least in as unmanaged a way as is possible with such organizations. In deciding whether and how to react, organizations seem to assess the political, economic, and organizational costs of responding, as well as the political and economic power of those expecting or demanding a response. The easier and cheaper the response, the readier organizations are to be helpful, even to relatively powerless constituents or other users, particularly if their responsiveness can be publicized, which adds considerably to the good will that can be claimed.

With an election always in the offing, politicians are sometimes even eager to be responsive. Normally it is possible to persuade a high-level politician or appointed official to come to a public meeting that will draw only a relative handful of citizens. Speech making is cost-free, and most politicians spend most of their evenings at such meetings even without an imminent election.

No one has yet computed how many letters, phone calls, petition signatures, or campaign dollars will persuade agencies or elected officials to be responsive to the different types of voter and lobby demands—or in the case of supportive letters, will encourage politicians to continue what they are doing. The general rule, which holds for commercial and political organizations and perhaps all large formal organizations, is that decision makers take notice when the number of letters, phone calls, or other reactions from the general public rises noticeably above the day-to-day average. A dramatic increase in news stories or editorials can have the same effect, on the assumption that journalists reflect the feelings of the general public.

Under the right conditions, the number of citizen communications does not even need to be very large. In 1984, 50 phone calls by constituents to each of 10 congressmen and -women made it possible to overturn a crucial Congressional vote on missile legislation. As the then president of Common Cause, David Cohen, pointed out, "It [impact] has to do with timing and the visibility of the issue. Suddenly, a congressional office gets 50 plus calls. The member senses that something's stirring out there . . . That worries any politician."[32]

In this instance the calls were instigated by lobbyists and went to 10 representatives who were "swing votes." However, spontaneous outpourings of calls and letters are usually more effective, simply because they are rarer. In 1974, approximately 100,000 phone calls, telegrams, and letters to the White House are said to have persuaded Richard Nixon to give up the Watergate tapes. This was far above the normal daily number of citizen communications to the White House although still a tiny percentage of all the people concerned with Watergate or in favor of the surrender of the tapes. Whatever that surrender meant personally to Richard Nixon, the decision incurred no political costs for the rest of the U.S. government and probably helped the reputation of the Republican party.

When the political costs rise, however, a much larger citizen reaction will not cause a change in policy. Marches, demonstrations, and other protests involving millions of citizens who sought an end to the war in Vietnam, including perhaps as many as a half million at one Washington march alone, did not achieve their aim, at least at the time of the march. Ending the war required drastic political and economic change by many parts of government, and besides, even at the height of the antiwar protest, many Americans continued to favor a victory in the war—and perhaps more than were opposed to that war.

Day in and day out, politicians are probably most responsive to "public opinion," and particularly to perceived changes in it. When and how public opinion affects politicians' actions is hard to pin down, however, because public opinion is hard to measure. Sometimes politicians will describe it as those opinions that back up their own actions or plans. Polls can supply numbers, but unless the questions identify obvious and rising discontent with a specific condition or the questions are directly relevant to current policies or strategies, as in campaign polling, politicians may be unable to infer what they should do or do differently. Since poll responses are reactive and respondents include people who do not care about the issues, politicians may ignore the results. Instead they identify public opinion from a higher than usual amount of citizen communication, news stories, and editorials, and above all from evidence of active discontent among their constituents. The number of citizens who express their discontent usually being small, their opinion may not even be the public's; it is, however, actively expressed and can therefore cause politicians who ignore it trouble.

Private industry is normally not required to be responsive except when consumer protection and similar legislation stipulate it. Car manufacturers often wait until the law requires them to recall deficient cars; manufacturers of processed foods are slow to provide fully honest labels until government regulations call for them; factories do not make expensive corrections of unsafe working conditions until federal inspectors have laid down the law. Easy and inexpensive responses may be made without prodding but there are few actions big firms can take easily and inexpensively.

One of the easier ways of responding is symbolic, for example, the hiring of token black and women executives before a firm is taken to court. Black fashion models and celebrities have appeared in commercials, and black quarterbacks on professional football teams, but they are more visible than executives and their presence can evoke fears of a negative reaction from white customers or fans. Every industry has a firm or two which is responsive without much pressure or acts in advance on the basis of conviction, but the typical response is to stall or resort to tokens.

Manufacturers of nationally sold goods usually establish customer service departments to maintain customer good will, although their responses to unhappy buyers are often as mass-produced as their products. When they are unwilling or unable to replace items or refund their price, they make symbolic gestures with coupons or letters or other kinds of "stroking." In most firms, customer service departments are on the margins of organizational hierarchies, so they lack the power to alter bad production practices. Only when sales drop precipitously are such drastic forms of responsiveness considered, although usually the first, and organizationally simplest, form of responsiveness is a price reduction.

Nonetheless, there are large variations between particular industries, depending both on their structure and on the implications of customer unhappiness. The purchase of the most costly items most families ever buy, the house and the car, is still based on an adversarial retail system in which each side tries to outwit the other, although the supplier generally beats the user except when protective government regulations and recall provisions are effective. Conversely, the television industry at times is unusually responsive. For example in 1987, 20,000 letters helped save "Cagney and Lacy," a detective mystery, although the network decision was influenced as well by a sharp rise in the ratings that followed the letters.[33]

The late Frank Reynolds reported that 36,000 letters by viewers supporting Vice President Agnew's implied criticism of his commentary in 1971 eventually led ABC to remove him from his anchorman position.[34] The national news media normally get a surprisingly small number of letters, and they, and the television industry in general, react like politicians: any sudden and drastic increase in letters is thought to be significant.[35]

Demoting a network anchorman and renewing an entertainment program with rising ratings for the usual 13 weeks are not very costly decisions, but when corporate responsiveness is expensive, it may not take place. The Johns-Manville Corporation resisted aiding or reimbursing its workers and customers who had contracted asbestosis for nearly 50 years, using a variety of legal and extralegal tactics, and then sought to escape responsibility by declaring bankruptcy.[36]

The Quality of Representation

The second substitute for participation is representation. Representatives act in place of and for those who elect them, but are not required to accede to or anticipate voters' demands and wishes. They are expected to decide what they think is best for the country and for their constituency as a whole, even if they do not always function in such altruistic fashion. Indeed, those who are unresponsive to their major constituents are not apt to be reelected.

Whether elected officials are being good representatives depends not only on what criteria are used to define good but also on which parts of a constituency are thought to be more important or deserving than others and, above all, on the country's goals a representative should support.

Whatever the difficulties of judging the quality of representation in the abstract, the people being represented seem to have ambivalent feelings. Since less than half the voting-age population casts ballots for the Congress during presidential election years and not much more than a third during Congressional election years, significant numbers of voters may not care much about their national representatives.

Although they reelect virtually all incumbent members of Congress, people do not seem very enthusiastic about the ways in which they are being represented, at least judging by how poll respondents answer questions that touch on various aspects of people's relationships with the government. A regular question that has been in the Center for Policy Studies election study schedule since 1964 asks, "Over the years, how much attention do you feel the government pays to what people think when it decides what to do?" and most people have always said it pays only "some." In 1984, 59 percent thought it paid "some" attention, 17 percent thought it paid "a good deal," and 24 percent "not much."[37]

Other questions ask people how well they are being represented, and generally 60 to 70 percent disagree with such statements as "The average citizen has considerable influence on politics" and "People like me have much to say about government."[38] In 1985, 61 percent agreed that "the public has little control over what politicians do."[39] Answers to these and related questions cannot be used to infer that people are unhappy about the particular politicians representing them, but they suggest a generalized dissatisfaction with how much the government is taking "the average citizen" or "people like me" into account.

One clue to the nature of their discontent concerns the class background of elected officials. Most Americans seem to have no intense objection to rich men and women running for office, but they appear to prefer "self-made" people. Perhaps they do not like to vote for politicians who might look down on constituents of lower status. When candidates listed in the *Social Register* run for office, they must generally prove at once that they are not snobs, having to exhibit "down-to-earth" lifestyle preferences and social habits in order to be acceptable.

People also seem to expect elected officials to live as if they earned approximately the same incomes as most of their constituents. They may want their representatives to know firsthand how it feels to live on a modest income and to be familiar with the resulting financial and other problems. In any case, legislation to increase the salaries of government officials, elected or appointed, always encounters strong opposition and is rarely brought up before an election. The pay increase for federal officials that President Reagan recommended in 1986 was put off until spring 1987, when Congress approved it. According to a January 1987 Gallup poll, three-quarters of the respondents were opposed to the pay raise.

Most of the poll answers that are critical of the governmental leadership or governmental policies cited in prior chapters could also be interpreted to reflect people's dissatisfactions with their elected representatives or with representation per se. However, many voters are unhappier with what their elected representatives do than with the representatives themselves, and sometimes they put the blame on government in general, making little distinction between appointed and elected officials. They could be unhappy about how representation is organized, and with its results rather than with the individuals who represent them. This possibility is suggested not only by the reelection rate of incumbents but by the opprobrium attached to the entire class of politicians.

Elected officials play the principal roles in the system of representation by definition, but others play indirect roles because they supply the elected representatives with information and guidance. These include pollsters who supply one measure of public opinion, and the news media, who supply others. Still, sometimes the most important players of the indirect role are lobbyists, for they are ever present to supply information, offer suggestions, and help draft legislation. Their lobbying organizations in turn represent constituents, although actually most of these constituents are yet other organizations, particularly corporations.

In 1983 there were 6,601 organizations in Washington that lobbied for or otherwise represented their constituents, and of these 52 percent represented corporations. Another 18 percent were trade and business associations, and only 7 percent represented citizens—9 percent if unions are included.[40] While some of the corporate and other business lobbies, and the further 7 percent which were professional associations, probably supported citizen concerns some of the time, the extent to which the interests of various citizen constituencies were brought before the Congress and the White House is minimal in comparison to those of corporate and other supplier constituencies.[41] These data may provide further explanation of why many poll respondents feel they receive too little attention from government.

Social Decentralization and Organizational Centralization

During the period of widespread optimism after World War II, there was hope that the shortcomings of political responsiveness and representation could be reduced because of an expected increase in the amount of citizen participation. Educated citizens believed that as larger numbers of Americans obtained more years of schooling, their political interest and activity would increase, which would help usher in a more democratic society.

That belief turned out to be wrong, however. There is no necessary connection between amount of education and commitment to democracy, particularly if people's various interests encourage some to favor nondemocratic solutions. Further, today's young adults, who are as an aggregate the best-educated population in the country, vote less, pay less attention to the news, and appear generally less interested in organized politics than other age groups, especially the old. True, they are basically not different from young people in the past, the mythology of yuppiedom notwithstanding, and some will change as they age. (Concurrently, small but committed groups of young people carry out much of the local community organizing and political activism taking place all over the country, they alone combining the needed idealism and lack of competing obligations.)

Some and perhaps even many of the apolitical young appear

to be joining with some of their elders in a trend that can be called social decentralization. In a step that goes beyond current forms of organizational and political avoidance, these people may be trying to move out of formally organized society as much as possible. To resurrect an old term, they may be trying to drop out of that society.

In the 1960s, the so-called "hippies" and other young people actually did drop out for a while, setting up alternative communities, in some cases with alternative economic arrangements. Contemporary dropouts, being culturally conventional, seek to establish new kinds of conventional communities and lifestyles in which there is more time for and emphasis on microsocial relations and less need for macrosocial ones.

Examples of social decentralization can be seen in the population movements of the last decade or two. One is people's never-ending search for areas of lower density—and more privacy—away from cities and now from established suburbs. In this process, people who can afford to do so are also heading for new communities where they can make a new social start, and where the formal organizations and the public facilities found in the Northeast, Midwest, or California are scarcer. There they can develop an even more home-centered life or a home-and-out-doors-centered one made possible by the geographical and climatic opportunities for year-round outdoor recreation available in Florida, Arizona, and others of the fastest-growing states.

The new communities are further distant from Big Government, Big Business, and Big Labor as well as from other disliked features of the larger society, including taxes. As a journalistic survey of some of these communities put it, "throughout the region, the prevailing philosophy was to promote individual enterprise and avoid government interference to a degree that was pronounced even for Arizona. There is a frontier quality to the area that the settlers seem anxious to preserve."[42]

The initial motive of people moving away from organized America is economic, for they are going where good jobs and new business opportunities are most often available. Consequently the mobile young initially moved to the economically growing parts of the Sunbelt, but after boom times ended there, they have headed for newer areas of economic vitality. In the mid-1980s some even located once more in older sections of the country, such as still rural parts of the Northeast.

The decentralizing trend is not new, for Americans have headed for the latest frontier since the 17th century. Some of the people who moved to suburbia after World War II were themselves dropouts, moving to new places to make a new start. Perhaps the major contemporary change is that more people and the companies that employ them can afford to be footloose and head for open spaces farther from the cities.[43] Sometimes it is the industries which prefer to be in decentralized locations, and sometimes it is their potential employees, forcing the industries to locate near the kinds of people they most want to hire. In either case, the new growth takes place at the edges of organized society, enabling the people who want the decentralized life to obtain it.

Another trend is in the opposite direction, for important formal organizations are becoming larger, with organizational authority becoming more centralized at the top. Economic activity per se is not being centralized, for most Americans still work in small firms and the number of small businesses has in fact increased over the last century.[44] The diversification of consumer demand and the decline of single-product mass production have led to the decentralization of manufacturing as well as the formation of new, smaller companies that specialize in catering to the newly diverse demands.[45]

Instead, what is being centralized is power. The decentralized manufacturing facilities remain parts of a single firm, and the eventual fate of successful new small companies is to be merged with or bought up by larger ones. Meanwhile, the domination of large firms over the economy as a whole rises continually. The share of total manufacturing assets held by the 100 largest manufacturing firms has been increasing about half a percent a year since the start of the century, and in 1984 it stood at nearly 61 percent.[46] In 1955 the 750 largest U.S. firms supplied 40 percent of private employment; by 1974 they supplied 55 percent.[47] In the late 1970s the stock of the 122 largest corporations comprised 41 percent of the market value of all common stock.[48] Although some other measures show concentration declining since the formation of the first giant corporations at the end of the 19th century, the large number of mergers and takeovers of the last two decades as well as the arrival of multinational corporations and conglomerates suggests that a new period of concentration is taking place.[49]

Although the new concentration expends untold billions of

dollars that could have been spent on productive economic growth, some of the increase in organizational size may be connected to the growth of the population. There is perhaps some relation between population increase, the need for more capital, and thus organizational size. The trend may even be affected by world economic conditions and could thus be necessary for the ability of American firms to compete, as some economists argue.[50]

When large firms grow larger, however, centralization of control is frequently a by-product, with a smaller number of offices and people at the top of the hierarchy obtaining more authority, power, and decision-making responsibility. This can also be true when firms decentralize their operating divisions and their administrative structures, for given the hierarchical nature of American industry and the capital and stock market pressures to hold one or two persons responsible, the top of the hierarchy in which control is finally lodged simply gets steeper, and ever more distant from the people in the middle and at the bottom of large firms.

The centralizing trends in the corporation may also spread to other formal organizations. As firms grow, so must labor unions, some surviving only as a result of mergers. Firm and population growth lead eventually to the enlargement of government and major nonprofit agencies that regulate, serve, or are otherwise tied to the firms and people.

The spread of growth and centralized control is further accelerated by interorganizational dynamics. Formal organizations find it easier to deal with other formal organizations, and large ones with other large ones, because they are cut from the same structural cloth. It is also cheaper for a firm or public agency to work with a small number of large firms or agencies than with a large number of small ones. As a result, a giant like the Pentagon ends up dealing with, or creating, other giants to supply its military weaponry. By the same process, highly centralized firms and agencies encourage those they work with to centralize also. Not only do top executives meet only with other top executives for the usual status reasons, but decision makers with final authority see no reason to meet with executives who must consult others before they can make decisions. The most extreme illustration of centralization comes from the small Western European welfare states, in which the representatives of government, management, and labor can meet in one room and agree on the major strands of their country's economic policy.

While growth and centralization of control may be more efficient in some respects, economies of scale have their limits.[51] So do the administration and politics of scale, for the handful of people at the top may have more difficulty supervising their organizations and, as the hierarchy becomes steeper, maintaining needed surveillance, feedback, and other communication mechanisms. As a result, overly centralized organizations also have problems in maintaining their ability to be responsive or representative. There are organizations that are so hierarchical that seemingly obvious empirical findings obtained through surveillance either no longer traveled up to, or could not be perceived properly at, the top of the hierarchy, producing very expensive decision-making failures.[52]

Political organizations encounter similar problems with representation, and even the relationship between citizens and political leaders is affected by greater centralization. When people look over presidential candidates, for example, they try to figure out which one they can trust most to represent them properly on crucial future national decisions. In the process they bring to bear many of the techniques and indicators they use in everyday life to determine which strangers are trustworthy. Until the last quarter century or so, many voters dealt with the problem by trusting whomever their party chose, or by the assessments they got from local party figures and "opinion leaders" they trusted.

As political parties have stopped choosing candidates and have turned into centralized campaign organizations and as candidates have done more and more of their campaigning on television, voters without party loyalties or without resort to trusted local politicians have increasingly had to infer from what they see on television and read in the newspapers which candidate is most trustworthy. In that process, people have to rely on campaign appearances, speeches, political commercials, and journalists' reports, must separate information from campaign hype, and then must infer trustworthiness from what they can perceive about a candidate's "character."

As a result candidates with clearly visible character failure do not survive, and dishonesty is a prime example of a clearly visible character failure. Lyndon Johnson, Richard Nixon, Gerald Ford, and Ronald Reagan lost their political trustworthiness for dishonesty on major political issues, while presidential candidate Gary Hart lost it in May 1987 for lies about his extramarital life, that being all the voters had to go on at the time. Although some observers felt he was being punished for turning his back on monogamy or on the country's Puritan heritage, a *Time* magazine poll reported that only 7 percent of the respondents were "bothered" by the possibility that Mr. Hart "had sex with [Donna Rice]" while 69 percent said they were bothered by his not telling the truth.[53] When a political structure is centralizing and distancing itself further from the voters, the latter have less than ever to go on in judging their leaders so that character and particularly honesty become ever more important. The *Washington Post* columnist David Broder quotes an "Ollie" North supporter who is ready to elect him president "as soon as he is out of jail," and her explanation touches on the core of the voters' dilemma. "We expect people in Washington to lie to us," she pointed out. "At least he tells you when he is lying and when he isn't."[54]

The decentralizing and centralizing trends may not be interrelated, but they are taking place at the same time. As a result, they suggest the possibility of an emerging society in which people are trying to put social and other distances between themselves and formal organizations and the formal organizations are adding to that distance by turning more hierarchical. The opposing patterns might even reinforce each other, producing a spiraling effect. As citizens see that large organizations are becoming more distant, they might react by yet less participation.

If the centralizing and decentralizing trends continue, and there is no reason to believe that they will stop, formal and informal organizations will perhaps also continue to move away from each other. One could imagine that sometime in the next century those Americans with enough security to afford self-sufficiency (other than with respect to work and income) might be able to avoid contact with most organizations of the larger society, except when their self-sufficiency or their more general welfare was disturbed. Concurrently, formal organizations that could afford the organizational equivalent of self-sufficiency would be able to avoid contact with and responsiveness to people.

What I have just sketched is a futuristic scenario based on a mechanical metaphor in which two elements of a societal machine move in opposite, or centripetal and centrifugal, directions. Societies are not machines, and futures are not scientifically predictable, so other scenarios with quite different effects are possible as well. For example, large corporations could exploit their economy of scale and their greater capital for competitive advantage by being more responsive than smaller firms, and some organizations will always have to be responsive, for market, political, and other reasons, whatever their size. With enough experience, hierarchical organizations should be able to develop new kinds of surveillance and feedback structures so needed information could move up and down. In a properly organized giant corporation, nothing should prevent its top officers from spending time at the bottom of the hierarchy to make sure that they got such information. In a democracy, political organizations must always perform some representative functions, and they too could learn, for example, how to overcome the faults of television campaigning. (Even now, candidates with enough time, money, and freedom to campaign in New Hampshire and Iowa can enable a few residents of at least two states to make trust and character judgments on a slightly more personal basis.)

A very different yet already familiar futuristic scenario calls for organizational decentralization, with small but beautiful economies, self-sufficient local governments, and the replacement or abolition of nation states. No indications exist at present, however, either that big organizations can be dismantled or that people are eager to obtain local self-sufficiency by taking over the functions of such organizations.

Even scenarios based on current trends are only predictions, and the tendencies toward greater centralization and decentralization could end. However, there are already enough imperfections in existing processes of political participation, responsiveness, and representation to give some cause for concern. Suppose, for example, that predictions about long-run economic changes are accurate and that many more American jobs will be lost to the very low-wage countries of the Third World as well as to computerization.[55] In that case, American unemployment and underemployment will eventually reach and surpass Great Depression levels, and perhaps remain there permanently. The conventional assumption is that political reverberations and corrections will also follow, that levels of participation and the quality of political responsiveness and representation will improve, and that, somehow, a latter-day form of the New Deal—or of an equally effective remedy—will be invented.

Unemployed people rarely become politically active, however, except for sporadic riots, and apparently "First World" societies can now operate adequately and without extended social unrest if they fail to act energetically to relieve unemployment. The U.S. has lived with a largely unemployed underclass for almost a quarter century now, its women and children surviving on below-subsistence benefits and its men surviving in ways that are for all practical purposes unknown.

Since some of these ways involve street crime, the existence of that underclass reduces the quality of everyday life for many other citizens, but as long as the underclass and the crime are for the most part concentrated in the cities, there is no significant political demand for national policies to deal with the causes of that crime. Nor are cities given significant aid to do so on their own. More prisons are built, adding to GNP, but a good deal of the problem is dealt with by private security measures that do not reduce crime. In addition, people console themselves with the belief that the underclass is morally, culturally, and otherwise undeserving. Because the urban underclass is thought to be largely nonwhite, latter-day versions of 19th-century concepts of racial inferiority are also being invoked. Both beliefs imply that the underclass does not deserve decent jobs and incomes.

The historical trends and the political conditions that brought about the New Deal may not come again—and, besides, it did not offer much help to the black rural proletariat, the ancestors of many of today's members of the urban underclass. Furthermore, the American pattern is not entirely distinctive. Unemployment is much higher in most Western European countries, but despite a strong socialist movement and labor party tradition, most of them are doing little more than the U.S. to reduce unemployment.[56] The jobless are politically inert there as well, but while many young people have never held a full-time job and may never hold one, crime rates are, for the present at least, much lower than in the U.S. All of the affected countries supply far more generous unemployment and welfare benefits than the U.S., however, so the incomes of the jobless remain close to the national median income.[57] This reduces the danger of underclass formation and is one explanation why crime rates are far below those of the U.S.

The contemporary American method of dealing with unemployment and the underclass is in part a result of the shortage of politically easy solutions, but it is also an effect of capitalist and other individualisms, including middle America's. That method results as well from current patterns of political representation in which the underclass is for all practical purposes unrepresented. Future additions to that underclass will, however, come to some extent from middle Americans who are or will be losing their jobs in declining industries and services, so that they too become victims of the country's individualisms and its patterns of political representation. Criticizing those individualisms and the representation system is relatively easy, but a more useful approach is to determine what could and should be done about them.

Five

Individualism, Community, and Society

INDIVIDUALISM has been criticized frequently over the years, and few ideas in modern American thought have been attacked as ecumenically. Beginning with de Tocqueville, who invented the term individualism, the attacks have come from secular and religious perspectives, as well as from the Right, the Left, and the Center. Virtually all the critics agree that people should sacrifice some of their individual strivings for more communal concerns.

The advocates of communal values, or community, disagree sharply, however, about the nature of that community, one major division being between those who want more communal consensus and action in the public interest, and those who fear that the community, or society, is falling apart and that greater order is needed. Some critics favor both more consensus and order, or believe that order is best achieved through consensus, but the advocates of order divide on who defines the disorderly and how they are to be controlled.

The Current Critiques of Individualism

For brevity's sake, the current critiques of individualism can be compressed into five types, all interrelated and all variations on old themes. I label them generational, medical, hedonistic, communal, and democratic (the latter to be discussed in Chapter 6), but it goes without saying that all are moral and political criticisms as well. They condemn individualism in nearly every sector of society, although the hedonistic critique is aimed particularly at middle America.

The generational critique goes back at least to Socratic Greece, when the younger generation was accused of behavior that might today be called individualism. The most recent manifestation of this critique could be said to have surfaced in August 1976, when Tom Wolfe published an article entitled "The 'Me' Decade and the Third Great Awakening." Although he dealt primarily with participants in some then popular religious cults who sought to transform their personalities—or "polish . . . one's very *self*" as he characteristically put it—his title quickly assumed a life of its own, writers of all stripes using it to indict young Americans for an allegedly new, unusual, and by implication pathological degree of selfishness.[1]

Journalists and also social critics frequently view moral failings and cultural change in America as occurring by decades. They also seem to need a catch phrase by which to label each decade, and perhaps they took over Wolfe's title because it could be contrasted neatly with the imagined altruism of the 1960s.[2] In any case, "the me decade"—or sometimes "the me generation"—enabled critics to accuse some people of moral dereliction and worry about what they might do to American culture, community, and politics.

The rules of social criticism do not require writers to be specific about exactly which populations are the targets of their criticism and why they should have become miscreants, although the young have always been a favorite target. An annual poll of college freshmen and -women became the empirical centerpiece of the me decade critique, because it showed that in the 1960s students were aiming toward public service and teaching jobs. Starting in the 1970s, however, more were becoming concerned with financial success and interested in business careers, a pattern that has continued in the 1980s. In 1985, 73 percent listed "being well off financially" as a top goal, as compared to 39 percent in 1970, while 7 percent wanted to teach as compared to 20 percent in the late 1960s.[3]

The critics who were taking over Wolfe's notion of the me decade did not consider that the students of the 1960s were reacting to the low unemployment and almost limitless optimism about the occupational future, while those of the 1970s and the 1980s were trying to cope with stagflation, economic uncertainty, the governmental cutback of public service jobs, and the subsequent revival of economic opportunities for the well-educated. Although the poll had no data on values or ethics, those who used the changed percentages for their critique treated them as the results of new values—and symptoms of the new national selfishness. They assumed further that this selfishness infected everyone, including the vast majority of Americans who were not first-year college students or who had never gone to college.

Wolfe's article dealt with a by-product of the striving for self-development, but he also described some bizarre side effects of cult behavior. Meanwhile, a number of clinicians and intellectuals began to view the search for self-development itself as pathological, associating it with a personality disorder they described as narcissism. Acting both as reporters of clinicians' judgments and as critics, Christopher Lasch, Richard Sennett, and others treat current expressions of individualism in part as a psychosocial sickness.[4] Unlike most clinicians, they call attention to the societal and cultural causes of narcissism, but whether they intend to or not, they ultimately contribute to a long American tradition of framing a social critique in medical terms.

Although neither the clinicians nor the critics present substantial data on who actually suffers from narcissism, they have developed theories of why this disease has become the psychopathology of our time. In the process their medical concept has also become a political one, which the critics have used to suggest that the best treatment is a transformation of American society in the particular directions they consider necessary.[5] Both Lasch and Sennett see narcissism as a source of cultural and other disorders, but they advocate very different kinds of community. Lasch appears to favor a modern version of a preindustrial and patriarchal form of society, while Sennett, opposing today's emphasis on intimate relations, finds his model in the public institutions—and forms of public communication—associated with, for example, the cultured classes of 18th- and 19th-century cosmopolitan European cities.

An extension of the critique of selfishness centers on a hedonistic theme: the excessive consumption of goods, usually termed materialism, which is, however, only one part of a generally amoral lifestyle. People who buy too many goods are sometimes thought to be pathological, and one cause of that pathology is the spread of individualism, which breaks down the social controls on consumption. The critique also has an esthetic component, for it accuses people of buying the wrong goods, although the interest in goods per se is sometimes thought to be an esthetic failure. This failure is not intrinsically a consequence of individualism, but at times it is related to the excessive freedom of choice made possible by individualism—and capitalism.

The hedonistic critique is largely about ordinary people, including middle Americans. The critics on the Right tend to argue that ordinary people are culturally or otherwise incompetent, those on the Left that capitalism has been accompanied by a mass-produced popular culture which gives people too many inferior choices but deprives them of significant ones.

The substance of the hedonistic critique is not new, for critics have attacked people for too much or the wrong consumption ever since the Puritans settled in America. The first accusers were advocates of religion, but they—and those who have come after them ever since—were also upset by the hedonism they perceived to exist among the lower classes.

America's first mass entertainment media, the "yellow press" and the movie, were initially most popular in urban low-income areas, and perhaps as a result, all subsequent mass media were attacked by critics of hedonism. After World War II, for example, comic books and television came under attack. Thereafter the critics condemned many other features of American popular culture and, in the 1950s, virtually all goods and practices associated with suburban living. As the critics branched out to find fault with the lower-middle class in addition to the poor and working class, they also put more emphasis on esthetic failures.[6] At times they became critical of people's seeming lack of interest in the quality of what they were buying, which was also ascribed to a failure of taste.[7] In the 1980s, the critics found a new target, the yuppies, that well educated middle class of young technicians and professionals, and their supposedly excessive spending for high-priced restaurants, vacations, electronic equipment, running shoes, and the like. However, yuppie became such a widely used pejorative that almost anyone young or single from the white middle class was being targeted. Even young middle Americans were occasionally labelled yuppies.

The critics' disapproval reflects not only their distaste for the general public's esthetic standards but their dismay over the declining respect for high culture and its reduced authority as a setter of national cultural standards. Concurrently, their unhappiness with American popular culture, which they call mass culture, reflects fear of cultural disorder, of a society being destroyed by the culturally undeserving in pursuit of individualism. This mixture of social and esthetic fears was first expressed by the European aristocrats and conservatives who initially formulated the mass-culture critique, but it has been voiced as well by American patricians and by Left intellectuals on both sides of the ocean.

The critics of the Left have worried less about cultural disorder—or hedonism—than that "mass culture" and the individualistic pursuit of consumer goods is destructive of socialist community building, removing workers from occasions of group consumption in which they could be politically active. For example, from an orthodox Left perspective, public housing is valued both for being group housing and for being publicly supplied. Once the workers become suburban homeowners, however, they are apt to think about property values and want lower taxes, and can become more conservative on other political issues as well.[8]

A somewhat different Left critique reflects the fondness of many Left intellectuals for ethnic and other kinds of past working-class cultures, as well as for even earlier peasant and worker folk cultures.[9] These were and remain preferable to mass culture not only on esthetic grounds but also because they may voice some socialist or presocialist ideas, and because, being communally created and used, they are neither commercial nor mass-produced. The evolution of the American working class into a set of customers for capitalist entertainment has been particularly hard to bear for those socialist intellectuals who had hoped that workers would join them in the development of a socialist but also modernist high culture.[10]

Despite the concern over individualism's potential for cultural disorder, it has probably been attacked most persistently for its harmful effects on community. The communal critique of individualism has taken many forms, but three are particularly significant. One, of European origin, is also an attack on industrialism and capitalism, and mourns the end of an idealized preindustrial community in which everyone shared much the same values and was more concerned with the common culture than with self.[11]

The other two critiques are more relevant to America. One

advocates collective solutions and argues that individualists deprive themselves of its many benefits of community, financial
as well as social. For example, a neighborhood playground offers
superior equipment and more playmates and also is cheaper than
what families can supply individually for their children in their
own backyards. More important, collective action using organized
protests and other means to persuade government to create jobs
is more effective than individuals going out on their own, especially if they compete with each other for an insufficient number
of new jobs.

The second relevant-to-America communal critique goes beyond collective action and faults individualism for its destructive
impact on the "sense of community," the communal bonding
and consensus that motivates citizens to work together altruistically and democratically for common goals. In our generation,
perhaps the most eloquent and thoughtful spokesperson for this
critique has been Robert N. Bellah, and a convenient prototype
of his general analysis can be found in the widely acclaimed
Habits of the Heart.[12]

Bellah's writing is based on the empirical research he and
his coauthors conducted among a sample of Californians and
others, almost all of them middle class people and better off
than middle Americans. Although Bellah supports some previously described critiques of individualistic selfishness, narcissism,
and materialism, he recognizes that American individualism is
not asocial. Indeed, he acknowledges the prevalence and the
importance of "lifestyle enclaves" and "spontaneous communities
of the like-minded," which are graphic terms for the informal
groups and networks I have described as microsocial. However,
Bellah finds both forms morally wanting.

For him, community is not just a functioning set of voluntary
relationships or the expression of a shared culture, but those
feelings, values, and actions which produce "serious commit-
ments . . . [that] transcend the lifestyle enclave and represent
genuine community."[13] Such community requires people's willingness to surrender their own individualism, but also many other
social forms of division and differentiation, including those of
class.[14] Bellah calls for other drastic economic and political changes
in which, for example, the corporation becomes a humanitarian
agency, with incorporation being "the concession of public authority to a private group *in return* for service to the public good."[15]

Bellah is not entirely clear about how genuine community is to be achieved, but it requires "personal transformation among large numbers . . . [and] the nurture of groups that carry a moral tradition,"[16] as well as "social movements which grow out of, and also influence, change in consciousness, climates of opinion and culture."[17] Although he models the social movements on the civil rights movement, Bellah does not consider how much the success of that movement was based on the right combination of personal transformation, moral tradition, professional organizing, and politically sophisticated planning of strategy and tactics.

In Defense of Popular Individualism

I find many of the preceding critiques unconvincing. Some are wrong about how middle, and other, Americans act and think; others are unconvincing because they are based on questionable arguments, while a few reflect values with which I disagree.

Increases in narcissism or even simple selfishness are difficult to substantiate, but Bellah himself reports that "if there are vast numbers of a selfish, narcissistic 'me generation' in America, we did not find them."[18] According to Lasch's analysis, narcissism has risen sharply among psychoanalytic patients in recent years, but that rise could also be due to patients with other emotional maladies heading for the many therapies that currently compete with psychoanalysis. Psychoanalytic and psychiatric patients as a group are not a representative sample of the country's population whatever their emotional problems, and these problems are not a reliable indicator of the country's problems.[19]

Lasch's conception of narcissism is far broader than that of the therapist, however, frequently resembling other-directedness, which David Riesman described as a new but not pathological cultural character type in The Lonely Crowd. At other times, what Lasch considers narcissism could also be interpreted as self-improvement, or self-improvement gone wrong.[20] Frequently Lasch weaves his own cultural criticism, for example of the bureaucratization and commercialization of sports, into his analysis of narcissism even though that criticism has nothing directly to do with narcissism.[21]

The critics have not been wrong, however, to notice and attack an increase of clearly antisocial individualistic behavior in the 1980s. Bullying, particularly of the racial variety, increased, in part because of the Reagan administration's lack of interest in civil rights and also because older racial antagonisms surfaced again as a result of economic tensions and high rates of urban black street crime created partly by these tensions.

Greedy behavior surely increased, changes in the national economy and the Republican control of the White House having combined to legitimize a permissive approach to business community morality. Opportunities for making large amounts of money were opened up in arbitrage and investment banking particularly, and as in the past when similar opportunities became available, people to exploit them quickly appeared. So did others who were willing to violate some laws in the hope of making even more money, including some high-level government officials.

Even the commercial exploitation of patriotic ceremonies that went on in the mid-1980s is not new. A good deal of huckstering by large corporations and small entrepreneurs—or what corporate advertisers now call cause-oriented marketing—took place in connection with the celebration of the 100th anniversary of the Statue of Liberty, but 19th-century hucksters were around when the Statue was built. In any case, greed is an expression of capitalist rather than popular individualism, and there is no evidence to suggest that middle Americans became greedier or richer during the 1980s.[22]

There is no evidence of an upturn in materialism, commodification, or hedonism among this population either. Some nouveaux riches—of all classes—have always shown off with outrageous consumption practices, and still do. So have some young people, and because there have been more young adults without family responsibilities and with more money in the 1980s than in the past, and because their boutiques are highly visible (some being geographically close to the urban haunts of the critics), America as a whole is being blamed for a new materialism.

As far as one can tell, middle American adults still buy primarily for increased comfort and convenience, although comfort now includes mass-produced versions of the gourmet foods and other specialty goods once available only to more affluent and educated consumers. In fact, the latter may complain when middle Americans "spoil" vacation sites and crowd European landmarks that only the well-off could afford in the past. Nonetheless, few middle Americans can be spending excessively, since, on the average, their real wages and salaries have been decreasing since the mid-

1970s. Too many critics seem to make their judgments about consumer materialism from television commercials and rock music videos, many of which lend themselves easily to apocalyptic analyses.

Hedonism, at least of the sexual kind, was probably practiced by a larger portion of today's young adults than in the past until the arrival of AIDS. Judging by the polls, however, adult America's sexual practices and attitudes, as well as the divergence between them, have not changed dramatically since World War II. As far back as the late 1940s, Alfred Kinsey and his coworkers found that 90 percent of the married men and half the married women had taken part in premarital sex, but the 1986 GSS indicates that 37 percent of the respondents still consider it "always wrong" or "almost always wrong."[23]

Drug use is significantly higher than in the past because marijuana has joined alcohol as an acceptable and socially used drug, although the use of either does not necessarily imply hedonistic occasions or motives. Drug use also becomes more visible every time a new drug is introduced, but if total drug use actually increases at that time, it declines again when the fashionable and the curious have stopped using the latest novelty. Perhaps the spread of heroin, cocaine, and various pills would never have occurred if marijuana had not been introduced, but in the end at least two-thirds of the population still relies upon alcohol.[24] There is also a proportion of the population that is addicted not only to drugs or alcohol but also to gambling, overeating, and compulsive buying—as well as to compulsive use of culture, low or high, and to overwork. Unfortunately, data on how many addicts live among us are not available; sadder still, effective cures for most addictions have not yet been found. However, very few addicts of any kind are hedonists.

Professionally trained critics exceed their bounds when they indulge in highly exaggerated or inaccurate depictions of American life. They also exceed these bounds if they insist that middle and other Americans must choose the same cultural and social activities they do. This insistence may be justified when the critics can demonstrate that the choices they advocate are absolutely necessary for the welfare of society and of the people they are criticizing. It is not justified, however, when ordinary people, lacking the education, income, and professional goals of the trained critic, simply prefer to make other choices. That middle

Americans, or others, are concerned with economic security in choosing careers does not make them selfish, and that they buy different or more goods—if in fact they do—than the critics does not turn them into materialists or hedonists.

A related critical misjudgment is the charge that many ordinary people cannot make individual choices but can only respond, sheep-like, to the goods, services, and ideas that commercial and governmental suppliers offer. Too many critics, on the Left and the Right, believe that "the masses" are essentially passive, accepting what is supplied them either because they are seduced by clever capitalists or because they are morally backward.

Describing a large number of people as a mass and deciding, a priori, that they are passive enables those who think this way to believe that they are among the elect few who are properly individual and who can therefore criticize the rest. It is a particularly distasteful way of thinking, for it denies others both the ability and the right to choose their own values and tastes. It implies that only experts, critics, and those saved from cultural heresy or false consciousness can judge how people should live their lives.[25]

Another critical shortcoming is to disguise criticism as a seemingly empirical fact about the past. For example, complaints about materialism frequently take the form of mourning for an alleged golden age in which people were crafts workers and obtained their satisfactions from pride of craft rather than from the pleasure of consumption. Surely such crafts workers once existed, although few were allowed to express their individuality, while the other 95 percent of the population toiled as laborers without time or the opportunity for pride in anything. Marx was as guilty of this nostalgia as conservatives of his time. Whether it comes from the Left or the Right today, and whether it puts the blame on individualism or some other element of modern life, this critique is often thoughtless. It is also wrong, because more people are doing work in which they have pride of craft today than ever before. Moreover, in all societies, most people who can afford comfort, convenience, and luxury indulge in all three, and perhaps nearly everyone is an occasional commodity fetishist when given the opportunity.

My perspective is different. It assumes that until proven otherwise, all people, educated or not, can know what they want and can make choices that reflect their individual preferences, except when they are unable to obtain or even know about the needed information, are in emotional straits, or under severe financial or social pressures that prevent them from choosing. Absent these kinds of conditions, I assume that adult individuals are the best—although not the only—judges of what they want and need. Furthermore, nothing is wrong with the way people satisfy their wants or needs unless these are demonstrably harmful to themselves, to others, or to the general societal welfare.

I do not deny that the pursuit of individualism and self-development can turn into the pursuit of self-interest, and even to a concentration on selfishness to the exclusion of all communal concerns. However, I doubt that selfishness is as widespread in middle America as some observers believe, or that criticizing popular individualism will produce a decline in selfishness. This does not negate appeals for more communal concern and public altruism, and it does not question the urgent need to attack poverty and other inequalities. Even so, sermons against selfishness and attacks on self-development, or merely on the desire for more comfort, are not likely to be effective. Practical ways of reducing poverty and inequality must be sought, but these cannot be practical unless they respect the middle American commitment to individualism.

Popular individualism is hardly beyond criticism, however, and its major fault is that, like all other individualisms, it creates victims.[26] Some people are hurt because they are unable to deal with the loosening of ties that is a part of individualism. Those who have lost ties, voluntarily or otherwise, but cannot develop new ones may suffer from levels and forms of social isolation that can lead to despair. Loneliness is unfortunately usually invisible and has therefore received insufficient attention from critics of individualism. The suffering of some victims of loosened ties can become socially dangerous if they panic and surrender their egos to religious cult leaders with secular ambitions and totalitarian methods, or to political cults.

Although individualism has been accused of being a significant cause of mental illness, evidence to justify the accusation is not now available. Historical studies suggest that rates of serious mental illness have declined over the last century and also during the last generation. Some recent contrary research proposes, however, that rates of severe depression have been rising over the last several decades.[27] So far, no causal analyses have yet been carried out and a nearly endless number of causes could be at work, but it is possible that the pursuit of individualism and the loosening of social ties it has helped bring about are among the responsible factors.

A rather different set of individualism's victims suffer when they explain their own behavior, and especially that of people and groups who dominate them, solely by factors which are distinct for every person, for example, motives and "personality differences." When social phenomena are described or explained in individualistic ways, proposals for the elimination of undesirable phenomena will also be distinct for every person. This could discourage solutions such as legislation or the alteration of financial incentives and constraints that attack the social roots of such phenomena.

When poverty is blamed on individual failure, antipoverty policy typically emphasizes intensive social work or educational schemes instead of policies that deal with the social roots of poverty, i.e., decent jobs and incomes. If affirmative action programs must wait for proof of individual bias against minority individuals or groups, they will wait a long time, since few people are likely to admit such bias. Further, what was called institutional racism in the 1960s can persist among racially tolerant people who establish nonracial entrance requirements that nonetheless end up excluding minorities. The 1987 Supreme Court decision that ignored studies showing capital punishment being mostly used for black criminals and instead required systematic evidence of individual bias in effect legitimized the existing pattern of execution for many blacks and life imprisonment for most whites.

The emphasis on individual explanation and solution unduly hurts the large numbers of people at the bottom of the socioeconomic hierarchy who require social solutions, while it unduly benefits those at the top who get personal credit for the successes of the organizations they head. Chrysler executive Lee Iacocca earned national fame (and $23 million in income in 1986) for being at the head of that auto company while government loan guarantees, big reductions in the number of workers, and wage and benefit givebacks by those not fired produced the Chrysler revival. Mr. Iacocca made a number of wise executive decisions in the process, but he did not save Chrysler all by himself any more than emperors, prime ministers, and generals personally achieve the military and other successes for which they are awarded historical immortality.

Individualism can disadvantage even the people who most

strongly endorse it. When American voters look for presidential character and become enamored of politicians who appear to be attractive personalities, whether the name be John Kennedy or Ronald Reagan, such voters can easily lose sight of the nature of those politicians' policies and pay insufficient attention to what the politicians have done rather than said. True, candidates not in a position to make government decisions until they are in the Oval Office must be judged to some extent by surrogate indicators such as character, but a politician already in that office has a staff to create the image on the basis of which voters must judge their character. When voters finally notice that the results of policies do not square with the niceties of the image, it can be too late.

By the same token, the middle American tendency to treat formal organizations almost as if they were families and to judge them by the moral norms by which families and their members are judged surely helps drive out the personally dishonest leaders and perhaps recruit more honest ones into these organizations. Even so, formal organizations are governed by rules, and the most honest executive operating with the wrong rules cannot possibly succeed. Untold numbers of Americans have been frustrated, disappointed, and hurt by their preoccupation with familistic morals for large organizations and their failure to insist on a change of rules.

Those who are disadvantaged or victimized by middle American individualism are drastically outnumbered by those who suffer the ill effects of capitalist individualism. Not only are entrepreneurs and corporate capitalists much more powerful to act on their ideas, but those ideas can affect people's livelihoods. Admittedly some of the regions and people who are losing their jobs to computers and poorly paid workers overseas are victims of worldwide economic trends, but the lack of effective help for these victims is a by-product of capitalist individualism and its influence on government. Middle Americans who are opposed to plant-closing legislation, heightened government efforts to save and create jobs, and the payment of more adequate and secure unemployment insurance are responsible as well, however. Those living by the values of popular individualism deserve criticism for supporting various other forms of governmental neglect, such as that of the underclass and racial minorities, but middle- and upper-middle-class advocates of individualism are equally to blame. It is hard to think of kinds of public neglect for which popular individualism is solely responsible.

The Communal Critique Revisited

Advocates of community who insist that individualists deprive themselves of the many benefits of collective action are obviously right. However, collective action requires a good deal of mutual trust and a commonality of interests and priorities, as well as the ability to pay the costs in time, energy, and patience for the hard work collective action requires. When people are similar enough socially—or know each other well enough—to possess that commonality, they are likely to develop sufficient trust as well. Collective action thus works best in small groups, and in fact most of the informal groups described in Chapter 2 engage in collective action without being aware of it.

In larger and formal groups or in communities where similarity of backgrounds, interests, and priorities is scarcer, collective action requires a sizable amount of interpersonal negotiation and compromise—and leaders who can apply personal skills that persuade people to ignore their differences. At times the viability of collective action may ride on the ability or charisma of the leadership— or on the charismatic qualities people attribute to it. Conversely, heavy burdens placed on leaders can also breed suspicions of their motives and thus impair attempts to work together.

The difficulties of collective action are sufficiently great that it arouses little enthusiasm except when success is clearly predictable. If success is unlikely, people resist because they doubt collective action can work, turning their doubt into a self-fulfilling prophecy that discourages subsequent collective action. Popular individualism deserves criticism for this kind of thinking because it helps middle Americans victimize themselves.

Nevertheless, liberal and other enthusiasts of collective action who keep insisting on its virtues without understanding its difficulties do not help their cause with middle Americans. Since collective action often fails, a more helpful approach would be to try to understand under what conditions it has been and can be successful and use that understanding to help make it work. Actually, middle Americans have often resorted to collective action for "negative" causes, such as keeping people or land uses of lower status out of their neighborhoods. An enemy on which all can agree is generally a useful ingredient for effective collective action.[28] Building on that fact and proposing collective action to achieve important positive middle American causes rather than the causes collective action enthusiasts think middle Americans should pursue may help too.

The two other principal forms of community advocated in the communal critique of individualism are harder to justify. The first, the community as a permanently cohesive body, essentially requires believers who cohere for religious or ideological reasons. Americans who are not believers will view that community as oppressive. The second form, community as "sense of community," is generally accepted as a periodic and temporary cohesion for bringing about collective action to cope with natural disasters and similar emergencies. However, Bellah's broader conception of sense of community, as well as the sensitive empirical work on which it is based, suggest that he and his colleagues may have identified a set of currently desired, and perhaps more permanent, communal values and feelings. The immense popularity of *Habits of the Heart* is further testimony to this possibility.

Bellah points out repeatedly, for example, that the people they studied have "tremendous nostalgia . . . for the idealized 'small town' . . . [and] wish for a harmonious community."[29] He notes, however, that "these feelings are belied by the strong focus of American individualism on economic success. The rules of the competitive market, not the practices of the town meeting or the fellowship of the church, are the real arbiters of living."[30]

The "marketplace" aspects of individualism cannot be ignored, but even so, Bellah underestimates the amount of cultural and social differentiation, the associated divergences of interests, and the resulting difficulties people have in dealing with these while working together communally. When they wish for a harmonious community, they probably would like to wish away these diversities and difficulties as well.

Bellah may also overestimate the extent to which people are ready to do more than wish, if only because he wants them to move beyond wishing. He is clearly discontented with how people actually live, judging by his repeated critical comments about their individualism, their "lifestyle enclaves," and their "communities of the like-minded." What he wants are "the practices of the town meeting" and the "fellowship of the church," but his idea that these could be "real arbiters for living" and deal successfully with the complexities of modern community life, especially in a heterogeneous community, is romantic.

When Bellah insists that genuine community is "an inclusive whole, celebrating the interdependence of public and private life and of the different callings of all," he simply asks too much.[31] It is hard to imagine the social movements and the personal transformations Bellah calls for developing among the people he and his colleagues studied, for these people display no interest in the quasi-religious community Bellah seeks. Thus, his transcendentalism is his own. It is also utopian in the sense that it requires not only a different society but possibly another kind of human nature. In addition it forecloses the possibility of a more secular sense of community achieved through more rational processes.

To be sure, Bellah does not ignore all rational processes. For example, he discusses national economic planning, although he does so somewhat reluctantly, because he believes that a cultural and moral transformation is required before even gradualist reforms can be carried out.[32] Similarly, Bellah is not reluctant to insist on the obligations and responsibilities of citizenship. The people he and his colleagues studied accepted these as well, but they also failed to act on them even if they appear to have felt guilty about that failure.

Because getting people to work together is extraordinarily difficult, Bellah, like other American reformers, has placed a heavy load of cultural and political expectations on community and on actual communities which neither can bear. The test of community cannot be high levels of participation and feeling or the emergence of a social movement, but whether, when problems arise, people do then come together, literally or figuratively, at least temporarily to solve the soluble problems effectively and democratically.[33]

Individualism and Society

Robert Bellah's search for genuine community is frustrated not only by his expectations but by a more fundamental social obstacle: that the residents of American communities lack the incentives and the facilitating institutions that would make them come together regularly. In small New England towns the town meeting once supplied both incentive and institution, although even then it was mainly a gathering where people endorsed the recommendations of local economic and political power holders.[34]

Today most towns are too large for even that function, and, in effect, government is the major representative of the residents in most communities.

These obstacles are magnified many times at the national level, by numerical and geographical size and also by another fundamental difficulty, that the national society does not exist as a body or entity that can undertake collective action. The nation is largely symbolic, and although decisions are constantly made in its name, they are made by the White House and other agencies which shape foreign policy. Many citizens pay little attention to these agencies until foreign policy decisions impact on their own lives, and may not even care about them except in wartime or unless they involve "American boys" in military adventures abroad.

Another collective entity is represented by the federal agencies and officials centrally involved in domestic policies and politics. The "domestic nation" is rarely a persuasive symbol because there are very few federal agencies that in fact represent everyone, and few policies that do not divide the citizenry. Presidents may nevertheless try to appeal to this symbolic nation, and even to patriotism, when they want popular support for their domestic agendas.

Society is the least visible collective entity. Sociologists think of it as an interrelated aggregate or collection of people, groups, and institutions within a set of spatial or other boundaries that separate them from other aggregates. These boundaries are often viewed as equivalent to those of the nation, and sociology texts commonly treat society as a synonym for the nation.[35] They do so not because sociologists are nationalistic, however, but because the term society is hard to define.

One of the definitional problems is that while people may describe themselves as members of society, they are not members in any formal way, for they have no explicit rights and privileges, obligations, or responsibilities in society as compared to the State. One may become a member of a club, a charitable organization, or the army, but one cannot take out a membership in society. Further, society lacks public or private agencies which represent people, and while people may think of themselves as citizens of their society, citizenship creates ties only to governmental and related political agencies. Being a citizen entitles people to governmental protections and benefits, but there are no societal equivalents to these.

One can of course argue that society does not really exist except as a symbol or concept. There is much to be said for such an argument, if only to discourage unnecessary social mysticism and vague causal analyses in which society is made responsible for deviant behavior or social problems. There are, however, a variety of institutions which are more than the sum of specific organizations, social processes that transcend the actions of particular individuals or groups, and norms, rules, and the like which guide social action and exercise social control even though they are not enforced by governments, other formal organizations, or informal groups.[36] These rules may exist and persist because they are internalized in people's minds, but they cannot be explained as products of individual minds. For this and other reasons, society is a necessary concept.[37]

Still, it is also a residual concept and before invoking it, researchers must see if they can identify the concrete organizations or other causal agents usually responsible for specific phenomena. In line with this argument, several questions can be raised about the nature of society which are sometimes used to criticize individualism. One question asks whether society can fall apart and if so, whether order is sometimes more important than freedom. A second is whether anyone speaks for society, and is justified in placing constraints on individualism in the name of society. A third asks whether society can be deliberately organized to reduce the power of the Market and State, as well as of the individualistic values which are said to legitimize them.

Long before modern sociology was invented in the 19th century, social analysts had asked what holds societies together and whether they can fall apart. Thinkers from many ideological camps have raised these questions, but conservatives have probably worried—and still worry—the most that society could fall apart, even if many were actually talking about the disappearance of a social order which they dominated.[38]

In conservative rhetoric, the disintegration of society is thought to take place when government, business, and other major institutions lose legitimacy, when there is widespread loss of faith in the rules and values that guide people's social lives, and if there is explicit disavowal of tradition. However, the prime danger is always explicit behavioral anarchy—the kind well imagined in Anthony Burgess's fantasy of rampaging underclass teenagers, *A Clockwork Orange.*

While societies have often endured lack of social peace and engaged in bloody internal conflict, few seem literally to have fallen apart. Genocides, wars, earthquakes, and other disasters can lead to the death or dispersal of such large numbers that the named societies no longer exist. Mythical or real, Priam's Troy clearly ended at the end of the Trojan War, at least until another population started anew on its site. When the Roman empire "fell," only its military and other central organizations disappeared; the rest of the country became a collection of rural settlements again.[39]

In modern times, various totalitarian governments, for example Hitler's and Stalin's, have tried systematically to destroy formal organizations and informal groups that opposed or could compete with them, but so far none has succeeded except by killing entire populations. The Holocaust and other genocides led to the disintegration of the societies of the murdered, but neither Russia nor Germany fell apart despite the immense toll that Stalinist and Nazi terror and World War II took on both countries. Likewise, the German inflation of the 1920s and America's Great Depression temporarily destroyed traditional assumptions about the value of money, work, and related kinds of resources, creating innumerable victims and tearing apart families and communities. In some countries such economic disasters have produced totalitarian governments, some of them hideously cruel. Still, the societies themselves did not fall apart, and most public and private institutions continued to function. It is hard to believe how many do so, and in a quasi-routine fashion, even while economic disaster or governmental terror takes place all around them.[40] The social and political chaos in which all reciprocity and trust disappear, basic institutions stop functioning, people kill each other, and society disintegrates seems to be found mainly in fictional dystopias.[41]

Consequently the periodic threat by supporters of the status quo—including Stalinists in Eastern Europe—that society could fall apart if people were given too much freedom must be rejected. Individualism cannot be used as an excuse either for the artificial preservation of a social order celebrated by conservatives or for the imposition of an authoritarian order to hold society together.

The second question about the nature of society concerns the issue of who can speak for it.[42] Since society lacks agencies that do explicitly speak for it, organizational spokespersons, doctors, ministers, and other experts, business leaders, and the like are ready and eager to speak for their society, for example to identify social problems that need solving or to encourage people—and governments—to behave and act differently.[43] Such speakers often feel they are entitled to represent the society because they have its best interests at heart.

Some are actually allowed to mount the societal podium. Presidents can step up to the "bully pulpit" to speak as moral leaders, and at times the same permission is given to authors, entertainers, and others, including social scientists, who have attracted a large audience for their work. In our time, journalists screen and select public figures who want access to the news media so they can claim to speak for society, and journalists themselves do so when, in their role as watchdogs, they have found evidence of previously unknown violations of laws by important organizations, including government.[44]

Sometimes society seems to speak for itself, at least figuratively, for particular values or even feelings are projected on it, generally in psychological ways. For example, society has been described as being "tired" after a period of political reform; unable to act because it is in a "middle-age slump" or because it "suffers from an identity crisis," and as favoring the restoration of capital punishment because it is "bloodthirsty and bent on revenge."[45] However, the most frequent figurative speakers for society are probably "the public" or a "public mood," the latter sometimes described also as a unified public opinion. These collective terms are generally invoked by identifiable individuals and agencies who propose, support, or justify a specific activity which they see, or would like to see, supported by "the public." (Actually, there is no single public of course, but only specific publics which are invoked around a specific matter, even if there is a polite fiction that it is always the same public.)

The public they invoke is an aggregate of undefined size and characteristics which seems to exist separately from the political process and which lacks an explicit voice. (The public mood is an even vaguer construct.) As a result, questions can and must be raised about this public, for example on what evidence it is perceived as existing, about its size and composition, how it has come together and with what intentions and mandates. Somewhat the same questions are appropriate to a public mood, and both sets of questions must be answered before a public or a public mood should be given any hearing. Last but not least, since influential individuals or groups could be deliberately constructing and hiding behind these collective images in order to pursue their own goals, it is also necessary to know whether the public or public mood is spontaneous or organized.

No empirical data can show that society is speaking for itself, although the individuals or organizations that create an anthropomorphic image of society may decide that there is such a widespread consensus behind a value or position, for example capital punishment, that it feels to them as if society as a whole was bent on revenge. The public and a public mood can, however, be identified, although hardly in direct ways. Their existence is generally inferred from poll data, letters to the news media, and especially communications to politicians or other organizational leaders. At times very small numbers of people are enough to convince some people, including politicians and journalists, that the public supports a particular opinion or action.

Publics and public moods are regularly and systematically organized by self-interested individuals and agencies using advertising campaigns, educational programs, and political rhetoric to create enough adherents or supporters to make the claim that a public or public mood exists credible. Spontaneous publics or public moods usually develop in reaction to a national crisis, a tragic accident or a sharp increase in a perceived social problem. However, even a highly organized campaign must attract voluntary (i.e., spontaneous) support from people; otherwise the resulting public will not be large enough. Conversely, the moment there is some indication of spontaneous enthusiasm for a person, product, or idea, these days someone is certain to try to organize it further, whether for profit, popularity, or influence. Book publishers and film distributors conventionally increase advertising budgets after they have evidence of spontaneous audience interest. Similarly, political candidates attract a far larger number of campaign contributors after they have evoked spontaneous support than they do before.

Business is probably the most frequent organizer of publics, and whenever a public mood develops to oppose particular taxes or a government regulation of specific consumer goods, investigative journalists later find firms or industries or their lobbyists that encouraged it. Government has done its share of organizing as well. Federal drug agencies created the first public alarm about marijuana beginning in the 1930s.[46] Politicians also try to engineer publics and public moods, and the Nixon administration was once discovered to have recruited supporters to flood the White House with favorable reactions to a presidential speech.

What size a public must be to deserve a hearing in a democratic society is a political question, but there are dangers in giving in too fast to those who claim to represent the public, to perceive a public mood, or to speak for society. Once values, claims, or demands are attributed to the public, or to the entire society, they are given greater legitimacy merely because of the attribution. Paying too much attention to those who claim to speak for society could lead to a majority tyrannizing a minority (or the reverse), to conformity pressures being mounted against unpopular ideas and acts, and to putting constraints on individualism without going through the political process. Societies cannot speak, and those who claim to speak for them and their claims must be treated with skepticism.

The third question concerns the ability of society to act as an adversary to Big Government, Big Business—and individualism. Although all ideological groups have claimed to speak for society, parts of the Left have always been particularly active insofar as both populists and millennial Marxists have identified society with "the people." As a result, militant protest by a handful of people to oppose a powerful economic or governmental agency is regularly viewed by revolutionaries as a first sign of the beginning of revolutionary fervor among "the people" even if there is absolutely no evidence for such a conclusion. Populists have been more realistic and look more toward local community organizations, but they too would like to believe that the successes of small groups of people are harbingers of a more populist future.[47] Understandably, any organization which believes it represents the people may feel justified to speak for society.

A related and highly sophisticated populism has recently been put forward among some writers who see society as an antidote to what they call the Market and the State. Alan Wolfe (no relation to Tom) has written that "The modern world . . . gave society the capacity to plan, to take fate into the hands of the people, thereby making society possible."[48] Sheldon Wolin has argued that "the revitalization of democracy must be undertaken primarily in society rather than through state-oriented institutions. . . ."[49]

So far these writers have not clearly identified the society in which they place their hopes, although its prime component for Wolfe is "ordinary people" and their "capacity for creative action and thought."[50] Wolin writes about "the craftsperson who respects what he or she is working with . . . not the administrator who 'creates' an organization," and he adds "countless community organizers and ordinary citizens."[51] He undoubtedly has in mind the activists of the liberal and socialist community organizations that have sprung up since the 1970s.

Wolfe's conception of society is more abstract as well as national in scope. He seeks a social structure "to accept such features of rational planning as economic growth and the welfare state yet to maintain simultaneously the *Gemeinschaft* virtues . . . individual freedom necessary to bring out the best in the person [and] . . . the collective planning necessary to bring out the best in society."[52]

Until such a structure can be developed, Wolfe's notions differ only slightly from some of those identified with Robert Bellah.[53] When Wolfe writes that "we must turn toward the ties that grow organically out of interaction with each other if we are to have an effective alternative to the ties from above . . . ," he is focusing on a communal rather than a national society.[54]

Such ties can also be found in families and informal groups that make up people's microsociety, but in middle America people seek to use and avoid rather than to replace Market and State. Nor are they eager to undertake collective planning. Wolfe, Wolin, and the local activists are, however, generally opposed to middle American and other contemporary individualisms and therefore propose a different society to achieve their plans.[55] The plans themselves deserve consideration, but there are better ways to deal with the excesses of Market and State.

Six

Individualism and Liberal Democracy

I<small>N</small> a democracy, all citizens ought to be represented directly or indirectly in the political system, exerting influence on its decisions and plans. Citizens ought also to have as equal an influence as possible, even if the one person–one vote rule of the Constitution cannot easily be applied in the non-electoral parts of politics or achieved in an economically unequal society.

A representative democracy becomes a liberal democracy when, through its own efforts and its impact on the economy, it encourages that economy and the class structure in general toward more economic and other equalities. A liberal democracy is basically an egalitarian welfare state.

Individualism is one of a number of obstacles to liberal democracy. It militates against the formation of a political community and even the consensus that would support a conception of the public interest emphasizing more equality. Individualism also justifies the existence of interest groups that further discourage this community. Pluralism, the doctrine with which America handles the representation of a multiplicity of interest groups, does not help either, for it is regressive, enabling those groups already politically and economically powerful to become more so.[1]

Marxists see individualism as encouraging false consciousness that makes workers and others accept inequality. Conservatives like to point out that it encourages another false consciousness, unreasonably high expectations that complicate the tasks of the governors.[2] Individualism is also inherently, if selectively, anti-government sui generis, and capitalist individualism particularly so. Still, it is not individualistic values but Big Business, and to a lesser extent Big Government, that do the most to divert the political system from becoming more democratic.

Middle American individualism contributes some additional and distinctive obstacles. If middle Americans continue their search for microsocial privacy and organizational avoidance by moving further away from contact with the major political organizations and if these in turn become more centralized at the top and less responsive to pressure, democracy is sure to suffer.

Democracy is likely to be hurt too by middle America's antipathy toward government. Some antipathy is unavoidable because government is the arena in which many of the country's class, racial, and other conflicts of interest must be resolved. As a result, government cannot satisfy many of America's political demands. When antipathy festers or when it becomes chronic, further obstacles are added to the citizen-government relation, with citizens unwilling to call on government when they need it, and government unable to reach citizens because of their suspiciousness. As a result, negotiation and compromise become nearly impossible—and any hope of cooperation illusory. Citizens are then tempted to withdraw further from politics and political situations, and bureaucracies will seek to insulate themselves from both citizens and politicians.

Liberal democracy, but also democracy itself, could be impaired by middle America's continuing faith in capitalist individualism—and in its hope for the return of past high levels of economic growth. The resulting, if usually silent, support of (or lack of protest against) many corporate policies adds to the political power of Big Business and to the increased powerlessness of those victimized by corporate policies. Middle America is also sufficiently unenthusiastic about long-term and democratic economic planning to enable Big Business and others to frustrate fledgling planning attempts, as in the short-lived industrial policy experiment of the late 1970s. True, most Western European and communist governments have not yet learned how to develop effective and democratic plans, and middle Americans have some right to be skeptical about the idea. Still, given the possibly harmful changes that could take place as a result of future postindustrial technologies and America's declining power in the world economy, further experiments in economic planning are necessary as simply one fail-safe mechanism.

Popular individualism is not, however, intrinsically hostile to liberal democracy, for middle Americans are not the enemies of greater equality they are made out to be. They are uninterested in abstract notions of egalitarianism and hostile to utopian leveling schemes, but like most other Americans, they are likely to be supportive of policies from which they themselves can benefit, including those which reduce poverty, as long as they are not expected to pay most of the bills.

Toward More Representative Democracy

The validity—and other virtues—of these criticisms notwithstanding, popular (and other) individualisms are by now so well entrenched in the structure of people's lives and in their beliefs that they are not likely to go away or even recede, except perhaps temporarily under conditions of extreme crisis. The same is true of middle American habits of political avoidance. Consequently, a different approach to democracy is required: one that makes it possible for political institutions to accept, and adapt to, popular individualism. Instead of trying to improve American democracy by demanding further participation and changes from its users, i.e., the citizenry, it is worthwhile to see what can be achieved by making changes among the suppliers in some existing political arrangements and institutions. To put it graphically, *if citizens cannot or will not come to political institutions to participate, these institutions have to come to them.*

In essence, political organizations must be made more representative so that government will become more responsive. Increased representation requires adding new people or processes to political organizations responsible both for finding out what citizens think and want and for standing in for the citizens. Increased responsiveness involves attending to the opinions and demands of the citizenry whenever possible. Citizens still need to communicate with those who represent them, but the challenge is to emphasize ways of political communication the citizens will use and to deemphasize those they now avoid.

In theory there are many ways to enhance political representation, both across the board and for those people now most poorly represented. Some require changes in existing political organizations; others are best achieved by new ones, but here the focus will be mainly on long-term changes in existing organizations. These changes should also lead to increased governmental responsiveness without, however, forcing government into the impossible task of needing to be responsive to all opinions and demands of all citizens. The proposals that follow are meant primarily to be illustrative. Several may be impractical in the short run but none are inherently or permanently impractical. However, none can be implemented without political support from the people who now avoid politics.

Five Proposals for Enhancing Representation

Perhaps the most obvious solution would be to help elected representatives, particularly at the national and state levels, do more representing by supplying additional paid staff who would reach out to constituents in ways that most elected politicians can no longer find time to do. Resembling in some respects old-time precinct captains as well, this staff would listen to citizens' complaints, hear their opinions, requests, and proposals, and transmit these to their employers and relevant government agencies. Above all, the added staff would get in touch with citizens who are normally reluctant or unable to contact politicians.

A variation of the scheme would assign such staff to the major political parties, which might help revitalize the parties, making it possible to reduce the emphasis on, and the money going to, television campaigning. Both schemes would, however, improve the ability of incumbents to get themselves reelected, since staff working for challengers could only make postelection promises.

Consequently, a wiser solution is to use nonelectoral organizations to improve representation. Accordingly, a *second* way to encourage representative democracy is through the broadening and diversification of lobbying. If the suppliers of goods and services, as well as other well-organized and affluent actors in the economy and polity, can support lobbyists to make their cases in Washington, state capitols, and city halls, why should the users of these goods and services not be equally represented? Customers and clients involuntarily pay for having many goods and services advertised to them. With the right legislation a part

of those funds—which firms deduct from their taxes anyway—
could be diverted to lobbyists who make sure that user interests
are represented alongside supplier interests when these diverge.
If companies doing business overseas can hire lobbyists to advance
their foreign policy interests, using tax-deductible funds to do
so, should not public funding be available for citizen lobbies on
foreign policy?

Civil servants and retired people as well as other senior citizens
already have lobbies, but perhaps there should be lobbies as well
for young adults and adolescents. More urgently needed are lobbies for hospital patients and for those who only need to see
doctors, particularly the chronically ill. Other lobbies might represent consumers of expensive goods, including car and home buyers as well as tenants. Workers not belonging to unions might
benefit from a variety of worker lobbies. Mass-transit users need
more representation than they now receive from municipal officials. Indeed, while business, industries, trades, and most professions create lobbies to support their own interests, their customers
and clients are on the whole limited to lobbies that further causes
such as world peace. Lobbies that represent people and their
prosaic day-to-day goals are much scarcer.

In theory, government regulation for the benefit of various
kinds of users and workers is supposed to preempt the need
for lobbies, but in many instances government regulators become
beholden to the industries and other suppliers with which they
must deal. Consequently, every large aggregate of people with
a common role or a common interest should be eligible for representation, especially those people who find themselves facing
powerful supplier lobbies.

The costs of establishing and running user lobbies could be
paid in part by the supplier organizations being opposed, the
private ones then deducting the resulting expenditures from their
taxes as part of the cost of doing business. Lobbies for citizens
who cannot pay these costs, notably the poor, should be publicly
funded.[2]

Nonetheless, people eligible for a particular lobby would have
to pay at least nominally for membership—as many people are
already doing for lobbies aiding popular causes. Membership contributions are needed not only to help fund the lobbies but to
indicate, and spur, member commitment. Despite the influence
of skillful lobbyists, citizen memberships remain a vital source

of lobby power. Lobby staff members can often win important victories with only a small number of active citizens providing letters, phone calls, and other forms of support, but a lobby must be able to demonstrate periodically that it can summon member support or it will lose its ability to win victories for its membership.

The idea that one lobby can represent a large aggregate or class of people is of course too simple, for any aggregate will consist of many—and even divergent—interests. In most instances, affluent users or constituents will have different interests than poor ones, and the latter stand the usual danger of losing out if not all interests can be accommodated. Some lobbies will be small and would have to join temporary or permanent coalitions to be effective.

Lobbies are not always attractive organizations. When members pay insufficient attention, their organizations can be co-opted by the opposition, especially if it has more money and influence. National lobbies may become bureaucratized, rigid, and unable to change with the times. Since "sponsored politics is never the same as spontaneous politics," a lobby can alienate those it represents even as it serves them.[3]

Nevertheless, because of the strenuousness of spontaneous politics, the attractions of political avoidance, and thus the virtual inevitability of sponsored politics, lobbies can give previously unrepresented people a greater voice in the political arena and more influence than they had before. Even if a lobby is frustrated or co-opted in 50 percent of its efforts, its clients still obtain 50 percent more political benefit than they had without the lobby.

Because of the declining role of political parties, lobbies may even be popular with the general public. In a 1983 poll nearly half the respondents agreed that "organized groups concerned with specific issues, such as business, labor, environmental and civil rights groups best represented their political interests," while only a third chose the political parties for this role.[4] No lobby can ever live up to the ideals of altruistic democracy, and adding many lobbies and lobbyists to all levels of government is hardly inviting. The only other equitable alternative, to abolish all lobbying, is even more impractical.

A *third* and more immediately applicable approach to broader representation is the extension of polling. When properly carried out, polling results in citizen input, not that of professional lobbyists. It also permits people to participate while enabling them to stay away from political organizations and politicians. Normally polling is far more representative than voting because all populations are sampled, including nonvoters.

To turn polling into an effective representational mechanism, it must become pluralistic, however, with greater diversity of questioners and questions than now exists. The current set of commercial and media polling organizations have become sufficiently close to the political and economic establishments that they ask questions mainly about current issues of concern to them. There are, for example, usually many questions about what the leading politicians are doing or planning to do about current issues but too few about what citizens think they should do about issues not on the politicians' agendas.

When the pollsters unduly limit their questions to issues that matter to the government, or to the corporations who hire them for commercial market research, it is possible that they are co-opting their respondents. Cornell University political scientist Benjamin Ginsberg has called attention to this danger, and has suggested that it has happened before. Indeed, the European political establishment invented polling when the political parties became too responsive to the lower classes, using it to co-opt these classes from actively protesting economic and political conditions.[5]

Americans appear to have been immune to such co-opting efforts so far, however. The polls of the 1960s did not discourage the civil disorders and widespread demonstrations during that decade, and as suggested in earlier chapters, poll responses toward the government are hardly favorable. Moreover, the answers are affected both by the health of the economy and by the actions of government. Polls about welfare state' programs indicate that people were not co-opted by the Reagan administration's hostility to such programs. On the contrary, the institutionalization of polling may have persuaded Americans whose ancestors were never consulted about national affairs that they are entitled to be consulted. Furthermore, as polling became ubiquitous, nervous presidents of the U.S. and other politicians have accepted this entitlement, sometimes wooing the pollsters in dubious ways to stop or hide the decline of their political fortunes.[6]

In order to make polling sufficiently pluralistic and properly representative, additional people must be asked additional questions even if both the people and the answers may be unpopular in Washington or city hall. For example, poor blacks—and poor whites—are too tiny a subgroup in current national polls, but so are Hispanics, family farmers, and middle American displaced workers. In fact, pluralistic polling means checking in regularly with an array of respondents chosen to take account of the country's diversity in people and ideas. Equally important, pollsters must spend more time asking people what is on *their* minds, what they want government and Big Business to do or stop doing for them and for the country and whether major institutions should be changed.

Admittedly, polling can distort representativeness, since it inevitably includes opinions from people who care little about particular issues and who may answer only to please the pollsters. Pollsters now know how to measure lack of interest—and knowledge—as well as intensity of opinion, however.[7] Respondents who supply pollsters with the conventional wisdom or with what respondents think they should say can be disarmed by proper questioning. Pollsters have long asked people to tell them both what the neighbors think and what they themselves think, for example. Polling must, however, become more sensitive to the distinctions people make between their own problems and needs and those of the country, and proper representational polling must enable people to make this distinction in their answers. Likewise, questions that require respondents to think more responsibly about questions involving policy issues and policy choices have to be developed.[8] Even so, probably the best way of reducing polling distortion in general is to make certain that the polls include questions that people care about and want to answer.[9]

Pluralistic polling can only take place, however, if there are changes in the structure of polling, notably through additional polling organizations which are free from the obligations and other ties in which today's well-known giants are enmeshed. In addition, the new pollsters and old who will carry out pluralistic polling must be encouraged to move away from the routinized dependence on standardized questions and narrowly precoded answers, and above all from a polling economy in which speed and cost frustrate the asking of detailed and searching questions.[10] Equally crucial are clients who need answers to questions that are not now being asked and who will be able to pay the higher cost of better questions.

Consumer goods manufacturers, other businesses, and political clients can be found to buy some polls with different questions, but public funding will be needed both for better quality polling and for the many organizations that lack the budgets required even for standardized polls. A Public Polling Service, modeled to some extent on the Public Broadcasting Service, could fund the polls for such organizations and carry out its own. Even so, additional monies must be available to allow impecunious organizations, journalists, researchers, and others to commission or carry out and report studies which are desirable for pluralistic and representative purposes but which include questions that might make even the Public Polling Service uncomfortable.

Additional polling would probably overload politicians and citizens with poll data, but while their overload could be a problem at first, it should lead quickly to more analyses of multiple polls, ending the current malpractice of drawing too many conclusions from one or two polls filled with standardized questions.

Pluralistic poll data and improved data analysis would allow politicians to know their constituents and to understand their opinions and demands more adequately. Politicians might thus be enabled to respond more adequately to these demands. Also, since most constituencies in America are highly diverse and full of conflicting demands, politicians who knew their constituents and these diversities better could turn conflicts into compromises more frequently. Further, they might not need to speak in generalities or "talk out of both sides of their mouths" quite as often. Constituents should then feel that they were being lied to less often and, all other things being equal, develop a little more trust in their elected officials.

Admittedly, better knowledge might help politicians manage and manipulate their constituents in a more sophisticated fashion and play more accurately on people's weaknesses than they have done up to now. Conversely, politicians could become so responsive to different groups that they would be unable to develop an integrated policy when it was needed. Campaigning politicians fell into this trap long before poll data were available, however, and they still have not lived down their traditional reputation for making different promises to different people.

The shortcomings of pluralistic polling only suggest the obvious: that poll results by themselves cannot and should not guide politics or policy and that such results must be combined with other citizen inputs. Voting has to come first by law, and other forms of direct citizen action will surely always weigh more heavily in politicians' thinking. Properly conducted polls could, however, enable elected officials to learn more about their mandate when only a small number of people were voting, and it would permit them to compare information supplied by and pressures exerted on them by lobbies (including the ones proposed above), which can be expected to exaggerate the number and feelings of their members and supporters.

Some political theorists are bitterly opposed to polling sui generis, since they see democracy as a deliberative process in which citizens have to talk with each other face to face. It is easy enough to agree with such critics in principle but difficult to find ways to satisfy them in a huge society; moreover, representational polling does not preclude establishing new deliberative institutions for citizens. There is always the possibility that when larger numbers of people are regularly asked questions, some will become interested in discussing issues they have previously ignored.[11]

A *fourth*, albeit indirect, means to enhance people's representation would be to encourage pluralism in the national and other news media. Journalists play a number of representational functions. Politicians watch how they cover and frame the news, looking for implicit attitudes that reflect or influence those of their audience. Thus the news is treated as an early version of polling. News stories supply politicians with up-to-date information about some of their constituents, and to the extent that news informs people, journalists are involved in the representational process by the information they convey to the citizenry. This in turn feeds back into what people tell the pollsters, even though they do not usually depend on the news to make up their minds.[12] The broadening of polling would thus be aided by broadening the news.

Consequently, additional news media with diverse ideological and audience perspectives would be helpful. Even a country as unideological as America needs to be served by more than four television network news organizations and news weeklies, fewer than half a dozen national newspapers, and a handful of national syndicates, all of them supplying fairly similar sets of stories framed in highly similar professional and political perspectives. Instead of pursuing the general news audience, the added media should supply news of particular interest to different audience segments that are not always well enough served now. These include older people, the jobless, those far removed from major urban centers, and especially the very large number of people, middle Americans included, who find present television and press news too complicated, hard to follow, or too often devoted to subjects of interest mainly to the well-informed.[13]

Additional news media would be costly, and would have to be established on a trial-and-error basis to see which audiences will actually want—and pay for—news that is more relevant to their living conditions and problems. Consequently, these news media would have to be developed by the cheapest means possible, using the least expensive print and electronic technologies and getting along with minimal news organizations to attract the minimal audience needed to survive economically. This might be accomplished by a supplementary "tier" of national, regional, and local newspapers and radio programs, supported by inexpensive television where and when possible. These news media would draw on the reportage gathered by the large national and local news media, using it for analysis, reanalysis, and commentary for their particular audiences, and from the points of view of these audiences and the journalists serving them. Some additional reporting would be necessary, but further large-scale professional news gathering, which requires expensive news organizations, would be kept to a minimum for economic reasons.

Most likely, even this low-budget tier of national media would require governmental or other subsidy, especially for the trial-and-error experiments and start-up periods. A National Endowment for News could be modeled on the existing Endowments for the Humanities and the Arts, which have been able to fight back virtually all attempts at political interference. Additional safeguards might be needed, however, to make sure that government funds but does not help select—or censor—the news.[14]

In view of the low level of people's interest in the news, the economic viability of a supplementary tier of news media is hardly certain. Whether enough readers, listeners, and viewers could be attracted is unpredictable, although news audience studies suggest that personally relevant news is of interest to people. Even if audiences were small, however, democratic representation would rise, and the more so if these media were to help inform poll respondents and also publish polls for which other news media had no room. Moreover, politicians can be counted on to pay attention to virtually all news outlets.

A *fifth* approach to broader representation is through the legal system, using the courts to argue that in a democracy, citizens are entitled to adequate representation. Not only must people be better informed of their rights but they must be able to obtain lawyers, both private practitioners and Legal Services or Legal Aid lawyers if they are poor, so that they have effective access to the courts. Class action and other suits can be used to fight inadequate representation or unfairly administered government programs and government programs which are unfair sui generis.

In addition, legal decisions, legislation and ombudsmen programs that strengthen people's rights can improve indirectly the way people are represented. For example, court decisions in support of affirmative action not only placed more women and minorities on public agency staffs but also meant that women and minority clients would thereafter obtain somewhat better representation in these agencies. Likewise, the Supreme Court's Miranda decision increased the rights of prisoners and also in the process forced the criminal justice system to pay somewhat more attention to prisoners in general. In the past, the extensions of suffrage, the abolition of the poll tax, and the passage of the voting rights legislation of the mid-1960s also had a considerable impact on representation. Turning previously disenfranchised people into potential voters makes sure that politicians will be more attentive and that subsequently, once disenfranchised populations will spawn their own politicians.

All five proposals require some additional governmental funds, but their cost will barely be visible in a trillion-dollar annual budget. They also add more bureaucracy to governmental operations—but this time for what should turn out to be a popular set of programs. Of course, none of the five suggestions are as idealistic or appealing as calls for a nationwide social movement to establish political community. They all reduce people's responsibility for making politics more democratic by their own efforts, even though they do not prevent such efforts from taking place. Nonetheless, new causes and inequities—and even old ones—will continue to give rise to new citizens' groups, some to press for new programs or solutions, others to march or otherwise demonstrate against old ones.

Furthermore, improving representation does not exclude attempts to improve participation as well, but proposals to do so must be drawn carefully, since greater participation does not automatically enhance democracy. Indeed, many schemes to increase participation are taken advantage of by those already most willing and able to participate. Facilitating more direct democracy in modern versions of town meetings is apt to bring out the better-educated, and they and other articulate people will probably dominate the discussion unless speakers are chosen at random. Voter registration campaigns are costly, are therefore usually undertaken by groups with the most political funds, and may end up registering mainly more of their own supporters. Consequently such campaigns could increase further the dominance of affluent voters in the electorate, unless current obstacles to registration that still exist in many states are removed. Public funds and public agencies would have to be used to give everyone an easy opportunity to register, including people from lower income levels at whom most existing obstacles are aimed.[15] Making voting easier will most likely bring out more of the present electorate too, particularly people with the most reason to vote—those whose concerns are already being represented by incumbents or voiced by challengers. All other things being equal, many conventional proposals to increase participation could actually add to the regressiveness of the political system.

As this suggests, even the most equitable methods of encouraging participation will not reverse the present high correlation between political participation and high income. Nor can such methods eliminate the political power that flows from economic power. Even if rich individuals, supplier lobbies, and large corporations could be prevented from spending money for political purposes, the economically powerful have other ways of expressing their political power. For example, corporations can influence politicians far more effectively by threatening to withdraw jobs or investment from an area—or from the country—than by making campaign contributions. The ability to abolish or add jobs also guarantees corporations special political representation, just as the ability to make or withhold political contributions guarantees individual "fat cats" better representation than other voters. Ultimately, some redistribution of wealth and income is necessary to democratize participation as well as representation. Genuine political democracy requires a good deal more economic equality than now exists in America.[16]

Too Much Democracy?

Proposals for better representation and more equitable participation are sometimes considered harmful to democracy because
they are alleged to have dangerous consequences for politics and
government. One argument is that any scheme to increase representation and participation will further split the country into separate interest groups or strengthen existing ones, making it yet
more difficult for the political leadership to pursue the public
interest.

This argument is not convincing because the notion that the
country has been, and can be, governed entirely in the public
interest is largely illusory. True, according to the conception of
altruistic democracy, politicians would govern in the public interest, pursuing either policies with which nearly everyone agrees
or those which so clearly add to the well-being of the country
as a whole that whether or not most citizens agree with them is
irrelevant.[17] In this ideal, group values, now sometimes called
"special" interests, would be considered only after the public
interest had been satisfied.

The ideal is most attractive to whoever defines the public
interest, or to those Americans who find that this definition coin-
cides with many of their own interests. The public interest promises seemingly automatic political cohesion, but except during
popular wars when victory is so clearly in the public interest
that it puts many interests—other than making money—on the
back burner, the public interest does not seem to provide sufficient
guidance to run the government. After international peace, national security, maintenance of the public order, garbage and
toxic materials removal, related public health measures, and continual economic growth, there are not many policies which fit
easily either conception of the public interest. Even some provisions of the Constitution, which ought to be in the public interest
by definition, have to be fought for, in the Supreme Court as
well as elsewhere. Moreover, declaring a policy to be in the public
interest does not, by itself, determine its priority or the amount
of money to be devoted to it. In the late 20th century, how much
is to be spent for the national defense turns out to be a more
relevant issue than whether that defense is or is not in the public
interest.

The list of public interest issues can be expanded, but many seemingly self-evident additions are not so self-evident. For example, holding or acquiring more public land for the benefit of future generations raises questions about how much our welfare should be reduced for that of our descendants. Everyone presumably agrees on the desirability of honest politics, but honesty is open to alternative definitions, and lying that supports yet more desired goals may not even be perceived as dishonesty. Then too, honest government has sometimes meant government by experts in administration who also favor low taxes for the business community and fewer public services for moderate- and low-income citizens. Apparently a number of Americans do not agree—by what they practice rather than what they preach—that the elimination of American starvation and the reduction of poverty are in the public interest, although both goals, as well as occupational safety, some form of full employment, and other kinds of economic security, deserve to be added to the Constitution as economic rights.

Once legislation is passed, enforcing and upholding the law is supposed to be in the public interest, but actually both processes continue to be struggled over politically. Laws unpopular with the majority somehow often fail to be enforced, and the enforcement of those disliked by influential minorities is liable to be sabotaged. Journalists who make headline stories out of laxities in the enforcement of the laws risk being attacked as dangerously liberal by conservatives who never made peace with the passage of the legislation.

Perhaps because of problems in agreeing about the public interest, rhetorical phrases are sometimes substituted for it, such as the desirability of progress, the national purpose, or an American mission. Like all general phrases, when they are specified, they often turn out to propose policies that are supported by only part of the population, or that will benefit a limited number. Progress almost always has victims even when it is generally desirable, and national purposes or missions can translate into expensive foreign policy ventures that take money away from needed domestic activities. Lip-service agreement about the public interest is easily achieved, but until more fundamental agreement about it can be hammered out, labeling a policy as being in the public interest remains a claim that requires discussion and struggle. Sometimes, it is a political appeal that claims to be above politics and can therefore be treated as rhetoric.

Although governing in the public interest would make it easier to reach decisions, the political system can also function on the basis of the current mix: some legislation in the public interest and a good deal more that is responsive to special interests, large and small. Still, none of the special interests should have so much political and economic power that they are able to pressure government to act in an undemocratic fashion.

Making democracy more representative need not interfere with the pursuit of the public interest. It will bring additional interpretations and specifications of that interest—as well as some new interest groups—into the political arena, but if such interest groups exist to begin with, a representative democracy ought to be representing them. The more interest groups that are represented, the better the chances of moving toward more extensive sharing of political power by roughly equal interest groups.

A second argument against increased representative democracy stems from the worry that it will end deserving public policies (claimed as being in the public interest) that are supported by a small number of organizations and voters—usually elite ones. Notable examples are some public subsidies with no practical payoff for most citizens in the short run, such as for basic scientific research or high culture, neither of which could survive without public funds.

This worry is largely groundless. The past century of democracy, here and elsewhere, has shown that nonelite populations understand the desirability of scientific research and other policies not of immediate benefit to them. They also retain considerable deference for elite policies sui generis, as long as these are not obvious schemes to enrich upper-class individuals or groups. Funding for high culture continues because of its public prestige and symbolic value as a community or national ornament even when most of the people who pay the subsidies obtain no personal benefit.[18] Should they decide to withdraw their support, however, it would be difficult to justify less representation and thus less democracy only in order to protect policies of and for various elites.[19]

A third argument, not unrelated to the second, fears that more democracy will only add to the power of ignorant and narrowminded Americans. In conservative fears, these Americans are illbehaved and profligate with public money; in liberal ones, they are likely to be racist and undemocratic. The implication is that any policy which reduces the influence of experts and other elites, who are assumed to be always democratically inclined and public-spirited, could endanger the country.

This argument is a political version of the mass culture critique, in which the masses ruin democracy instead of culture. While some Americans surely act in ways that might justify conservative and liberal fears, their numbers are far smaller than imagined. In addition, this argument ignores the existence of the courts, as elite institutions and usually as bulwarks against violations of constitutional democracy, particularly by the kinds of people that evoke these fears.

The fourth, perhaps most frequently heard, argument against representational schemes is that they will add too many additional demands and pressures to the decision-making process.[20] Too much representation will impair democratic decision making, it is alleged; it will interfere with the recruitment of politicians and political leaders and ultimately harm rather than further democracy.

This prediction has been put forth by incumbents every time suffrage has been extended or new interest groups have entered the political arena, but newcomers are always suspect. Undoubtedly, increasing representativeness will complicate government and politics, particularly if political agendas thereby become more diverse. Taking more points of view into account is an additional burden on politicians, parties, and the decision-making bodies in government, whether elected or appointed. Politicians must keep more constituents in mind, and their need to deal with added points of view and demands makes it harder for them to act. Since they are apt to disappoint more people with every action, their credibility could suffer as well.

Nevertheless, despite all the fears about too much diversity—and democracy—political and governmental institutions somehow continue to "muddle through." While some members of Congress now decline to stand for reelection because their work is becoming much harder and the need to raise money for television campaign commercials never ends, there is no dearth of candidates to replace them. Still, most incumbents choose to run again, and almost always win again. Americans vote less for a party slate these days and more for individuals, but party loyalty continues to prevail in Congress for a variety of reasons.

Above all, decision makers are still making decisions. Many have coped by hiring more advisers, including policy analysts, while others pay more attention to lobbyists than they did before. (This alone is justification for the democratization of lobbies.) If decision-making bottlenecks do develop, a large variety of proposed structural changes in the polity are available. The difficulties of more representation not only seem surmountable, but are less harmful than the injuries to democracy resulting from the status quo.

None of these observations suggest that American democracy should become totally representative, for that could enable all majorities always to silence or harm all minorities. More so than other democracies, the United States is a constitutional democracy in which the Bill of Rights requires governments to respect individual rights against tyrannies of majorities and minorities. Needless to say, laws to further representative democracy are also subject to constitutional requirements and constraints. The legitimacy of the Supreme Court—and of juridical democracy in general— would be enhanced if those portions of government that are supposed to be representative were in fact properly so.[21] Consequently, there need be no inherent conflict between constitutional government and representative democracy, even if there must be conflict today, when the laws are passed by a politically inegalitarian legislature operating in an inegalitarian economy.

User-Friendly Government

Making democracy representative should encourage greater government responsiveness to the citizenry, requiring public agencies to pay more attention to what various constituencies of users want from government: that it help them improve their lives and pursue their goals. In short, government would become friendlier toward the people who are the users of its services.[22]

That responsiveness could be sought even now. If today's elected and appointed officials wanted to reduce some of the avoidable hostility that middle Americans feel toward them, they could encourage user-friendliness in government virtually at once. They might try harder to reduce lines in the Post Office and ensure greater helpfulness by clerks in Social Security and other offices. A user-friendly government could even try to reform the Internal Revenue Service to make it less forbidding and less adversarial toward the many taxpayers who are not out to cheat the government. A less suspicious IRS could even collect more in taxes in the long run, for at least some citizens who owe only modest amounts in taxes might be inclined to follow the rules in the future.

User-friendly public services will cost more than the present ones. If government clerks are grouchy because they are over-worked, staffs will have to grow, but taxpayers may be ready to pay the cost if the result is a more responsive bureaucracy—and that result is visible to them. When the bureaucracy is grouchy because anticorruption laws require it to consider all its clients guilty until proved innocent, or because it has a monopoly and clients have no place else to go, more basic alterations are neces-sary. Among other things, public agencies will have to behave more like, or outdo, those private firms that need to satisfy custom-ers in order to be profitable. In some cases public agencies may have to compete with each other so that clients have some choice, and agencies some incentive to satisfy their clients.

How such competition could best be achieved will vary across services and with users. In some cases, different governments could supply alternative versions of the same service. State gov-ernment might, for example, compete with local government, as it already does where students can choose between attending a city or state university. Government might add services to public facilities that users value—and that would encourage them to keep coming. Libraries now lend best sellers and tapes; museums have added blockbuster exhibits and revitalized their stores in order to make themselves more popular—and profitable. Urban parks have recently increased attendance with rock and classical music concerts. They could add to it further and on a more regular basis by including some attractions associated with commercial amusement and adventure parks.

Further, government can compete by offering otherwise un-available services—for example, hospitals organized around pa-tient, not staff, needs, and nursing homes that are more than storage facilities for the infirm elderly.[23] It can build safer or longer-lasting cars than currently come out of Detroit, and single-family as well as apartment housing that departs from the handful of styles supplied by private builders—if sufficient demand for these products can be shown to exist.

In some cases, government would make friends among users by turning some activities over to private enterprise entirely. Un-der optimal conditions, privatization can result in goods and services tailored more to what people want, or to their opportunity for choice—provided that government retains some power to regulate against user exploitation and that it, or private enterprise, makes funds available to those who cannot pay for the privatized goods or services out of their own pockets. Too many privatization schemes are, however, calculated to transfer public programs to politically influential businesses, without improving the services supplied or ending the monopoly under which they are supplied. Instead, the aim is to achieve an actual or symbolic reduction of government spending while awarding a politically connected entrepreneur a chance for profit. In too many instances the profit in privatization comes from "loadshedding," the private suppliers shedding costly clients, notably the poor, reducing the wages of service workers, or cutting corners in the quality, provision, or delivery of services.[24] Under those conditions, privatization is not justifiable.[25]

None of these suggestions can deal with all obstacles to user-friendliness. The IRS cannot charge more for kinder treatment, shed its monopoly, or be privatized. Some shortcomings of public agencies, most of which are shared by private ones, reflect employee biases toward clients of lower status. Welfare clients are unlikely to encounter user-friendly social service agencies unless they win new legal rights, or obtain political power or some other scarce resource that makes people respect them.

Some services should neither be privatized nor kept by government, but wherever possible should be performed by informal groups, with government providing financial help to those needing it.[26] Relatives and neighbors already supply most of the day care actually used by working mothers, and if government offered grants to all low- and moderate-income working mothers of preschool-age children, they could then decide to opt for formal day care, informal relative or neighbor care—or for doing the caring themselves instead of working. Public funds are already being used to help the incapacitated elderly stay in their own apartments until informal care is no longer sufficient and only a nursing home can handle them. Government should provide some regulation of informal arrangements, but only to prevent demonstrably harmful practices. Neighbors who hurt children while supplying day care are harmful, but those who lack professional degrees or fail to play games popular among upper-middle-class experts are not.

When all is said and done, however, the most effective way of increasing government's friendliness, especially for middle Americans, is expensive financially and politically: to build up the sustenance policies described in Chapter 2, so that people feel they can rely on the government for economic security if and when all else fails. That means, for example, the provision of jobs when private enterprise falters, and the payment of unemployment insurance for longer periods and on a more secure basis. It requires better government regulation of job quality and work safety, and the provision, or subsidization, and regulation of related facilities and services including among others housing, higher education, and health services.

Many of these proposals run at once into political difficulties. Affluent people who purchase their own services in the private market are unwilling to pay taxes for public sustenance services for their fellow citizens. Even middle America would prefer that government underwrite its economic security without higher taxes and, for some, without government intervention that can be made to appear socialistic. Government can probably not supply quality goods or services more cheaply than, or as cheaply as, private enterprise because it must usually obey laws, satisfy interest groups, and honor political obligations that private enterprise can avoid. Cultural facilities like libraries, parks, and museums are defended by dedicated supporters who believe that they must remain "unspoiled" by commercialism other than the kind they themselves initiate in the face of rising costs. Conversely, government is generally restrained from supplying popular services because private enterprise will brook no competition for activities that are profitable, using its political influence to maintain a division of labor in which government supplies unprofitable activities and serves only unprofitable users.

In some respects that division of labor is even necessary, for as long as private enterprise shuns such activities and users, government must step in. Nonetheless, the notion that many public services exist only or mainly for the poor, to improve either their character, their behavior, or their standard of living, is not likely to improve government's political base or its budget. Services for the poor are almost always funded poorly, and universal multiclass services are usually better for everyone, including the poor, even if some have to be internally segregated until the nonpoor are accustomed to the use of multiclass services.

"Nonpolitical" Representation

If middle Americans do not participate in politics, they should not be expected to be politically active in the economy. Therefore, greater representativeness is also needed in the private economy as well as in the semipublic or nonprofit sector, and some of the prior proposals can be applied here.

Workplace democracy and worker control are well known in America, but they have not been tried as much in America as in Europe. Worker control has usually been installed as a last resort in firms deserted by their capitalist owners, and workplace democracy has generally been limited to giving workers some power over their own role in the manufacturing process, particularly in assembly-line reform. Participation in running the workplace, most widely practiced in Yugoslavia, is barely known in the U.S. As a result, few workers have been eager to become workplace politicians. A large majority of workers have extended political avoidance habits to the workplace, treating it solely as a source of income and letting unions function as their representatives. Whether more democratic workplaces can operate with enough efficiency to survive in capitalist or, for that matter, socialist economies is not yet known.

With all its faults, the union movement still remains the best representative for workers. In industries and regions in which unions have been forced out or not allowed in the first place, workers could perhaps substitute lobbies. Concurrently, however, workers should be placed on corporate boards of directors. Actually both are needed, since neither will provide enough representation. Today's small corporate boards lack room for the several skill levels and other divisions among workers, and besides, these boards are normally voices of management to begin with. Worker representation would also have to be accompanied by customer representation, if only to prevent a recurrence of the silent agreements made by managements and unions to pass wage increases on to customers during the years of post-World War II affluence.

Local lobbies and board representatives can help workers in nonprofit institutions as well. Price and other competition being virtually absent in these institutions, however, management and labor might decide to make a deal, and clients need to be represented as well. For example, the perspectives of patients and their families need to be heard more widely in all hospitals, clinics, and nursing homes. If representatives spoke for students and their parents on a more regular and broad basis than PTAs or citizens who attend school board meetings can do, elementary and high schools might provide a little better learning experience, despite the immense diversity among students and in parent expectations. If all welfare departments had to listen regularly to client representatives, welfare might be a little less punitive. The client case should also be made in relevant professional associations such as the American Medical Association, the American Hospital Association, the National Association of Social Workers, and the like. Other clients could benefit from the same kind of representation inside relevant professional associations, including scholarly ones.

The pluralistic polling suggested earlier would also have a place. Indeed, when organizations are under no compulsion to listen to anyone's representatives, polls of patients, students, and other clients would at least provide exposure for their attitudes. Public polls among the customers for a variety of products would make their discontents more visible than secret market research, and firms depending for their profit on good will would have to act quickly—more quickly than nonprofit institutions or government. News stories in the second news media tier could not hurt either.

Ultimately, however, workers, customers, and clients have very little legal standing in private firms and the nonprofits, so that these organizations do not have to pay any attention to democratic methods. As a result, people have to rely on the rights and power they possess as citizens, expressing their demands, preferences, and grievances in the political process. This is why various basic economic rights should be added to the Bill of Rights as constitutional amendments. Such rights include, among others, the entitlement to a job, a humane minimum wage, the education and job training needed for a job in today's economy, as well as protection against being fired without cause. Additional rights will have to be won through class action suits, legislation and other forms of representative democracy. Even all these cannot accomplish very much until the law of the land recognizes that being a worker, customer, and client is in part a political role, and that representative democracy is often relevant outside the political system.

The Future of Liberal Democracy

American democracy should move toward greater representativeness, but it must also become more liberal, creating a welfare state that emphasizes egalitarian principles and economic security as its key ingredients. Actually, were improvements in representation to be achieved, government would probably become more liberal almost by itself because low- and moderate-income groups, who have the greatest need for welfare state programs, could voice their demands and opinions more effectively than is now the case.

Despite, yet partly as a result of, the renewed affluence of the 1980s, the U.S. is becoming economically more unequal than before. According to the U.S. Census, the share of all family income going to the poorest fifth of the population has declined from 5.2 percent in 1979 to 3.8 percent in 1986; that going to the richest fifth has risen from 41.7 percent to 46.6 percent during the same period.[27]

The inequality of incomes is underscored by the even greater inequality of wealth. A 1986 federal study indicates that in 1983, 68 percent of the total net worth of all households was owned by the richest 10 percent, while the 400,000 households that make up one-half of 1 percent of the population owned 27 percent of the country's net worth.[28] These figures would be even steeper if home equity were not counted as wealth. For most Americans, their home is their only wealth, although it must also serve as their shelter. The basic figures have not changed drastically since the end of World War II, although various tax reforms—including some provisions of the 1986 Tax Reform Act—have helped the very richest increase the degree of inequality.[29]

While poll respondents generally complain about the rich and the political favors they can obtain, effective moral outrage over the degree of economic inequality has never been widespread, and egalitarian proposals have not received much support. Equality can probably not be expected to be a popular policy in an individualistic society. Consequently, advocates of greater equality must take a different approach than they have done in the past. They have to accept the fact that Americans will continue to press for more resources and rights than they already have, but these advocates must recognize that when that pressure comes from people low in wealth, income, and *rights*, it is a *de facto* demand for more equality.

Further, while the goal of an egalitarian welfare state must be the reduction and eventual elimination of poverty, political logic suggests that as long as the poor lack political power, this goal is not easily achieved even when economic times are good. Whatever the number of Americans who tell pollsters that government must help the needy, politically significant proportions have been cool to "welfare" and to policies that would enable poor people to compete for jobs, housing, and status with better-off citizens. Election campaigns that center on pity for the poor are not likely to be successful.

For this and other reasons, a liberal democracy must provide economic aid both to the poor *and* to moderate-income Americans, especially the approximately 35 percent of all families who earned below $20,000 in 1984, as well as nonfamilial households in an equivalent economic position. Moderate-income Americans have a little more political influence, so the poor can benefit from the spillover effects of that influence.

If the centerpiece of liberal democracy is to be economic security, the best spillover program continues to be full employment, not only because it provides jobs to the jobless but also because it raises the wages of the already employed if and where labor becomes scarce. Full employment can thus help not only the poor but people further up the socioeconomic ladder. Unfortunately, however, full employment appears to be turning into a utopian goal in America. While the official jobless rate has declined from the double-digit figure it reached early in the 1980s to about 6 percent at this writing in the summer of 1987, the actual rate rises if all jobless people are included. For example, in 1985, "discouraged" workers who were known to have given up the job hunt made up 1 percent of the labor force, and there were undoubtedly many others who could not even be reached by the Census.[30] A further 4 percent of the labor force reported having stopped looking for work, going to school or keeping house instead. Most likely the actual jobless rate is double the official one. Moreover, people who are involuntarily working part-time must also be included in some way, and they numbered 5 percent of the labor force in 1985.

Full employment has generally been set at 3 percent joblessness, and even if this figure may become difficult to achieve, government and private enterprise can try much harder than they have for the last quarter century, for example through the encouragement of labor-intensive economic activity by private enterprise and enhanced opportunities for public employment. Ideally the goal should be full employment at decent wages, but because ever-larger numbers of the new jobs created in the U.S. are at low wages, other policies may be needed to prop up the incomes of the affected workers. The minimum wage has to be raised on purely moral grounds, for no adult should be asked to work for so low a figure. Even then, the minimum wage is unlikely to supply its recipients with a decent income, but it and other substandard wages or salaries can be supported by various kinds of tax relief, including relief from Social Security taxes and expanded earned income tax credits (a form of income subsidy) for those too poor to pay taxes.[31] People unable to find work are entitled to longer-lasting and more generous unemployment insurance, with those condemned to involuntary part-time work obtaining partial insurance payments.

Unemployment insurance should be set high enough to give every jobless family or other household at least half the median income, with the proviso that the insurance may become permanent for people who can never find work again. Half the median income is a more modest figure than the 60 to 70 percent or more that most Western European countries have been paying their less fortunate citizens. Eventually the U.S. must also reach at least the 60 percent figure.

Long-run plans for full employment and unemployment insurance programs are hard to think about because no one can now even guess at the employment effects of future economic change. As I suggested previously, unemployment could rise drastically if the loss of American jobs to the computer or to low-wage countries increases further. Alternative possibilities are further increases in lower-wage jobs in the U.S., or a rising replacement of full-time by part-time work.[32]

Whatever the future holds, an egalitarian welfare state should emphasize a job-centered set of policies, for virtually no Americans, including the poor, want to be on income grant programs if they can avoid them.[33] (If a permanent job shortage is in the offing by the 21st century, an across-the-board work-time reduction, or worksharing policy, is a far better solution than a society in which a privileged minority of the labor force can retain full-time jobs and the rest are relegated to varieties of part-time work.[34] In either case, however, government is going to have to help people obtain income additional to that earned from work.)

Even a job-centered welfare state cannot be limited solely to work but must also include previously mentioned sustenance programs, notably in health, education, and housing. Such programs not only are essential to economic security but have other constituencies whose political support will be needed. Public services that fall in the quality-of-life category cannot be totally ignored as long as they are user-oriented and attract political support. Since these services are almost always labor-intensive, they are sources of jobs as well.

The most urgent question about the welfare state is not programmatic, however, but political: where will the needed money and political support come from? Years of existing and proposed welfare state schemes, including unpopular ones for which middle Americans were nevertheless expected to pay a large share of the bill and supply the votes as well, have badly damaged all redistributionist proposals. Further, during a decade in which immense deficits have been created by the Reagan administration's military spending, the normal political difficulties inherent in funding new government responsibilities have only worsened.

Until American democracy becomes more representative and the American economy becomes healthier, viable solutions are hard to invent. Still, desirable ones have to be proposed as trial balloons, especially by people, including academics, whose jobs are not on the line if the balloons are shot down. In this spirit, several proposals follow.

First, in a capitalist economy private enterprise must continue to bear the major responsibility for people's economic security—and the needed jobs. Government's role is crucial, however, in encouraging and pressing firms to achieve greater productivity. Government must also have the power to make sure that the fruits of that productivity do not flow into unreasonable profits, but into investments and taxes that will help bring about full employment. If higher productivity results from machines that replace workers, or from exporting American jobs overseas, private enterprise must be required to create new jobs here. If a growing proportion of private economic growth must be capital-intensive, some of the resulting profits must go into additional unemployment insurance and public job programs.[35]

Second, in a liberal democracy, government must insist that one of its major purposes is redistribution, but it must start with redistributionist policies for which it can obtain political support. Full employment is an obvious first candidate, since it is a popular policy and probably not even now thought of as redistributionist. In addition, government must find or invent politically feasible redistributionist tax reforms. Poll after poll has shown that there continues to be considerable sympathy for higher taxes on the very rich and on business. That sympathy has so far not been translated into political support, mainly because people with moderate and median incomes fear that tax reform will eventually be diverted in a regressive direction and end up raising their taxes.

That fear is not unrealistic, since the power of the rich to deflect progressive tax proposals is obvious, parts of the 1986 Tax Reform Act notwithstanding. A more representative democracy would surely produce progressive tax reform; meanwhile, complete public funding of all election campaigns could move tax policy in that direction even now. However, raising the taxes of the very rich must be combined with tax reduction in middle America and with safeguards so that tax reform will not endanger economic growth.

How much redistribution is possible is a political question with no permanent answer, for that answer will depend on what the relevant public finds desirable and what the holders of economic power will accept. In view of the traditional nervousness about redistribution, progressive tax reform must probably begin on a small scale—perhaps nothing more than a sales tax on large yachts and other goods bought only by the very rich. A more productive possibility is a tax surcharge on the income and especially the wealth of the top 1 to 2 percent of the population, with some of the funds earmarked for antipoverty programs. Another alternative is to end more of the regressive tax provisions and loopholes, for example, tax and mortgage interest deductions for high-priced housing and the income and wealth still sheltered by the very rich and unusually profitable businesses. Nonetheless, the supply of very rich people has limits, and private enterprise cannot be "soaked" regularly for large amounts of money. Tax reform probably has to remain secondary to raising productivity and channeling it into progressive directions.

Third, some funds should eventually become available through a reduction of the defense budget. Although this is easy to say and to wish for, I believe that in the long run both the U.S.S.R. and the U.S. are going to have to spend less on arms for reasons of economic self-defense. In a competitive world economy, even superpowers will be unable to afford all that unnecessary military preparedness and must divert a good deal of manpower and metal to more productive uses. In the U.S., reduced defense budgets could initially result in increased joblessness, but once the funds are invested in peaceful uses, these will also produce new jobs.

Fourth, welfare state programs must be designed and administered to exclude, in highly visible fashion, as many of the government practices which upset people as possible. For example, if public funding of all elections would also include monies to maintain the political parties, as it should, some of the current "waste," such as "no show" government employees who are party workers and graft, such as contract kickbacks that pay party expenses, can perhaps be decimated if not eliminated. Likewise, a way must be found to minimize the compulsive and costly safeguards against petty dishonesty that contribute to the widespread disapproval of "bureaucracy," especially those safeguards that are most often encountered by the majority of citizens, but that vanish for some citizens—and firms—whose thefts are on a grand scale and who also have political influence.

Fifth, whenever possible government programs must head in a user-oriented direction. Sometimes the most user-friendly solution is for government to give money, rather than services, to people, especially if the money is sufficient and the market such that people can buy their own services if they so choose. (This solution is also called income redistribution.)

A compromise solution is a voucher directed to a specific need but user-oriented enough to maximize people's choices, including in some cases the choice to spend the money for other purposes. The best example is a generously funded housing voucher that low- and moderate-income people can use to rent or buy better housing in an area of their choice or to reduce their present housing bill if it is an unreasonable proportion of their incomes. Likewise, user-oriented medical and education vouchers would enable peo-

ple either to widen their choice in the private market or to find
public agencies which could employ the vouchers to help fund
the programs chosen by voucher recipients. The disadvantages
of vouchers must, however, be minimized. They cannot be used
to create a captive market, for example, for landlords who could
raise rents in response to a housing voucher scheme, and they
should be designed to include government regulation against
other forms of exploitation of recipients.

Sixth, redistributionist programs have to be structured in such
a fashion that some present material or nonmaterial gaps between
social and economic classes remain and people do not begin to
fear having to compete with "lower" classes and status groups
for significant amounts of prestige or resources. As long as people
feel the need to identify inferiors from whom they must distinguish themselves, redistribution can apparently succeed only
within some form of the existing class hierarchy.

Liberal Democracy and the Underclass

In today's America the greatest challenge for liberal democracy
is the underclass, the more or less permanently poor people who
have been driven to the furthest margins or entirely out of the
contemporary labor market. At best they work in the worst-paid
dead-end jobs both in the formal and in various informal or off-
the-books economies. Although today's stereotypical representative of the underclass is the unmarried mother with several children who survives on welfare, she is often merely the visible
adult in a stable or serial nuclear family in which the man with
whom she is involved is the true "member" of the underclass.
Unable to find work at decent wages, he is unable or unwilling
to support the family. Most of these men are probably among
the ranks of discouraged workers or those whom the U.S. Census
cannot reach.

The goal of a redistributionist welfare state must be to reintegrate as many people from this underclass as possible into the
economy, public and private. Despite facile conceptions of the
underclass as carriers of a disease called the culture of poverty
or as actual and potential criminals, many only need steady work.
They could be reintegrated into the economy if it needed their
work, if the requisite job training were made available, and if
employers as well as coworkers would accept them.

Others, notably the victims of one or more generations of mental illness and people beset by drug or alcohol addiction, irrevocable despair, loss of even minimal self-confidence, or paralyzing anger, may be beyond help even if an economic need for them existed. Although their number is probably still small, it has been growing over the past quarter century. One cause of that growth is a self-fulfilling prophecy, for as long as there is no economic need for the underclass, one solution is to stereotype everyone in it as culturally or morally diseased and thus not entitled to help. No wonder then that the number who are truly beyond help rises.

Most likely the private economy of the future will also not need many of the people who can still be reintegrated. The political support for making public service jobs available to them may be difficult to create, especially if joblessness increases. Some of the workfare experiments that began in the mid-1980s can reintegrate a portion of the underclass if the work being supplied can function as entry-level employment leading to regular jobs; if the needed financial, emotional, and other supports can be provided the workers and those who hire them; and if there is enough political patience to allow the programs to survive despite initial mistakes or failures.

Still, many eligible people will not be able to get into workfare or be reintegrated into the labor market in other ways. They need welfare payments that come up to at least the official poverty line so that parents have enough money to start their children on the better life they want for them. Some relief from the economic crises and the stigma associated with welfare would give more of the children hope for the future and reason to stay in school. Actually, welfare ought to be abolished and the permanently jobless made eligible for unemployment insurance, for it will always be more generous and secure as well as less punitive. After all, people's economic difficulties are directly or indirectly results of the failure of the economy to offer them work.

It is hard to imagine, however, that the millions of taxpayers who work at unpleasant jobs for insufficient pay will soon permit the extension of unemployment insurance to people afforded the seeming luxury of never having to work at all. These taxpayers might feel somewhat differently if they knew that whatever is saved by minimal welfare payments is spent many times over to protect them from the additional people who end up in the mentally ill, addicted, or criminal sectors of the underclass. More likely, however, the best way to extend unemployment insurance or to raise welfare payments to the poverty line is through the previously mentioned surtax on the rich.

The economic, political, and other problems of reintegrating and otherwise helping the underclass are complicated further by racial issues.[36] Because the black and Hispanic people in the underclass are, rightly or wrongly, viewed as the major sources of crime, pathology, and immorality, racial fears have increased the anxiety and hostility of white America and have even discouraged some middle American blacks and Hispanics from helping the less fortunate members of their communities. Although high unemployment rates among racial minorities are conventionally explained by their lack of needed job skills, many are actually jobless because employers want only white workers or fear the loss of white employees if they hire members of racial minorities.[37]

Despite the complicated interplay of class and racial factors in both the formation of the underclass and the fears of the rest of America, a liberal redistributional policy must focus primarily on class-related, i.e., economic, policies. Racial fears are always in part class fears, and they begin to decline when poverty and subsequently the crime and pathology associated with poverty are reduced. The ethnic history of the 19th and early 20th centuries indicates that when Italians, Jews, Greeks, and other members of the "swarthy"—and allegedly dangerous—"races" achieved middle American economic status, they were then also no longer seen as swarthy or dangerous. The elimination of racial stereotypes through economic policies cannot be accomplished as easily for blacks, so antidiscrimination programs and policies must also be pursued. Even so, they have to be complementary to "class" policies. The political catch, that the racial minorities in the underclass will not be helped economically until white Americans become less fearful and hostile, might be reduced if the underclass were better represented in the polity—but miracles should not be expected even in a perfectly representative democracy.

The Role of Liberals

By liberals, I mean people who actively support liberal democracy and the egalitarian welfare state, if not necessarily my own conception of these. Due to the contemporary diffuseness of the term liberal, some of them are also thought of as Left liberals. Others may be democratic socialists who have given up their faith in traditional socialist policies, for example, the nationalization of industry and across-the-board public ownership.

Since liberals are too few to bring about liberal democracy by themselves, they need help from many quarters, including that of middle Americans—individuals as well as whatever organizations that can speak for them. Liberals and middle Americans have more common interests than either population realizes, but if these are to be expressed politically, liberals have to work harder than in the past to appeal to middle America.

One traditional stumbling block is class, for most liberals have higher incomes, more schooling, and better jobs. They are in fact largely upper middle class, and upper-middle-class people are often unpopular in middle America.[38] Liberals cannot hide or mask their class position, but they can try to end some practices that help cause resentment. They must, for example, never assume that because they are better-educated, they are therefore wiser and have better values. They should advocate liberal values and policies, but they must refrain from claiming special moral expertise, guard against moral inconsistencies, and make sure their positions are defensible. They must, for example, distinguish between whites who are demonstrably anti-black and those who are fearful about local street crime committed mainly by blacks. White liberals cannot advocate racial integration in the cities if they live in lily-white suburbs. They have to desist from moral judgments about matters of culture and taste which make middle Americans out to be cultural inferiors. Liberals have a right to support public television, but they should not treat those who prefer commercial television as less worthy. Liberals should also guard against criticizing other people's differences with pseudo-scientific analyses. Middle Americans and others who are unenthusiastic about collective action are not necessarily victims of atomization, alienation, or anomie.

Further, liberals need to broaden liberal beliefs and adapt them to the needs of other classes. Liberal feminism must learn to speak to the middle American suburban housewife who works at dead-end jobs because the family needs the money but who in the absence of a good job would just as soon stay home. When electoral candidates are chosen, liberals have to understand that upper-middle-class politicians are normally unlikely to excite middle American voters. The candidates who run well on New York City's Upper West Side, Chicago's Lake Shore Drive, or in academic sections of Cambridge, Mass., may not win many votes elsewhere.

As professionals, liberals often design public programs, draft legislation, and supply public services. As political liberals they must, however, transcend these supplier roles, learn how policies and services look to people who are users, and then correct those which mistreat users. Liberals must insist on school busing programs that protect the rights of both black and white students, as well as the concurrent rights of parents to retain as much control as possible over their neighborhood schools.[39] Asserting the rights of homosexuals need not exclude the parallel assertion of the rights of heterosexuals. The same principle applies to singles and families so that neither group feels left out, especially if both can be accommodated.[40] When accommodation is impossible, differences can sometimes be negotiated. Some liberals might accept a minute of religious silence in the public schools if more significant attempts to violate the separation of church and state were halted in return.

Obviously any coalition between liberals and middle Americans must begin by emphasizing what they have in common: a belief in the sustenance policies of the welfare state. Liberals have been selfless in fighting for legislation that advances the economic security of middle Americans along with those of people of lower income. They should continue to insist that the drastic reduction and eventual elimination of poverty must remain their first priority. However, the antipoverty programs themselves have to be so designed that the programs do not take place at middle America's expense.

The liberal–middle American coalition can be aided further if liberals continue, with their union allies, the use of collective-action strategies. They should not, however, expect middle Americans to therefore see the virtues of collective action over political avoidance, and they must surely refrain from preaching these virtues to people who actively dislike being preached to, especially by the better-off.

At the same time, liberals must not confuse collective action with collective solutions. Some middle Americans may support liberals who carry out collective action that benefits middle America, but they will not support some of the collective solutions of which liberalism is fond, for those conflict too often with popular individualism or produce the almost universally disliked effect of forcing people to mix involuntarily with others they do not like, including those of lower status.[41]

True, liberals must insist on the collective solutions they feel very strongly about, for example, public education, but they must not press for those that are clearly unacceptable to most other people. Liberalism suffers every time liberals propose that people who own or who are desperate to own single-family houses should live in apartment blocks, whether for their or the community's benefit. Even if collective solutions are cheaper, as they often are, liberals must realize that middle Americans—like everyone else, including liberals—will pay extra for what they value most.

Perhaps the basic conflict is best illustrated by the liberal notion of private affluence vs. public squalor. Liberals are especially concerned with reducing the latter; middle Americans seek above all to secure the former. Liberals might respond that private affluence is in some instances increased by attacking public squalor, because they see a democratically guided public sector as improving the health of the economy. They can try to persuade middle Americans, but if they are unsuccessful they must realize that worrying about public squalor is easier for people once their private affluence has been secured—and middle Americans are still trying to secure it.

Last but most important, liberals have to accept the legitimacy of popular individualism, respect its major aims, and understand the reasons for its persistence. People who lack reasonable control over their environment and power over their employers and the holders of political office, and who doubt that they could change society even if they could organize, calculate that relying on their own efforts and the people they trust may get them close to what they want. Unable to risk the failure of collective action, unwilling to be dependent on organizers and political leaders who may ask them to rearrange their routines of living, conform to the organizational needs of the group, and consider new political values, they choose self-reliance with all its faults. In terms of their own, middle American values, their calculus is rational more often than not![42]

Upper-middle-class liberals have more economic security and greater control over their lives. Thus they need to bank less on self-reliance. Actually, most liberals are themselves individualists, but their upper-middle-class individualism is different enough from the middle American form that liberals may not see its similarities. Class-related cultural and esthetic differences hide the similarities further.

On this matter as on others, it may be unfair to expect liberals to transcend their class position as well as the perspectives and cultural convictions that go with it. Besides, they have never been very good compromisers. Like everyone else, liberals retain the right to remain principled. If liberal democracy is to be furthered, however, liberals must understand how and why middle Americans are different, and then figure out how to work together with them on a continuing basis.

Needed: A Vision of Liberal Democracy

Liberals must also help to develop a vision, an inspirational summary of a political program that inspires and attracts people. That vision must be centered around middle American individualism, but it has to include a societal component. The nature of that component is actually far more significant, for it must depict an acceptable egalitarian welfare state that can promise the economic security people want while also minimizing the bureaucracy and taxes they do not want. Concurrently, it must leave room for a capitalistic economy that can provide growth and jobs, as well as a government that regulates this economy to eliminate exploitation and that supplies more jobs and additional economic security to boot. All this must be incorporated in a democracy that is fully representative but enables people to avoid political participation much of the time.

I have tried to make some proposals toward the start of a political program. What is needed next is a set of workable policies that can begin to obtain political support, are sufficiently feasible and visible to create some momentum, and lend themselves to a vision that inspires people. The policies and the vision must also combine individualistic values, workable forms of collective action, and solutions for the most urgent problems of both people and country. If liberals can join with middle Americans and others to put all this together, America could yet become a liberal democracy.

Appendix—
On Methods and Other
Social Science Matters

THE basic methodology of this study is an adaptation of one part of my fieldwork method— the method participant-observers use who do research by being and talking with, observing, and informally interviewing the people they study. The data of fieldwork are written down and stored in field notes, but this time instead of writing field notes, I wrote notes to myself about the books and articles I was reading, polls I was looking at, as well as hunches and ideas. These I filed by topics, as I do with field notes, and they became the raw material for the book. The rest was endless reorganizing of the file materials, as well as continued additions to them, and writing, rewriting, and further rewriting.

When I had completed what I thought originally would be the final draft, two of its readers suggested that the book was short on evidence and could use more. I had already been relying on poll data, both from major works using polls, such as Lipset and Schneider's *The Confidence Gap* and one regular poll, the *New York Times*–CBS News poll.[1] Now I reviewed a number of other polls and surveys with the help of a couple of research assistants, looking for data to illustrate my generalizations, the general argument, and specific points in it.[2] I read through reports of national polls like Gallup and Harris, but I relied the most on NORC's *General Social Survey Codebook* because it collects in one volume answers to many hundreds of questions on diverse topics asked in the annual GSS polls.[3]

The Pros and Cons of Poll Data

If I had had large amounts of time and money, I could have undertaken fieldwork, living in one or more representative American communities to collect data about and test the ideas in this study. Lacking that time and money, I decided to rely on existing polls. I also made that decision because many of the pollsters' questions inquire into how people think and feel about general issues of social life in America and about fundamental moral, ethical, and social values. I discovered quickly that when polls deal with such values, and sometimes also when they ask about topics currently in the news, the basic American individualism generally comes through clearly. (It can also be found in the answers to the kinds of ideological questions asked around July 4th, but I stayed away from intentionally or otherwise loaded questions.) What comes through too is people's desire to be left alone by Big Business, Government, and Labor, as well as by most experts—intellectual and moral—who tell them what to think or do. When one has looked at polls on thousands of questions, as I did for this study, one gets a good sense of how people apply that basic individualism to many diverse issues, problems, and spheres of life.

My reading of the polls left two other impressions. One is how comparatively infrequently people's answers varied significantly by class, gender, race, and other background characteristics. When people's economic interests are directly affected, the class variations increase at once, but even then they usually remain smaller than I would have expected. This either testifies to the limited usefulness of poll responses or indicates once more how clearly the polls report a basic American consensus at the level of general attitudes, even if that consensus may sometimes be superficial—or misleading when current events produce bitter economic or political conflicts.

Most of the time I assumed that the polls, or at least the polls and questions I chose to study, express such an attitudinal consensus. This is one reason for reporting the poll results for the entire sample rather than for middle Americans alone, and for not comparing middle Americans with others more often. Since I was using the data for illustrative purposes only, I felt I could assume that because of their numbers, middle Americans would be included in the majorities whose responses are reported in the book. I looked at enough class and other breakdowns of poll data to feel assured that my assumption is generally valid, though I know that at times it is not.

The other impression left by the polls is how sensible most respondents are most of the time. People usually get at the crucial ethical and policy issues in topical matters of the day although they frequently know few of the factual details about an event or headline-making problem. While somewhat too beholden to conventional wisdoms, they are generally able to distill reality from hype and nonsense. The majorities reported in these polls are culturally, politically, and socially too conservative for me, and too divergent in many of their lifestyle, leisure, and taste preferences from my own. They are also too punitive toward people of lower status, darker skin, and deviant ways of living— but I was not studying the polls to find out why people disagree with me.

I used the polls with varying degrees of trepidation, however. Ideally, polling can produce data that are almost as reliable and valid as fieldwork, provided the pollsters can ask many questions about every topic and can probe for specifics and details with individual respondents. Current polls, which have to be done as quickly and economically as possible, cannot come up to this ideal. They can obtain general answers to general questions, but they cannot report thoughts and feelings in any detail, especially those about complex situations or issues.

When read properly, polls are probably most useful for understanding people's general values. Consequently, I looked mainly at polls about various kinds of attitudes that directly express or stand for general values. I concentrated on attitudes from the last five or so years and sought out questions that pollsters have been asking for a long time, because both changing and unusually stable answers to such questions are useful clues to important attitudes.[4] Here and there, I used polls with distinctive or unusual attitude questions and at times I looked at questions about behavior that might illustrate a point I was making. However, I generally avoided questions about behavior and especially questions about behavior patterns, which ask people to generalize about their behavior. I am not sure how good respondents are at generalizing since most of them have not been trained in it.[5]

Even attitude questions have to be analyzed cautiously. Because pollsters have to interview large numbers of people—and usually a national sample—they can only ask questions about general attitudes that many people can agree or disagree with. These attitudes are not necessarily the same ones people express when they are talking to family members or friends, however. The pollsters' attitudes are frequently abstracted or disconnected from those in everyday life. As a result, the questions used in today's polling can at best provide hypotheses about people's thoughts, feelings and the values behind them; hypotheses which can be tested with more detailed and intensive interviewing or through fieldwork, which is best for studying people's everyday life and everyday attitudes.

Furthermore, the data in today's polls come from answers to questions drafted by others, and respondents may only be able to choose between precoded standardized answers to these questions. Thus, poll answers are not bits and pieces of a consistent set of values because people have no control over the questions and because, unlike social scientists, they are not required to be consistent. Their enthusiasm for individualism is, as I have often noted, combined with the continuing approval of a variety of New Deal and even quasi-socialist policies.

Polls also have to be read carefully because many other factors can affect people's answers, including the way the questions are worded. For example, when people are asked how they feel about helping the poor, they are generally favorable. Such answers must be discounted somewhat because few respondents want to look heartless to an interviewer; in addition, they can be altruistic because a poll does not raise their tax bill. The moment the word welfare is used in questions about poverty, however, whites become less altruistic because then the questions seem to evoke images of "welfare cheaters," unmarried teenage mothers, and the black underclass. Question wording affects many poll answers, and answers can be understood only in relation to the questions producing them. In addition, polling has to be a polite venture or else respondents may ask interviewers to stop. Consequently, questions are politely worded, which could discourage angry or profane responses even if an honest answer requires them. Also, in view of the way most polls are analyzed, there are rarely codes for angry and profane answers—and for that matter, for iconoclastic and otherwise deviant ones.

Probably my hardest task in reading the polls was to try to

figure out how people would answer questions if some unwitting biases were left out, or if pollsters assumed less respectful postures toward government and other authority figures, or if the questions were put in colloquial English rather than the now increasingly international and artificial language of polling, or if interviewers and respondents had enough time for however long a proper answer takes. In effect I was trying to figure out what the answers might look like if the questions were asked by a fieldworker rather than a pollster.

Metaphors and Models

When I was writing the paper "What Is Society?" with which I began this study, I realized once more how many social scientists, myself included, were relying on metaphors and models to picture society—and how many of these come from physics and other natural sciences.

Probably the most useful metaphor and model for my study was Edward Shils's picture of society as consisting of a center and a periphery.[6] The distinction itself goes back at least to early-20th-century ecological ideas about the central city and its hinterland. Shils applied it as a societal model, however, in which the center "houses" a society's most important values, sacred and secular, ultimate and primordial, as well as the institutions and elites which formulate, implement, and defend these values. The periphery encompasses the ordinary population and the prosaic institutions and concerns of the society.

In his most concise definition of the model, Shils notes that

> The center consists of those institutions (and roles) which exercise authority . . . and of those which create and diffuse cultural symbols. . . . The periphery consists of those strata or sectors of the society which are the recipients of commands and of beliefs which they do not themselves create or cause to be diffused, and of those who are lower in the distribution or allocation of rewards, dignities, facilities, etc.[7]

Shils makes it clear that he believes the center is and should be the most important part of any society, and the periphery, marginal. Consequently, he suggests that the people on the periphery should take guidance from and support the values, functions, and personnel of the center almost as if the latter were high priests, although he is not blind to their faults.[8]

Shils's model, which I have oversimplified here considerably, was helpful in two ways. First, his emphasis on the sharp difference between center and periphery helped me visualize the cultural and social distances between informal groups and formal organizations, between microsociety and macrosociety. Second, both his analysis and his value judgments illustrated graphically that middle Americans see the world very differently from those who consider the elite more important to society than the general public. While middle Americans may accept, or be resigned to, the authority and power of the center, they turn Shils's model upside down or, since it is a circle, inside out. They believe, or act as if they believe, their families, friends, and the rest of their microsociety to be at the center. For them, business, government, and most other formal organizations are on a periphery which is sometimes necessary or useful, but more often troublesome and therefore to be avoided whenever possible. In an ideal world, moreover, these organizations and leaders ought to be serving them.

Although middle Americans probably endorse many of the values that Shils identifies with the center, they do not accept the superiority of the people who supply them. Shils is of course aware that the people he thinks are peripheral may feel no allegiance to those of the center, although he makes that point from the perspective of the center, noting (and perhaps criticizing) "the limited capacity of many people to sustain a direct, continuous and intense relationship to the center of their society."[9] That middle Americans usually view bureaucrats, politicians, and most experts—including sociologists—as peripheral may be troubling to *them*, but that view is an important perspective on America.[10] It also inspires and organizes many of the middle American values described in this book.

At times I sought to picture the various metaphors I encountered during the course of this study, especially those used in societal models. I decided, for example, that Shils's center-periphery model is a tower-like hierarchy, for the people of his periphery seemed to me to be looking up to the values and elites of his center. The social system of functionalism I saw as a well-designed and well-oiled machine with a large number of differentiated but interdependent parts, and the social system of network analysis as the wiring pattern of a highly complicated appliance of the precomputer era. Both images are caricatures, but as such they emphasize that the question of how systemic social systems really are and how well they hang together can only be answered empirically. I am skeptical of models that give the impression that society is a unit or a fairly completely interdependent system.

My preferred images of society are borrowed mainly from what I now recall of the high school astronomy and biology of the 1940s. One pictures society as a universe without definite boundaries, consisting of many types of astronomical bodies, all in motion and all floating in space. The larger bodies, which could be likened to governmental, economic, and other formal organizations of various sizes, influence and may even dominate the shape and motion of the millions of asteroids and other tiny ones (read informal groups), while the various regular and predictable movements, as well as the pushes, pulls, crashes, and explosions, can be likened to what goes on in the "human universe" when groups interact and more powerful ones push the less powerful ones around. Nonetheless, because there is so much space in the universe, even the tiny bodies are able to exist with some degree of freedom and independence.

The biological image comes from what I remember seeing in the high school microscopes of the early 1940s, in which organisms of varying shapes and sizes were bumping into each other, the bigger ones also pushing the smaller ones around, but again with some empty space between them to provide a little freedom of movement for the latter. Neither my astronomy nor my biology bear any relation to those of professionals in the field, but both are useful to set against overly mechanical images of social life.

A final metaphor that I have found helpful is perspective, by which I mean the angle and distance used in studying social phenomena. In the late 1970s, sociologists began to use the Bateson-Goffman concept of frame, which I take to be the overall combination of values, assumptions, and concepts (and perspectives) with which we approach the people and structures we study empirically, and which is a more complex and subtle version of the common-sense concept frame of reference.[11] I think, however, that perspective should be separated from frame, because the angle and distance from which we look at social phenomena has an independent effect on what we see even when the rest of the frame is the same.

In some respects perspective is analogous to camera angle. The metaphor comes once more from the physical sciences, but human beings are holding the cameras. In fact sociologists have begun to study the effects of the camera angles used by photographers on the resulting pictures, for example in television news.[12]

Insofar as researchers stand at a particular angle to what they are studying, their results will be affected. For example, if one looks at a firm or public agency from the bottom up, the differences between middle and top management begin to recede. In fact if the researcher does his or her study only from that perspective, he or she may come to the same conclusion—and value judgment—as the employees at the bottom, that they have a large number of bosses all seeming to go continuously to meetings but not to do any "productive" work.

Likewise, in a mobile society, researchers doing their research at the top of the class hierarchy will see lower orders moving up and can therefore fall prey to the notions held at the top that those who are coming up are bringing moral decline with them. From very high up, the people at the bottom almost always appear to be a dangerous class, whatever their actual behavior. Because anything at the top is usually considered better than anything at the bottom, the countries that are placed at the top of maps have a symbolic advantage over those placed at the bottom.[13]

Distance can have as significant effect as angle, and researchers' pursuit of higher levels of abstraction is sometimes achieved by distancing themselves from what they are studying. Then trees turn into forests, separate organizations and groups melt into a social system, and human agents are replaced by seemingly impersonal forces. If America is studied from India, American poverty is minimal and may be hard to find. Family members see almost all the differences and certainly all the conflicts in their family, but may think that all government bureaucracies look alike.

Where researchers stand—from what kinds of angles and distances they look at what they study—is a function of intellectual, social, and usually also economic and political factors that themselves require study.[14] Still, the metaphor of the camera angle is useful just by itself as a first cut at learning the perspectives from which a particular study has been carried out. As a result, that image portrays in dramatic fashion issues in the sociology of empirical research that need further attention.

That all of the metaphors and images I have discussed here have come from one or another of the natural sciences is no accident, since sociology has always treated the natural sciences as its role model. Today's young sociologists are sometimes trained in humanist approaches to research, and when society is likened to a discourse, it cannot also be a machine. Even so, other young researchers are discovering new mechanistic models, including some taken from classical economics. I wonder what would happen to empirical research and theorizing if more of sociology's metaphors were borrowed from artists, poets, novelists, filmmakers, composers, and others of that ilk. The late Erving Goffman took a highly influential first step at giving up mechanistic models by looking at social life as if it occurred on a stage, and following his lead more often would have beneficial effects on the social sciences.

Users, Suppliers, and the Social Sciences

My interest in and qualified advocacy of popular individualism reflects a personal set of values about the rights of middle American and other "ordinary," i.e., nonexpert, nonintellectual, people to pursue their own destiny as long as they carry out their responsibilities in a properly representative democracy. This set of values, details of which can be read in and between the lines of this book, also has implications for the kind of social science—including sociology—I consider desirable. I call it *user-oriented*, but to describe it properly I need to return to my earlier distinction between suppliers and users.[15]

Suppliers are roles, people, and institutions that produce, distribute, and sell or give away goods, services, ideas, and the like. They are not only manufacturers, sellers, and advertisers, however, but also professionals who supply education, legal services, health care, and social research; artists who supply art and intellectuals who supply analysis and criticism; and public officials who supply government with policies and decisions. Users are the people, institutions, and roles at the receiving end, but I think of the term as applying particularly to people such as middle Americans who are mainly users and only rarely suppliers.

Like all dichotomies, this one has all the shortcomings of dividing the world into two slices. The terms describe a role, and actual people and institutions perform other roles as well, can be suppliers and users concurrently, and sometimes are neither. General Motors is a user of parts from its various subcontractors, but this user role only contributes to GM's overall role as a supplier of cars. Little is gained by calling the people working on GM's assembly line suppliers, since all they are doing is some of the company's dirty work. GM's executives are, however, acting as suppliers.

Although the terms are taken from market exchange relationships, they are actually more helpful in describing cultural divisions of labor, power relations and conflicts, and economic struggles that are not purely financial. As such the dichotomy can add social factors to the analysis of modes and relations of production and distribution, and can be applied in comparative studies of institutions that seem, on their face, to be totally different. For example, suppliers of artistic and intellectual products, but some others as well, usually set performance standards for themselves and their users which the latter may not appreciate or follow. Being users, they have different interests and see the product, service, or idea supplied them quite differently. One result is the cultural and political conflicts between artists and audiences, teachers and students, authors and readers. High culture steadfastly upholds the standards of artists and authors, while popular culture exists mainly to satisfy users. Folk culture was probably somewhere in between, although in theory its artists and audiences were supposed to share the same standards. Parents supply upbringings to their children and are displeased when the latter fail to live up to parental standards. (Some child-raising experts may agree with the children in this case, but then supply their own standards for bringing them up.) Doctors are upset if their patients do not follow their orders, and campaign managers who supply political strategy to candidates complain because their users go off on impulsive tangents. Detroit engineers treat the car as a machine, while the design and sales departments want a vehicle to attract the user. Likewise, reporters frequently have a different conception of a news story than editors, whose job it is to keep the interests of the audience in mind. Thus, medical journalists are apt to report a medical research story from the perspective of their researcher sources, while the editor typically will want to know what the research will eventually mean to patients.

The supplier-user distinction is even helpful for understanding ideologies and the unwillingness of most people to be ideological or to be enthralled by ideologists. For one thing, most ideologies are supplier-oriented. Capitalist individualism exists first and foremost to serve entrepreneurs, corporate executives, and small businessmen and women, while democratic socialism and liberalism are the ideologies of intellectuals and government officials who believe that supplying people with the right government programs is the best way to create the good life for them. Revolutionary communism and radical conservatism are ideologies of vanguard parties that aim to change society, read users, to behave in accordance with their conceptions of the good society. Once in power, communists rarely worry whether the public ownership of the means of production will actually get more resources to the users in whose names they rule, just as liberals and democratic socialists often do not think sufficiently about how well their favorite government programs actually serve the users for whom they are in theory intended.

Peter Saunders has pointed out that Marxism has perceived people only in their worker roles and has not paid attention to them as users.[16] Not to do so made good sense during the 19th and early 20th centuries, with their terrible working conditions, but it makes less sense today when these conditions have improved and most workers, at least in America and much of Europe, can treat work mainly as a source of income for other parts of their lives. Before the recent advent of the market economy in state socialist societies, the central planners were still almost entirely concerned with production and, except for keeping prices of basic necessities low, showed little interest in the consumers and the kinds of goods they were getting. Marxism's persistent supplier orientation has helped explain the decline of support for it among workers both in the West and the East.

Middle American individualism is a user-oriented ideology. Unwritten and uncodified, it puts forth the values and interests of people who are mainly users. It does not seek to supply anything to anyone or, lacking professional ideologists, even to supply itself to anyone as a desirable ideology or political program. Moreover, popular individualism does not support, favor, or justify particular suppliers. If anything, it is apt to be suspicious of all suppliers until they have proved themselves innocent of harming users.

Needless to say, treating suppliers or users as homogeneous

populations is inadequate and possibly dangerous. Suppliers come in various types because, for example, creators of art may have different interests than sellers. Users may be less diverse, if only because they are at the receiving end, but those with money to spend are in a different position than those without.

Furthermore, the supplier-user distinction does not do away with more directly economic or political concepts, but adds some sociological and cultural qualifications. That organizations or individuals own or control major resources remains more important in most analyses than that they supply goods, services, or power. Although suppliers tend to have more money and influence than users, the dichotomy does not substitute for analyses of class and power.[17] Also, it cannot replace looking at religion, race, and other factors that unify and divide people, institutions, and societies. Suppliers and users are not always adversarial, however, for suppliers who earn profits by satisfying users will side with users for that purpose. Still, users are apt to see the relationship as a source of profit for commercial suppliers and not as a reason to make alliances with them.[18]

Sociologists, like other social scientists, can themselves be studied as suppliers and users. The academic majority among them are paid mainly for supplying insights and findings to students and others in society. When they are doing research, social scientists have more often been on the side of suppliers than of users. Whether they are academics working as consultants or sociologists in "practice" positions, they typically do studies for government and industry, and may in fact be hired to supply research about users.[19]

Academics doing scholarly research usually remain independent, working with scientific grant funds or none at all. Still, the choice of research topics can never be value-free, for these topics may unintentionally favor the points of view of one or the other group. Once they have chosen their topic, however, academics usually take a detached and distanced position, trying to look at their object of study from socially "far away," and therefore in a sufficiently abstract manner that it is "above" whatever differences of interests may exist between the suppliers and users being studied. Nevertheless, precisely because the perspective is from above the fray, the researchers may be looking at the phenomenon from the top down. As a result they may be taking one of the perspectives used by organizational planners, or be developing theory and data that are most salient to planners, especially those working for decision makers in large organizations who look at their organizations from the top down. When the researchers' view is from the top down, or comprehensive enough to embrace entire organizations, or when the research is operating on minimal funds, the researchers are also likely to depend on existing sources of information. These usually come from suppliers, users not being data collectors or employers of research departments.

Social scientists are also asked, or volunteer, to function as experts, and in this case they normally work for suppliers. No matter for whom they work, experts sometimes confuse their personal interests with their expertise, including these in the expertise they supply. If this confusion leads them to impose their own interests or those of their profession while functioning as experts, or even if they decide what lay goals and values are best for lay people and mix that into their expertise, they are once more taking supplier roles rather than serving users.

Toward User-Oriented Social Science

The social sciences need to become, not totally user-oriented, but far more so than they are now. Their work and perspectives ought to be more salient to ordinary people who spend most of their lives being users—and workers. Since "user" is itself an abstraction to describe people doing an immense variety of different things, this proposal is not concrete enough to be a guideline. It means, however, that social scientists should be aware of and report both supplier and user interests in all organizations and social phenomena they study. As researchers, they should make sure they look at the empirical world from user as well as supplier perspectives, especially where suppliers and users are in conflict. If they choose to take sides, they should tilt to the side of the users, if only because suppliers can usually avail themselves of so many research and advisory resources. If they stay neutral, they must make sure that they are not taking sides implicitly, by the perspectives they employ, the topics they study, and the data they rely on.

Still, the most urgent task of user-oriented social science is research that aims to understand the people whose relations with formal organizations are mostly as users. For example, a good deal is now known about large and complex organizations, but too few of the studies have dealt with their users—with the ways people use, exploit, manipulate, and fight with these organizations, and how they are exploited, manipulated, and used by them. Likewise, researchers in public administration and policy have looked extensively into the "delivery systems" by which complex organizations like cities deliver services; but these studies tend to look at such systems from the suppliers' angle, as funnels down which they slide what they supply. Research at the end of the funnel is needed to discover what users actually get, think they get, and what they do with it. Such research would also have to look at how users feel and what they do when they have little say over what comes down the funnel and cannot choose what they want. Sometimes, they attempt to establish their own delivery systems through user-dominated cooperatives, self-help schemes, and barter arrangements. More often they are unhappy with government.

The same general approach can be applied to all organizations and institutions in which supplier-user relations take place, whether the study is about supplying new jobs to laid-off steel workers, television news to viewers, nursing home care to mentally alert old people, or undergraduate courses to college students. This approach would add some new insight into how people deal with formal organizations they need and cannot avoid, for example, by the informal motors and havens described in Chapter 2 which protect people from some of the exploitative and manipulative policies of formal organizations. Concurrently, other studies would examine the suppliers in these organizations, seeing how they perceive the users and how they try to discourage—or encourage—user avoidance patterns, either by being responsive or unresponsive. Similarly, organizations must be studied to learn how supplier strategies and other activities in them are influenced directly and indirectly by the users and supplier perceptions of these users.[20]

Studying users is more difficult, time-consuming, and expensive than studying suppliers, since the latter are usually clustered in one place, are often able and even eager to supply data about themselves, and may now even be employing social science research in their own work. Users, on the other hand, are apt to be scattered and thus have to be contacted in small groups and even as individuals. Studying them calls for interviews and/or ethnography.

In the past, American sociology has been distinctive in going out into "the field" studying the ordinary people I have described here as users, while economics and political science have emphasized studies of suppliers, often using their data or government statistics. There is no reason, however, why economists and political scientists cannot use interviewing and ethnographic methods to study the people who function as users in the economy and in government. A handful now employ these research methods, but they are still considered deviants in their disciplines. Historians have stopped looking only at the suppliers of government, war, and the like, and are doing history "from the bottom up," which involves searching for archival materials left by ordinary people both as workers and users. Anthropology is currently in transition because, while it has begun to move its ethnographic methods from overseas to the United States, many anthropologists are searching for American equivalents of the preindustrial small societies and tribes their predecessors studied overseas. Such studies may be important, but not as important as studies of ordinary people more in the American mainstreams.

Members of the general public have not paid much attention to the social sciences, partly because of their technical languages, jargon, and preference for quantifiable data, but also because of their frequent lack of relevance to problems concerning that public. More user-oriented research would probably help the social sciences obtain more public support.

Be that as it may, more studies of and among users also means more research in middle America. Such studies are also needed in connection with the themes and proposals discussed in this book. If democracy is to be more representative, we need to learn much more about the user role called citizen, to replace the prevailing civic textbook romanticism about citizenship, among other reasons. Advancing liberal democracy requires concerted research on the various kinds of welfare state policies various Americans want, need, and will pay for. We—and they— need to know, for example, exactly what people want government to do to help them pursue economic security. The most important research topic may also be the hardest: whether American democracy can actually become more representative and liberal.[21]

Notes

Chapter One

1. Although I appreciate the objections of Canadian and Latin American readers to the terms America and Americans in references to the United States of America, I shall have to use them, because so far no one has invented an adjectival form of "United States."

2. See for example, Theodore D. Caplow et al., *Middletown Families: Fifty Years of Change and Continuity*. Minneapolis: University of Minnesota Press, 1982. This third study of Muncie, Indiana, emphasizes the continuity since the Lynds' initial studies of the 1920s and 1930s.

3. For a good review of the major expert individualisms, see Steven Lukes, *Individualism*. Oxford: Blackwell, 1973.

4. Peter Clecak, *America's Quest for the Ideal Self: Dissent and Fulfillment in the 60s and 70s*. New York: Oxford University Press, 1983.

5. The GSS is an annual poll. One of its regular questions asks people how easily they could find a job with "approximately the same income and fringe benefits [they] now have." In 1986, a further 39 percent thought it would be "not easy at all." James A. Davis and Tom W. Smith, *General Social Surveys, 1972–1986: Cumulative Codebook*. Storrs, Conn.: NORC-Roper Center, 1986, Question 179, p. 211.

6. The term has been used by a number of social scientists, but I borrow it from Richard P. Coleman and Lee Rainwater, with Kent A. McClelland, *Social Standing in America: New Dimensions of Class*. New York: Basic Books, 1978, Chapter 9.

7. Bureau of the Census, *Statistical Abstract of the United States 1987*. Washington D.C.: U.S. Government Printing Office, 1987, Table 919, p. 536.

8. Pink collar workers is an apt term coined by the late Louise Kapp Howe for a variety of factory and service jobs, most of them unpleasant and poorly paid, held exclusively by women. See her *Pink Collar Workers: Inside the World of Women's Work*. New York: Putnam, 1977. Since then, Ralph Whitehead has

coined the term new collar to describe some of the factory, office, and service jobs created as a result of technological and other innovations in the economy in the last quarter century. In addition, he wanted to debunk the idea that all of these jobs were professional—and held by yuppies—but above all he was hoping to find a new occupational category to explain voting and other political changes. See Timothy Noah, "Birth of a New Idea," *The New Republic*, December 30, 1985, pp. 20–22. At the start of the computer era, program designers were sometimes called no collars, presumably because of their unwillingness to abide by workplace dress and other codes.

9. Bureau of the Census, op. cit., Table 197, p. 121.

10. Ibid., Table 199, p. 122.

11. Computed from Bureau of the Census, "Money Income and Poverty Status of Families and Persons in the United States in 1984," *Current Population Reports*, Series P-60, No. 149, August 1985, Table 5. The statistically middle-income population, i.e., families from the 25th to the 75th percentile, earned between $12,500 and $40,000 in 1984.

12. Coleman and Rainwater, op. cit., p. 126.

13. Most Americans do not agree, however, for according to the 1986 GSS, 43 percent of the respondents said they were working class and 47 percent, middle class. Poll respondents must usually respond to the pollsters' categories, but many working-class Americans prefer to call themselves "working people." Davis and Smith, op. cit., Question 184, p. 218. In 1974, Andrew Levison demonstrated that in terms of occupation, America is not a middle-class society. Although the book needs updating, his analysis is still basically correct, and an important antidote to conservative opponents of the welfare state who like to depict America as more comfortably off than it actually is. See his *The Working Class Majority*. New York: Coward, McCann and Geoghegan, 1974.

14. The erosion of sharp differences between the working and middle classes and between factory and office workers was a major finding of the third study of Middletown, Caplow et al., op. cit. That erosion is also reported by a very different study using national survey data, Mary R. Jackman and Robert W. Jackman, *Class Awareness in the United States*. Berkeley: University of California Press, 1983, p. 93.

15. Bureau of the Census, *Statistical Abstract*, op. cit., Table 1303, p. 723.

16. Jonathan Schell reports on some inconsistencies among Milwaukee middle Americans in his *History in Sherman Park*. New York: Knopf, 1987. For sociological analyses see Eugene Litwak, Nancy Hooyman, and Donald Warren, "Ideological Complexity and Middle-American Rationality," *Public Opinion Quarterly*, Vol. 37, No. 3., Fall 1973, pp. 317–322; and Donald Warren, *The Radical Center: Middle Americans and the Politics of Alienation*. Notre Dame, Ind.: Notre Dame Press, 1978.

17. In fact, most sociologists argue, and rightly so, that how people act or have to act exerts a major influence on the values they develop or alter.

18. This is even true among some of the very first Americans. Bernard Bailyn, *The Peopling of North America*. New York: Knopf, 1986.

19. Acculturation includes both the process of giving up the old-country culture and that of constructing a new identity from the available American

culture, but in what follows I am concerned mainly with the move away from the old-country and immigrant cultures.

20. Popular individualism appears to exist in England, and in a form not very different from the American kind. R. E. Pahl, *Divisions of Labor*. Oxford: Blackwell, 1984, pp. 325–327.

21. Middle Americans are slowly but surely becoming as ready to move out of the parental household prior to marriage as more affluent young people. Calvin Goldscheider and Frances K. Goldscheider, "Moving Out and Marriage: What Do Young Adults Expect?" *American Sociological Review*, Vol. 52, No. 2, April 1987, pp. 278–285, especially Table 1, p. 281.

22. Gallup polls have been reporting that about 40 percent of their respondents say they attend religious services every week for a number of years, but the March 1987 *New York Times*–CBS News poll reported a figure of 31 percent.

23. For working-class families, churches are one place in which to practice upward mobility, principally by regular church attendance and active participation in church social clubs and voluntary associations.

24. The irony is that these workers obtained higher wages and job stability largely as a result of working in unionized industries. Richard B. Freeman and James L. Medoff, *What Do Unions Do?* New York: Basic Books, 1984.

25. David Halle, *America's Working Man*. Chicago: University of Chicago Press, 1984, pp. 171–180.

26. These observations are based particularly on my research among working class people in the West End of Boston at the end of the 1950s.

27. The importance of education in upward mobility is emphasized by two major sociological studies of the 1960s and 1970s. One is Peter Blau and Otis D. Duncan, *The American Occupational Structure*. New York: Wiley, 1967. The other is David L. Featherman and Robert M. Hauser, *Opportunity and Change*. New York: Academic Press, 1978.

28. The climb has, however, been steady. Bureau of the Census, *Statistical Abstract of the United States 1985*. Washington, D.C.: U.S. Government Printing Office, 1985, Table 120, p. 80. Bureau of the Census, *Statistical Abstract 1987*, op. cit., Table 123, p. 80.

29. Perhaps the frequent use of therapeutic language reported by Robert Bellah and his colleagues in their study of a fairly well-off middle class population reflects in yet another way the process and problems of coping with individualism. Robert N. Bellah et al., *Habits of the Heart: Individualism and Commitment in American Life*. Berkeley: University of California Press, 1985, especially Chapter 5.

Chapter Two

1. Davis and Smith, *General Social Survey, 1972–1986*, op. cit., Questions 349 C and D, p. 358.

2. Reported by Seymour M. Lipset, "Roosevelt and the Protest of the 1930s," *University of Minnesota Law Review*, Vol. 69, No. 2, January 1984, pp. 501–526, at pp. 506–507; and William Schneider, "Half a Realignment," *The New Republic*, Vol. 191, No. 23, December 3, 1984, pp. 19–23, at p. 21.

3. The supplier-user distinction is discussed further in the Appendix, pp. 165–169.

4. Davis and Smith, op. cit., Question 182, pp. 212–213.

5. The classic study is Eli Chinoy's *Automobile Workers and the American Dream.* Boston: Beacon Press, 1955.

6. Among lower white collar workers, 69 percent wanted to go into business in 1939, while only 28 percent wanted to do so in 1976. There was not much change among the jobless, however, 59 percent indicating such a wish in 1939 and 52 percent in 1976. Kay L. Schlozman and Sidney Verba, *Injury to Insult: Unemployment, Class and Political Response.* Cambridge, Mass.: Harvard University Press, 1979, Figure 6–8, p. 158. David Halle found that the factory workers he studied fantasized about going into business but noticed that their colleagues who had tried also usually failed. *America's Working Man,* op. cit., pp. 165–167.

7. Davis and Smith, op. cit., Question 181, p. 211.

8. H. Roy Kaplan, *Lottery Winners.* New York: Harper & Row, 1970.

9. Davis and Smith, op. cit., Question 175, p. 208.

10. James R. Kluegel and Eliot R. Smith, *Beliefs about Inequality: Americans' Views of What Is and What Ought to Be.* New York: Aldine de Gruyter, 1986, Table 6.4, p. 165.

11. Seymour S. Lipset and William Schneider, *The Confidence Gap: Business, Labor and Government in the Public Mind.* Baltimore: Johns Hopkins University Press, Revised Edition, 1987, pp. 170–173.

12. Advisory Commission on Intergovernmental Relations (ACIR), *Changing Public Attitudes on Governments and Taxes 1983.* Washington: The Commission, 1983, Table 7, p. 13.

13. Nearly 40 percent considered it fair. Lipset and Schneider, op. cit., Table 13–2, p. 423. This poll was carried out before the 1986 tax reform legislation was passed, however.

14. ACIR, op. cit., Table 2, p. 8. However, this study did not ask respondents whether levying higher taxes on the business community or the very rich would make the tax fair.

15. In the 1970s, the local property tax was thought to be the least fair, until inflation forced people into higher tax brackets and increases in the federal payroll tax combined to reduce the progressivity of federal taxes considerably. Ibid., Table F-1, p. 40.

16. Recreation and cultural facilities and services are normally the first candidates for budget cutting when pollsters ask respondents to indicate which services they want increased or decreased if budgets have to be reduced. See, e.g., ibid., Appendix Table N, p. 54; and Davis and Smith, op. cit., Question 350, pp. 360–361. Space programs usually fall into the luxury category as well, and except in times of Cold War tensions, so do military ones. For a good summary of polls on these topics over the years, see Richard F. Hamilton and James D. Wright, *The State of the Masses.* New York: Aldine, 1986.

17. A somewhat overly optimistic analysis of popular support for welfare state services during the Reagan years is Thomas Ferguson and Joel Rogers,

Right Turn: The Decline of the Democrats and the Future of American Politics. New York: Hill and Wang, 1986. An earlier and more comprehensive review of studies can be found in Lipset and Schneider, op. cit. For a good review of data on the popular opposition to "welfare" for the poor, see Kluegel and Smith, op. cit., pp. 152–163.

18. Lipset and Schneider, op. cit., p. 88.

19. There have been attempts over the years to create user-oriented playgrounds, for example the adventure playground, but they soon lose their attractiveness to youngsters as well. Baseball diamonds and the like always draw, but many suppliers of public recreation services do not consider them to be playgrounds.

20. Robert E. Lane, "Market Justice, Political Justice," *American Political Science Review*, Vol. 80, No. 2, June 1986, pp. 383–402, quote at p. 388.

21. Louis Harris, *Inside America.* New York: Vintage Books, 1987, pp. 356–358.

22. "Exercise Industry Sees Spurt in Sales to Homes," *New York Times*, May 21, 1984, pp. D1, D4, quote at D4.

23. Computed from John Herbers, *The New Heartland: America's Flight Beyond the Suburbs and How It Is Changing Our Future.* New York: Times Books, 1986, p. 188.

24. Bureau of the Census, *Statistical Abstract 1987*, op. cit., Table 1293, p. 716.

25. TRB (Michael Kinsley), "Megabucks 1985," *The New Republic*, November 11, 1985, p. 4.

26. Samuel P. Huntington, *American Politics: Promise of Disharmony.* Cambridge, Mass.: Harvard University Press, 1981, p. 33.

27. Lipset and Schneider, op. cit., Table 3–4, p. 87. These data are for 1977.

28. ACIR, op. cit., Table 1, p. 7.

29. Reported in Lipset and Schneider, op. cit., p. 346.

30. The 1980 poll is cited in Kluegel and Smith, op. cit., Table 6–1, p. 183, the 1985 one in Davis and Smith, op. cit., Question 349D, p. 358.

31. Lipset and Schneider, op. cit., p. 346.

32. Davis and Smith, op. cit., Question 358C, p. 366.

33. Lipset and Schneider, op. cit., pp. 222 ff.

34. Ibid., p. 235.

35. Davis and Smith, op. cit., Question 358B, p. 365.

36. Lipset and Schneider, op. cit., p. 241.

37. Kenneth E. John, "More Americans Are Lending a Helping Hand," *Washington Post National Weekly Edition*, June 22, 1987, p. 37.

38. Kluegel and Smith, op. cit., Table 5–2, p. 112.

39. William Form, *Divided We Stand: Working-Class Stratification in America.* Urbana: University of Illinois Press, 1985, Table 8–1, pp. 172–173.

40. Kluegel and Smith, op. cit., Table 64, p. 165.

41. Davis and Smith, op. cit., Question 337, p. 346.

42. Ibid., Question 76, p. 108.

43. See e.g., Lee Rainwater, *What Money Buys: Inequality and the Social Meanings of Income*. New York: Basic Books, 1974, Chapter 8.

44. Davis and Smith, op. cit., Questions 79–84, pp. 110–115.

45. Ibid., Questions 123–136, pp. 157–163.

46. Ibid., computed from Questions 128, 128A, and 128B, p. 160.

47. A graphic study of white middle American fears of and reactions to poor blacks is Jonathan Rieder, *Canarsie: The Jews and Italians of Brooklyn Against Liberalism*. Cambridge, Mass.: Harvard University Press, 1985. However, he found that the white violence was not a community response but had been staged by ultra-right-wing organizations in the area.

48. My favorite, albeit somewhat extreme, example of the distinction between organizations and individuals comes from that part of New York City's off-the-books economy which deals in stolen goods. According to Craig Castleman, who is conducting a study of this economy, sellers in it will work with "honest" thieves, those who steal from large stores and institutions, but they refuse to deal with "dishonest" ones, those who steal from individuals. (Personal communication.)

49. I developed the concept of altruistic democracy while studying and identifying the basic professional values of journalism, but believe it is more widely shared—or else journalists could not be credible to their audiences. Of course, middle Americans, like all others, do not mind if a politician deviates from altruism—or honesty—if that is necessary to satisfy their demands. For a fuller discussion of altruistic democracy, see Herbert J. Gans. *Deciding What's News: A Study of CBS Evening News, NBC Nightly News, Newsweek and Time*. New York: Pantheon Books, 1978, pp. 43–45.

50. Lipset and Schneider, op. cit., Table 2–1, pp. 48–49.

51. Ibid.

52. Ibid., pp. 421–422.

53. The question is one of several asked regularly in the biannual election surveys of the Center for Political Studies of the University of Michigan. The answers from 1964 to 1980 were taken from Hamilton and Wright, op. cit., Table 88, pp. 364–365; that for 1984 was computed from the Center's 1984 codebook. The decision to treat this question as an indicator for altruism is mine, not the Center's.

54. Other questions that I consider relevant as indicators of altruism are "Do you think people waste a lot of the money we pay in taxes . . . some of it or [not] . . . very much of it?" and "Do you think that quite a few of the people running the government are crooked, not very many are, or . . . hardly any . . . ?" In 1984, 66 percent thought that there was a lot of waste, while 33 percent thought that "quite a few" government officials were crooked.

55. Lipset and Schneider, op. cit., pp. 61–66.

56. S. M. Lipset and William Schneider, "Confidence in Confidence Measures," *Public Opinion*, August–September 1983, pp. 42–44.

Chapter Three

1. Raymond Williams has described the British equivalent of organizational avoidance as "mobile privatization," feeling that modern automotive and other new technology have led to the "unprecedented mobility of . . . privacies." Raymond Williams, *The Year 2000*. New York: Pantheon Books, 1983, p. 188.

2. Alexis de Tocqueville, *Democracy in America*. New York: Vintage Books, 1954, Vol. II, p. 104. De Tocqueville does not make this observation approvingly, although in the sentences that precede and follow it, he is much harsher toward selfishness, which stems from "depraved feelings," whereas individualism "proceeds from erroneous judgment."

3. A graphic description of middle American informal groups at work and after hours is in Halle, *America's Working Man*, op. cit., Chapter 2.

4. Peter V. Marsden, "Core Discussion Networks of Americans," *American Sociological Review*, Vol. 52, No. 1, February 1987, pp. 122–131.

5. Michael Burawoy, *Manufacturing Consent*. Chicago: University of Chicago Press, 1979.

6. Robert Zussman, *Mechanics of the Middle Class: Work and Politics among American Engineers*. Berkeley: University of California Press, 1985. Other recent examples of organizational motors in the factory can be found in Harley Shaiken, *Work Transformed: Automation and Labor in the Computer Age*. Lexington, Mass.: Lexington Books, 1984.

7. Sunshine laws which require all meetings to be public have discouraged these motors or, more often, driven them further from public scrutiny.

8. The classic study on this topic is by Edward A. Shils and Morris Janowitz: "Cohesion and Disintegration in the Wehrmacht in World War II." *Public Opinion Quarterly*, Vol. 12, No. 2, 1948, pp. 280–315.

9. I borrow this term from Lee Rainwater's "Fear and the House-as-Haven in the Lower Class," *Journal of the American Institute of Planners*, Vol. 32, January 1966, pp. 23–30.

10. Donald F. Roy, "Quota Restriction and Goldbricking in a Machine Shop," *American Journal of Sociology*, Vol. 57, No. 5, March 1952, pp. 427–442.

11. Arlie R. Hochschild, *The Managed Heart: Commercialization of Human Feeling*. Berkeley: University of California Press, 1983.

12. Fred Siegel, "Notes on the New Right," *Commonweal*, May 8, 1981, pp. 269–272, quote at p. 271. The concept of antagonistic cooperation is David Riesman's.

13. However, Europeans belong to more organizations with economic purposes and functions. Kay L. Schlozman and John T. Tierney, *Organized Interests and American Democracy*. New York: Harper & Row, 1986, p. 59.

14. Davis and Smith. *General Social Surveys, 1972–1986*, op. cit., Question 172, pp. 201–205.

15. Thus, 63 percent of professional workers, 30 percent of clerical workers, and 35 percent of crafts workers reported memberships in organizations other than unions, but only 23 percent of "operative" blue collar workers and 13 percent of laborers did so. Adding union memberships to the analysis reduced but did not eliminate the class skew. Schlozman and Tierney, op. cit., Table 4–1, p. 60; and pp. 60–63.

16. Reported in *Public Opinion*, February–March 1982, p. 22.

17. Likewise, 37 percent of business office workers as compared to 20 percent of manual workers reported volunteering.

18. Reported in *Public Opinion*, November–December 1986, p. 26.

19. Intentionally or not, "60 Minutes" devotes most of its exposés to local organizations, enabling the audience to compare these to their own experience and perhaps thereby adding to the program's credibility and popularity.

20. Freeman and Medoff, *What Do Unions Do?*, op. cit., p. 30.

21. Steven M. Cohen, *American Modernity and Jewish Identity*. New York: Tavistock, 1983, Table 3–2, p. 56.

22. The other four rituals at home were observing Passover's special dietary rules, fasting on Yom Kippur, placing a *mezuzah* on the front door, and lighting Sabbath candles. Thirty eight percent of the sample reported synagogue membership, and 32 percent synagogue attendance at times other than the high holidays. Ibid.

23. Robert Lekachman has argued just the reverse, that viewers know that the executives of "Dallas" and "Dynasty" are exaggerated, and therefore view the programs as escape or as a criticism of capitalism. Robert Lekachman, *Visions and Nightmares: America after Reagan*. New York: Macmillan, 1987, p. 132.

24. I do not mean to suggest that the viewers necessarily see the programs in that way, however. Moreover, Esther Shapiro, the creator of "Dynasty," suggested in a 1984 seminar at Columbia University that her main interest was in establishing a popular television program in which women were as powerful and therefore also as good or bad as men. See also Joe Klein, "The Real Star of 'Dynasty,' " *New York*, September 2, 1985, pp. 32–39.

25. Michael Schudson, *Advertising, the Uneasy Persuasion: Its Dubious Impact on American Society*. New York: Basic Books, 1984, Chapter 5.

26. Sussman analyzed a 1986 *Washington Post*-ABC News poll about Salt II and concluded that only 3 percent of the respondents thought they knew a good deal about it, while 67 percent suggested that they knew "not much" or "nothing at all." Barry Sussman, "Think of Those Three Monkeys Covering Their Eyes, Ears and Mouths," *Washington Post National Weekly Edition*, August 11, 1986, p. 37. Even so, respondents were able to offer opinions on the basic issues. In the summer of 1987, several polls reported that majorities or near majorities of poll samples could not describe Nicaragua's location or indicate which side the Reagan administration was supporting, but people had no difficulty in deciding whether the U.S. should aid the "contras," or send American soldiers to fight in Nicaragua. For a brief summary of these polls, see Richard Morin, "The Best of the Worst of the Summertime Surveys." *Washington Post National Weekly Edition*, September 21, 1987, p. 37.

27. The figure is from a February 1985 *New York Times* poll.

28. The frequency figures differed somewhat between the networks but generally speaking, an additional 4 to 8 percent of the viewers saw 13 to 16 programs a month, so that on the average and across all networks, about 10 percent saw 13 to 20 news programs during this period. The percentages were computed from the A. C. Nielsen Company's "National Audience Demographics Report," May 1987, Table 3. Total audience data are from Table 4A. I am grateful to William Behanna of the A. C. Nielsen Company for supplying the data. These figures were collected from viewer diaries, a method which was replaced by the "people-meter" in the fall of 1987.

29. Lipset and Schneider, *The Confidence Gap*, op. cit., pp. 130–151.

30. *Ibid.*, Figure 5–1, p. 131. Respondents are also asked to judge both matters for a time "five years from now," and during the 1970s and 1980s have been yet more optimistic for their own future, that average ranging between 7.1 and 7.5. Assessments of the country's future varied between 5.0 and 6.2 in the same period. *Ibid.*

31. The two polls are cited in Hamilton and Wright, *State of the Masses*, op. cit., p. 366. People make the same distinction between their personal finances and the country's economy. According to the July 1987 edition of the monthly "ABC News Consumer Comfort Index," 55 percent of the respondents reported their personal finances as excellent or good, but only 42 percent rated the national economy in this way, the remaining 58 percent judging it not so good or poor.

32. Reported in *Public Opinion*, August–September 1982, p. 24.

33. Only the two other possible causes—"lack of good leadership" and "too much commitment to other nations in the world"—seem inapplicable to family and informal group relations.

34. Bellah et al., *Habits of the Heart*, op. cit., p. 250. Both Presidents Carter and Reagan, like others before them, portrayed themselves as running against the government when they were candidates and representing the country, the nation, or the American people instead.

35. Needless to say, this does not stop politicians, lobbyists, and others from using nationalistic appeals for their own, instrumental, purposes.

36. The broad conception of national pride among Americans may help to explain why levels of pride are far higher here than in other countries. According to the *New York Times* international poll, "Trust in Government and National Pride," also carried out in 1983, 87 percent of Americans said they were very proud of their nationality as compared to 65 percent of Spaniards, 58 percent of the British, 44 percent of Italians, 42 percent of the French, and 20 percent of West Germans.

37. European and most other nations have national athletic teams, which at times seem to help their citizens cope with national humiliations and other problems.

38. For another comparison, see Bruce Bawer, "Ronald Reagan as Indiana Jones," *Newsweek*, August 27, 1984, p. 14.

39. Quoted in "Perspectives," *Newsweek*, August 4, 1986, p. 11.

40. In the Netherlands, "Queen's Day"is also the occasion for a nationwide "garage sale," in which children sell their families' discarded household goods and knickknacks on the major streets of their communities.

41. Robert Y. Shapiro and Harpreet Mahajan, "Gender Differences in Policy Preferences: A Summary of Trends from the 1960s to the 1980s," *Public Opinion Quarterly*, Vol. 50, No. 1, February 1986, pp. 42–61.

42. Fred Siegel has in fact implied that American working-class patriotism derives from a kind of family loyalty. Siegel, op. cit., p. 271.

43. Presumably overseas Americans miss the goods and services that make everyday American life convenient and comfortable for them, as well as the kinds of equality of opportunity and treatment and other features of the social structure that have remained distinctive to the United States for over a century. A study of homesick overseas Americans, particularly whites, might identify what else they miss, thus offering an unusual research opportunity for glimpsing a national culture which is so difficult to see inside the United States that some observers doubt that a single national culture that is actually nationwide can even be found.

44. Obviously, Toennies's dichotomy is far more complex than I here suggest. See Ferdinand Toennies, *Community and Society: Gemeinschaft und Gesellschaft*. New York: Harper & Row, 1963. The book was first published in 1887.

45. True to their times and the then topical issues, these analysts were also comparing models of social life dominated by emotion versus reason, competition versus cooperation, "natural" versus deliberate behavior, and several other such contrasted pairs.

46. Eugene Litwak has analyzed the division of labor between informal groups and formal organizations, demonstrating that the former perform distinctive functions that supplement or substitute for those of the latter. His work is also policy-oriented, showing when each type of group, or a combination of both, best achieves the intended purposes. See, e.g., Eugene Litwak, *Helping the Elderly: The Complementary Roles of Informal Networks and Formal Systems*. New York: Guilford Press, 1985.

47. Allan Silver has developed the most insightful analysis of the two social worlds and the divisions of labor as well as conflicts between them. He writes, "Modern citizens live in two increasingly differentiated worlds: one in which efficient, task-oriented performances are expected of them, and one in which they seek the fulfillment of emotional needs and social gratifications. The former set of arrangements is concerned with the production and allocation of goods and services, and with the administration of welfare functions and the bureaucratically-managed maintenance of social peace. Personal relationships—of family, locality, subculture, friendship—which previously dealt with at least some of the collective tasks requiring a degree of efficiency and impersonality—become unprecedently privatized in function. The disjunction in modern society between the sphere of the personal, the voluntary, and the affective on the one hand, and the impersonal, efficient, and remote on the other, helps set the stage for what may be described as the seemingly boundless cultural and emotional expectations generated by modern society." Allan Silver, "Family, Politics and Labor Markets in Modern Society: Preliminary Notes," unpublished paper prepared for the Committee on West Europe of the Social Science Research Council, October 1977, p. 8.

Chapter Four

1. Mancur Olson, *The Logic of Collective Action*. Cambridge, Mass.: Harvard University Press, 1965.

2. The term strenuous is Allan Silver's.

3. Harold D. Lasswell, "The Structure and Function of Communication in Society," in Lyman Bryson, ed., *The Communication of Ideas*. New York: Harper, 1948, pp. 37–51.

4. W. Russell Neuman, *The Paradox of Mass Politics: Knowledge and Opinion in the American Electorate*. Cambridge, Mass.: Harvard University Press, 1986, Table 6–4, p. 149. The source for the table is C. Richard's Hofstetter's 1975 report to the American Enterprise Institute, "Television and Civic Education."

5. The figures on Western Union messages come from Daniel Schorr, "Washington Notebook." *The New Leader*, October 19, 1987, p. 5.

6. Sidney Verba and Norman H. Nie, *Participation in America: Political Democracy and Social Equality*. New York: Harper & Row, 1972, p. 28. This summarizes the findings of Lester Milbrath, *Political Participation*. Chicago: Rand McNally, 1965, pp. 16, 21.

7. Neuman, op. cit., pp. 170–171.

8. Davis and Smith, *General Social Surveys, 1972–1986*, op. cit., Question 172D, p. 202.

9. Likewise, 22 percent of those earning over $25,000 in 1981 claimed membership as compared to 12 percent in the $15,000-to-$24,000 income category and 7 percent of those earning less than $15,000.

10. Bureau of the Census, *Statistical Abstract 1987*, op. cit., Table 418, p. 243.

11. Ibid.

12. Bureau of the Census, "Voting and Registration in the Election of November 1984," *Current Population Reports*, Series P-20, No. 405, March 1986, Tables F and 13.

13. The determinations are based on checking what people tell interviewers against election board reports.

14. Bureau of the Census, *Statistical Abstract 1987*, op. cit., Table 420, p. 244.

15. Ibid. Employed blue collar workers vote less often than white collar ones as well. Bureau of the Census, "Voting and Registration in the Election of November 1984," op. cit., Table 11.

16. *Statistical Abstract 1987*, op. cit., Table 420, p. 244.

17. Frances F. Piven and Richard A. Cloward, *Democracy Thwarted: Why So Many Americans Don't Vote*. New York: Pantheon Books, 1988.

18. Some of the objections to the presidential candidacies of Jesse Jackson reflect the fact that he has represented the poor and has spoken to the issues they consider to be important to them.

19. People who become active because they are discriminated against because of race, class, or ethnicity and thus are barred from conventional ways of upward

mobility are, however, not unusual. In this case, the society that discriminates against them should be considered unusual.

20. Harold D. Lasswell, *Psychopathology and Politics*. Chicago: University of Chicago Press, 1930.

21. I continue to be surprised that neither social scientists nor physiologists seem to have done research on this topic.

22. For a detailed study of these and other problems of participation in social and protest movements, see Michael Lipsky, *Protest in City Politics*. Chicago: Rand McNally, 1970.

23. Perhaps the most optimistic advocate of these organizations in Harry Boyte. See, e.g., Harry Boyte, Heather Booth, and Steve Max, *Citizen Action and the New American Populism*. Philadelphia: Temple University Press, 1986. For a more empirical analysis, which looks at shortcomings and problems as well as successes, see Gary Delgado, *Organizing the Movement: The Roots and Growth of ACORN*. Philadelphia: Temple University Press, 1986.

24. Schlozman and Verba, *Injury to Insult*, op. cit., pp. 156, 158. This may be a partial free-rider rationalization, since people making such a judgment know that until others become politically active and jobs are created as a result, they themselves cannot be free riders. However, the people studied had not been active politically in any way before they became jobless.

25. Terry F. Buss and F. Stevens Redburn, *Shutdown at Youngstown: Public Policy for Mass Unemployment*. Albany: State University of New York Press, 1983, p. 125. Also, Leonard Perlin and Carmi Schooler have found that relying on others can sometimes increase stress, so that self-reliance can become the emotionally most comfortable solution. "The Structure of Coping," *Journal of Health and Social Behavior*, Vol. 19, March 1978, pp. 2–21.

26. The data on the 1984 vote of the jobless are from the 1984 CBS News Election Poll. I am grateful to Dr. Kathleen Frankovic of CBS News for supplying me with the figures.

27. I draw here on Lily M. Hoffman and Barbara Schmitter, "Community Responses to Unemployment: The Case of Home Mortgage Foreclosures," an unpublished paper presented to the Society for the Study of Social Problems, August 1983.

28. Barry Sussman, "The Porcupine Theory: Explaining Contradictory Opinions," *Washington Post National Weekly Edition*, August 5, 1985, p. 37. Sussman argues that these poll respondents are displaying porcupine-like passivity even though they take the view, as did 57 percent in the Washington Post–ABC News poll to which he is referring, that "the justice system in the United States favors mainly the rich."

29. A movie can do well at the box office during the first week, but if the word of mouth from the initial ticket buyers is unenthusiastic, that film will begin to "die" in the second week.

30. Sandra Salmons, "P&G Drops Logo: Cites Satan Rumors," *New York Times*, April 25, 1985, pp. D1, 8.

31. On the media practices of the Carter White House, see Michael B. Grossman and Martha J. Kumar, *Portraying the President: The White House and the News Media*. Baltimore: Johns Hopkins University Press, 1981. The Reagan White

House is emphasized in Martin Schram, *The Great American Video Game: Presidential Politics in the TV Age*. New York: Morrow, 1987, Part 1.

32. Michael Pertschuk, *Giant Killers*. New York: Norton, 1986, p. 222.

33. Lisa Belkin, "Viewers' Pens Mightier than the Ax," *New York Times*, June 18, 1987, p. C26. In 1986, NBC indicated that it renewed "Remington Steele," another detective series, in response to 10,000 calls and letters protesting its planned cancellation. "The Spy Who Loved Too Much," *People*, August 11, 1986, p. 87. Again, other factors were involved as well. In this case the program's male lead was being considered by moviemakers for the James Bond role at the time.

34. Barbara Matusow, *The Evening Stars: The Making of the Network News Anchor*. Boston: Houghton Mifflin, 1983, pp. 178–180. At the time, ABC was an unprofitable third in the network competition and allegedly hoped to increase its income and stature in conservative regions of the country by openly supporting the Nixon administration.

35. In 1975 I analyzed all the letters viewers wrote to the NBC's evening news program during October and estimated that the program received about 4,600 that year. In the mid-1970s, *Time* received about 60,000 letters per year, *Newsweek* close to 40,000, but they publish letters columns. Gans, *Deciding What's News*, op. cit., pp. 227–229. In 1985, when *Time's* total circulation had risen considerably, the number of letters had declined to 47,000, presumably because fewer readers were angry about current events or *Time's* coverage of them. "Looking into 1985's Mailbag," *Time*, February 17, 1986, p. 16. Conversely, Senator Daniel P. Moynihan of New York announced that his office estimated receiving over 500,000 letters in 1986.

36. Paul Brodeur, *Outrageous Misconduct: The Asbestos Industry on Trial*. New York: Pantheon Books, 1985.

37. Warren Miller et al., *American National Election Study, 1984: Pre and Post Election Survey File*. Ann Arbor, Mich.: Inter-university Consortium for Political and Social Research, 1986, Question L6, p. 548. Responses to questions of this type have gone up and down over the years in much the same pattern as that to questions about people's confidence in national leaders described in Chapter One. However, the former questions have evoked even less enthusiasm than the latter. In 1964, only 32 percent thought the government paid a good deal of attention to people, and by 1980, the figure had sunk to 8 percent. Lipset and Schneider, *The Confidence Gap*, op. cit., Figure 1–3, p. 25.

38. Davis and Smith, op. cit., Question 348, pp. 356–357.

39. Ibid. Other statements about representation, such as "I don't think public officials care much what people like me think" or "People like me don't have any say about what government does" go back to 1956, when 28 and 27 percent agreed, respectively. Agreement with the former statement reached a high of 46 percent in 1978 and declined to 33 percent by 1984; agreement with the latter climbed to 55 percent in 1980 and stood at 41 percent in 1984. The 1984 figures are from Miller et al., *American National Election Study, 1984*, op. cit., Questions 7Lb and 7La, p. 459; the earlier data are in Hamilton and Wright, *State of the Masses*, op. cit., Table 8–8, pp. 364–365.

40. Schlozman and Tierney, *Organized Interests and American Democracy*, op. cit., Table 4–2, p. 67, and Chapter 4, passim.

41. Large corporations are likely to be members of several lobbies. General Electric, for example, belongs to more than 80 trade and other business associations. Ibid., pp. 71–73.

42. Herbers, *The New Heartland*, op. cit., p. 124.

43. John Kasarda, "The Implications of Contemporary Redistribution Trends for National Urban Policy," *Social Science Quarterly*, Vol. 61, December 1980, pp. 373–400.

44. On the continuing smallness of the workplace, see Mark Granovetter, "Small Is Bountiful: Labor Markets and Establishment Size," *American Sociological Review*, Vol. 49, No. 3, June 1984, pp. 323–355.

45. Workplaces are heading for the same areas, in part because they are following their most sought-after workers, but also because many of these areas feature weak unions or none at all. Toffler and other popular prophets have predicted an even more extreme form of workplace decentralization, people working for their employers on a computer in their homes, which Toffler calls the electronic cottage. Alvin Toffler, *The Third Wave*. New York: Morrow, 1970, particularly Chapter 16. I find this prediction hard to believe, since most work will still have to take place or be supervised in groups.

46. Michael Useem, *The Inner Circle: Large Corporations and the Rise of Business Political Activity in the U.S. and the U.K.* New York: Oxford University Press, 1984, pp. 34–38.

47. Ibid.

48. Lars Osberg, *Economic Inequality in the United States*. Armonk, N.Y.: M. E. Sharpe, 1984, p. 34.

49. Edward S. Herman, *Corporate Control Corporate Power*. New York: Cambridge University Press, 1981, Chapter 6. The contrary trend data are at pp. 191 and 192.

50. For example, Yale Brozen, *Mergers in Perspective*. Washington: American Enterprise Institute, 1982.

51. Michael J. Piore and Charles F. Sabel, *The Second Industrial Divide: Possibilities for Prosperity*. New York: Basic Books, 1983. Walter Adams and James W. Brock, *The Bigness Complex: Industry, Labor and Government in the American Economy*. New York: Pantheon Books, 1986.

52. This seems to have been one of the factors in the failure of Time, Inc., to launch a national magazine for cable television viewers. Christopher M. Byron, *The Fanciest Dive: What Happened when the Media Empire of Time–Life Leaped Without Looking into the Age of High-Tech*. New York: Norton, 1986.

53. *Time*, May 18, 1987, p. 26. The poll was done by Yankelovich-Clancy-Shulman. An August 1976 Hart poll which asked people for one or two qualities "that Americans want in their leadership" showed that 56 percent mentioned a president "who was honest with the people and played by the rules." Ten percent more mentioned "a strong leader and take charge person."

54. David S. Broder, "When North is Up," *The Washington Post National Weekly Edition*, July 27, 1987, p. 4. Several months later, of course, the contragate investigations revealed that Col. North also lied quite often without telling anyone that he was doing so.

55. See, e.g., Barry Bluestone and Bennett Harrison, *The Deindustrialization of America: Plant Closings, Community Abandonment and the Dismantling of Basic Industry.* New York: Basic Books, 1982; and Wassily Leontief and Faye Duchin, *The Future Impact of Automation on Workers.* New York: Oxford University Press, 1986.

56. Sweden, Austria, and Switzerland have used government policy in an effective fight against unemployment, and jobless rates have so far stayed below 5 percent in these countries.

57. Even so, members of some ethnic and racial minorities appear to be headed for virtual exclusion from the economy, and thus may turn into recruits for underclasses.

Chapter Five

1. Tom Wolfe, "The 'Me' Decade and the Third Great Awakening," *New York*, August 23, 1976, pp. 26–40.

2. During the late 1960s, few writers described the antiwar protestors of that time as altruists.

3. Alexander Astin, *The American Freshman: National Norms for Fall 1986.* Los Angeles: American Council of Education and UCLA, 1986.

4. Christopher Lasch, *The Culture of Narcissism: American Life in an Age of Diminishing Expectations.* New York: Norton, 1979. Richard Sennett, *The Fall of Public Man.* New York: Knopf, 1977.

5. For an incisive political critique of these critics and earlier ones in the same vein, see Elizabeth Long, *The American Dream and the Popular Novel.* Boston: Routledge & Kegan Paul, 1985, Chapter 6.

6. A historical analysis of this critique can be found in Patrick Brantlinger, *Bread and Circuses: Theories of Mass Culture as Social Decay.* Ithaca, N.Y.: Cornell University Press, 1983. For a more critical analysis of the critique see my *Popular Culture and High Culture: An Analysis of Taste.* New York: Basic Books, 1974, Chapter 1. A historical analysis of the critique of consumer behavior which indicates that nothing has really changed in that critique in the last century is Daniel Horowitz, *The Morality of Spending: Attitudes Toward the Consumer Society in America, 1875–1940.* Baltimore: Johns Hopkins University Press, 1985.

7. To the extent that a decline in the quality of goods has actually taken place, it is partly a matter of taste, because middle Americans may not want to buy goods of such permanence. However, it is also a matter of economics, since people may be unable to afford them. (The higher cost of quality is a consequence both of the rise in wages and the prices of materials.) Middle Americans who are nostalgic about the decline of quality probably do not remember that their ancestors subsidized quality goods with the low wages they received.

8. Halle, *America's Working Man*, op. cit., especially Chapter 11.

9. My favorite of the many books along this line remains Richard Hoggart, *The Uses of Literacy.* London: Chatto & Windus, 1957.

10. This theme suffuses the work of Dwight Macdonald, but can be found in the writings of other socialist intellectuals who were and are fighting in

behalf of modernism in culture while at the same time advocating socialism for society. Dwight Macdonald, "A Theory of Mass Culture," in Bernard Rosenberg and David M. White, eds., *Mass Culture: The Popular Arts in America*. Glencoe, Ill.: Free Press, 1957, pp. 59–73.

11. This is originally a European romantic ideal and is reflected in Toennies's concept of *Gemeinschaft*.

12. His coauthors were Richard Madsen, William M. Sullivan, Ann Swidler, and Steven M. Tipton. Bellah wrote the final draft, however.

13. Bellah et al., *Habits of the Heart*, op. cit., p. 74.

14. At this point, Bellah's argument is similar to the traditional socialist one, although his analysis is by no means socialist or neo-Marxist.

15. Bellah et al., op. cit., p. 290. Emphasis in text.

16. Ibid., p. 286.

17. Ibid., p. 275.

18. Ibid., p. 290. A 1986 Harris survey reported, however, that sizable numbers of Americans believe that a considerable increase in greed, materialism, hedonism, and overall selfishness has taken place. Unfortunately, the questions were framed as applying to "yuppies," and the answers may therefore indicate only that the respondents absorbed the contemporary stereotype about and concurrent dislike of the people labeled with this term. Harris, *Inside America*, op. cit. pp. 147–149.

19. Paul L. Wachtel, *The Poverty of Affluence: A Psychological Portrait of the American Way of Life*. New York: Free Press, 1983, pp. 234–241.

20. In the summer of 1976, Christopher Lasch wrote an article in the *New York Review of Books* on the new narcissism, which was critical, among other things, of the then novel self-improvement cults. I disagreed with part of his analysis and wrote him that "my own impression of [the cults] is that they are only the latest expression of the search for individualism and individual fulfillment on the part of people whose opportunities for individualism emerged only in recent years." Christopher Lasch, "The Narcissist Society," *New York Review of Books*, September 30, 1976, pp. 5–13.

21. Lasch's style is often so intensely condemning that both his cultural critique and his clinical analyses appear to be devoted to the exposure and punishment of sin. Whether he is writing about mental illness or sin, however, many people seem to share his feelings, at least judging by the number of Americans who buy his books. No one knows if the buyers of his books seek to read about America's troubles or their own narcissism, or whether they are making sure that they do not suffer from it. The latter is possible because Lasch's style is sufficiently hyperbolic that some readers could feel reassured that *they* are reasonably healthy.

22. *Time's* 1987 set of cover stories on the decline of ethics and the rise of "mindless materialism" in America sees the problem as a national failing, but all of the villains are from one or another elite. *Time*, May 25, 1987, pp. 14–29.

23. Davis and Smith, *General Social Surveys, 1972–1986*, op. cit., Question 217, p. 236.

24. At least that percentage reports drinking "sometimes." Ibid., Question 173, p. 205. A 1985 Harris poll of teenagers showed that 93 percent said they had used alcohol in the past year. Harris, op. cit., p. 76.

25. Classical Marxists, Maoists, and others like them often portray the workers as passive so that they can be mobilized by a vanguard. For a brilliant and bitter critique of this portrait, see Aileen S. Kraditor, *The Radical Persuasion: Aspects of the Intellectual History and the Historiography of Three American Radical Organizations*. Baton Rouge: Louisiana State University Press, 1981.

26. So of course do socialism and communism, but one injustice does not excuse others.

27. The principal historical study, which argues that a reduction of mental illness has occurred over the last century, is Herbert Goldhamer and A. W. Marshall, *Psychosis and Civilization*. Glencoe, Ill.: Free Press, 1953. Its basic finding is supported by Leo Srole and Anita K. Fischer, "The Midtown Manhattan Longitudinal Study vs. 'The Mental Paradise Lost' Doctrine," *Archives of General Psychiatry*, Vol. 37, February 1980, pp. 209–221. The contrary argument is based on less firm empirical grounds, but see, e.g., Gerald L. Klerman et al., "Birth Cohort Trends in Rates of Major Depressive Disorder among Relatives of Patients with Affective Disorders," *Archives of General Psychiatry*, Vol. 42, 1985, pp. 689–693; and Elliot S. Gershon et al., "Birth-Cohort Changes in Manic and Depressive Disorders in Relatives of Bipolar and Schizoaffective Patients," *Archives of General Psychiatry*, Vol. 44, 1987, pp. 314–319. I am indebted to Prof. Bruce Link for these references.

28. Middle and other Americans actually learned by the late 1960s to use the successful protest and other techniques of the civil rights movement.

29. Bellah et al., op. cit., p. 251.

30. Ibid. Bellah and his colleagues devote considerable attention to the argument that the people they studied lack the language to implement their wish. I still believe that language remains a tool, however, which people are usually able to invent if their wishes require it and when conditions to use the language for these wishes are favorable.

31. Ibid., p. 72.

32. Ibid., pp. 267–270.

33. Currie makes a strong case for a different community to prevent crime and recidivism: one that provides both caring and economic support. Elliott Currie, *Confronting Crime: An American Challenge*. New York: Pantheon Books, 1985.

34. Michael Zuckerman, *Peacable Kingdoms*. New York: Knopf, 1970.

35. Curious as to how sociologists define and write about society, I reviewed about a dozen introductory sociology textbooks written between 1940 and the 1980s. The study sample was chosen unsystematically, but since it consisted of texts in my own library and that of several colleagues, it was reasonably random. I discovered that all the texts, including the ones which used "Society" in the title, defined the term briefly and cursorily and then went on to other matters. Most authors saw it as a community writ large, with a population sharing a bounded territory and sometimes also a common culture, and generally

the boundaries of the territory and the culture were the same as those of the nation.

The relative lack of interest in defining the term may be wise, since it allows sociologists to avoid the agonies which anthropologists suffer in trying to define culture. Instead, we—sociologists and others—use society variously. We use it as a residual term, to describe the many phenomena and groups inside national boundaries that cannot be classified as economic, political, cultural, psychological, etc. Sometimes we also use society as a summary term for everything that happens inside those boundaries, encompassing economy, polity, culture, etc.; or we use it as a noun that follows a much more important adjective, as in industrial society or fascist society. At times we treat the term as a simile for an informal but large group which has one characteristic in common, for example, the society of stamp collectors. I have used the term in all these ways in this book myself.

36. While society may be a scholarly concept relevant to understanding social life, every parent of an American teenager must have wondered at times about what processes suddenly make one rock group or piece of clothing a huge seller all across the country despite the fact that dozens of seemingly similar rock groups or pieces of clothing are being promoted equally energetically at the same time.

37. In "The Field of Sociology," Simmel has written that "society . . . is an abstraction . . . it is no *real* object" (his emphasis), but adds that abstractions are necessary, and that "the alleged realism that performs this sort of critique of the concept of society, and thus of sociology, actually eliminates all knowable reality." Kurt Wolff, ed., *The Sociology of Georg Simmel*. Free Press: Glencoe, Ill., 1950, pp. 4 and 7 respectively. I am grateful to Eviatar Zerubavel for sending me back to Simmel's work and pointing his observations out to me.

38. Liberals sometimes worry about fragmentation and Marxists see contradictions, although they do not fear these.

39. The idea that Rome "fell" has always seemed to me an example of the centralist and militarist bias in the conventional studies of civilization. The medieval Italians who lived just after the end of the Roman state may not have been "civilized," but whatever the condition of their cultures and formal organizations, they seem to have killed fewer innocent people for military and other purposes.

40. Few of the disasters have ever occurred in the United States. As a result, Americans, Native Americans excepted, are not even familiar with the possibility of social disintegration. During the 1960s, the ghetto disorders and the militancy of antiwar radicals persuaded some that America was in danger of falling apart, but in fact the social peace was disturbed in only a few communities for brief periods, and most Americans, other than blacks, experienced the events wholly through the news media. Television reported mainly the dramatic highlights, as it always does, but the events themselves were dramatic because none like them had taken place for several decades.

41. The belief that societies which are not facing mass destruction can fall apart assumes society to be a holistic, intensely interdependent social system in which all parts are so functionally interrelated that disturbing a few elements can topple the entire social structure. Such a view not only caricatures functionalism but conflicts with all that is known about the systemic qualities of modern

societies. This caricature of functionalism also encourages the conservative taboo against trying anything new or different. When everything is alleged to be related to everything else, unintended but always dreadful consequences will follow, at least according to conservative doctrine.

42. There is also the question of who can act for society. Governments can do so, and they can delegate others as well. "Unauthorized" actors are sometimes tolerated because there is no one to stop them unless they are taken to court, although someone will probably "authorize" them if they have widespread public support.

43. Bernard Beck points out that the identification of social problems requires and presupposes the existence of society. See his "The Politics of Speaking in the Name of Society," *Social Problems*, Vol. 25, No. 4, April 1978, pp. 353–360.

44. Jeffrey Alexander argues that journalists do speak for the society as a whole, although I do not believe they or anyone else can speak for an entire collectivity, whatever the claim. "The Mass News Media in Systematic, Historical and Comparative Perspective," in Elihu Katz and Tamas Szecsko, eds., *Mass Media and Social Change*. London: Sage, 1981, especially pp. 17–23.

45. These are examples of a genre I have found in a variety of popular magazines and newspapers over the last several years. Even so, scholars are not exempt from personalizing society, for example, those who search for cycles and swings in society as if it experienced psychological ups and downs, biorhythms or what one historian has called basic swings in human nature.

46. Howard S. Becker. *Outsiders: Studies in the Sociology of Deviance.* New York: Free Press, 1963, pp. 135–146.

47. The right-wing populism that developed toward the end of the 1970s seeks identification with or leadership of "the people" in order to obtain the support of middle Americans for conservative or ultraconservative Republicanism. This populism emanates mainly out of Washington organizations such as the Heritage Foundation, which were established with, and are supported by, corporate monies. Some of their expertise and technical work comes from ambitious young intellectuals and analysts of middle American origin who consider themselves populist because of their origin. Although solidly laissez-faire, most obtained their educations from tax-supported public and private universities and are now working for nonprofit foundations which, being tax-exempt, are thus subsidized by other taxpayers. In addition, the big corporations that fund these organizations deduct their contributions from their own taxes. Ironically, 40 to 50 years ago, anyone who praised "the people" was suspected of being a communist, and was likely to be investigated by the conservative politicians of that time.

48. Alan Wolfe, "Is Sociology Dangerous?" *Tikkun*, Vol. 1, No. 1, Summer 1986, pp. 96–101, quote at p. 100. Wolfe praises 19th-century sociology as the originator of an antimarket and antistate conception of society and believes it to be a more radical discipline today than I think it actually is.

49. Sheldon Wolin, "Editorial." *democracy*, Winter 1983, p. 5.

50. Alan Wolfe, op. cit., p. 98.

51. Wolin, op. cit., p. 5.

52. Alan Wolfe, op. cit., p. 101. These ideas are developed in more detail in his *The Ties That Bind*. Berkeley: University of California Press, forthcoming.

53. Wolfe is further to the left than Bellah, however, and in some respects his work is closer to the ideas of Paul and Percival Goodman, for example in their *Communitas: Means of Livelihood and Ways of Life*. New York: Random House, 1947.

54. Alan Wolfe, "Is Sociology Dangerous?," op. cit., p. 101.

55. Wolfe's advocacy of "individual freedom . . . to bring out the best in the person" might be supportive of individualism if individuals could decide what was best in them, but not if that decision was made for them by others. As always, the right of definition is crucial and who defines best has at least the ideological power to affect people's lives.

Chapter Six

1. Theodore J. Lowi, *The End of Liberalism: Ideology, Policy and the Crisis of Public Authority*. New York: Norton, 1969, p. 291.

2. Public funds will also be needed to enable poor citizens to take time off from work and to pay for transportation to Washington, state capitols, or other places where their presence is needed to support their lobbyists.

3. Theodore J. Lowi, personal communication.

4. Advisory Commission on Intergovernmental Relations, *Changing Public Attitudes on Governments and Taxes 1983*, op. cit., Table 9, p. 15.

5. Benjamin Ginsberg, *The Captive Public: How Mass Opinion Promotes State Power*. New York: Basic Books, 1986, Chapter 2.

6. Bruce E. Altschuler, "Lyndon Johnson and the Polls," *Public Opinion Quarterly*, Vol. 50, No. 3, Fall 1986, pp. 285–299.

7. Conversely, it would be possible to design a polling system that would screen out those who do not care; in that case, the polls could become a mechanism to transmit the results of the griping discussed in Chapter 4.

8. One approach is to ask people hypothetical questions about how they would feel and act under different conditions, giving them a variety of actual policy options. They would still not need to feel responsible for their answers, but if polling became a widespread and diversified practice associated with policy and politics, many people might answer more carefully than they do today.

9. This might also reduce the pollsters' problem of declining response rates.

10. The real need is for open-ended questions which enable respondents to give their own answers. Such questions are so costly to ask and analyze, however, that today's commercial pollsters can virtually never use them.

11. The continuing invention of new interactive communications technology, by which people can now talk back to television programmers and "vote" from their television sets, suggests that someday the technology for using the TV set as a polling device will be available. The idea is tempting but only if questioning random samples under diverse auspices with diverse questions remains possible. Otherwise, interactive television will become only a new way

to pack the house. The same danger attaches to face-to-face discussion among citizens on television, since politicians struggling for political advantage would also pack the screen with their supporters. Traditional polling, door to door or even by phone, turns out to have impressive democratic virtues.

12. I believe that journalists cannot tell people what to think or, with some exceptions, even what to think about. Journalists are currently viewed in some quarters as agenda-setters for the audience, but in order to get the audience's attention, the journalists often report stories about subjects that people are already thinking about or have been know to think about in the past. Thus, the audience also sets the journalists' agenda.

13. John P. Robinson and Mark R. Levy, with Dennis K. Davis et al., *The Main Source: Learning from Television News*. Beverly Hills, Calif.: Sage Publications, 1986.

14. "Second tier" news media already exist—for example, in the form of white ethnic and black publications, union newspapers, and a variety of magazines, papers, and newsletters for many other "special interests." A more detailed discussion of these news media and government funding for them can be found in my *Deciding What's News*, op. cit., Chapter 10.

15. Piven and Cloward, *Democracy Thwarted*, op. cit.

16. I have not altered the opinions I expressed on this topic in my *More Equality*. New York: Pantheon Books, 1973.

17. The two conceptions of the public interest are my summary of the five developed by Edward C. Banfield, "Supplement: Note on Conceptual Scheme," in Martin Meyerson and Edward C. Banfied, *Politics, Planning and the Public Interest*. Glencoe, Ill.: Free Press, 1955, pp. 303–329.

18. Actually, they probably obtain some benefits, not only from tourist income but also because achievements in high culture seem to contribute to feelings of national pride. Further, support for high culture also counteracts the guilt that some upper-middle- and middle-class people feel for avoiding it.

19. For a more extreme version of this position, see Edward C. Banfield, *The Democratic Muse: Visual Arts and the Public Interest*. New York: Basic Books, 1984.

20. This argument is often identified with Samuel Huntington. See Michael Crozier, Samuel P. Huntington, and Joji Watanuki, *The Crisis of Democracy: A Report on the Governability of Democracies to the Trilateral Commission*. New York: New York University Press, 1975, pp. 59–118.

21. Lowi, *End of Liberalism*, op. cit., pp. 311–312.

22. I do not include as desirable kinds of user-friendliness nepotism or other kinds of illegal and questionable kinds of favoritism.

23. Some voluntary and proprietary hospitals have already begun to offer patients what they call "guest relations" because they have too many empty beds. A truly patient-centered hospital would be even more costly. If it were supplied by government, extra user charges would surely be required. However, government already levies such charges for higher-quality services, for example on the first-class cars of passenger trains on Amtrak and other publicly owned lines.

24. Mark Bendick, "Privatizing the Delivery of Social Welfare Service," Working Paper 6 in *Project on the Federal Social Role*. Washington: National Conference on Social Welfare, 1985.

25. Privatization is also unjustifiable under many other conditions, such as for services which are used only or mainly by the poor and thus cannot possibly be profitable; and for facilities in which government cannot share its monopoly with private enterprise, such as prisons, police forces, and other institutions involving the administration of justice.

26. Litwak, *Helping the Elderly*, op. cit., see also Peter Willmott, *Social Networks, Informal Care and Public Policy*. London: Policy Studies Institute, Research Report 655, 1986.

27. Frank Levy, "The Middle Class: Is It Really Vanishing?," *Brookings Review*, Vol. 5, No. 3, Summer 1987, pp. 17–21. The 1986 data come from Robert Pear, "Poverty Rate Dips as the Median Family Income Rises," *New York Times*, July 31, 1987, p. A12.

28. James D. Smith, "Wealth in America," *ISR Newsletter*, Winter 1986–1987, p. 3.

29. Ibid., p. 5.

30. A more accurate rate would have to include joblessness among illegal immigrants, who cannot report their status to Census Bureau interviewers for fear of deportation. The rate would also have to factor in off-the-books employment and unemployment, which cannot be reported either.

31. Alvin Schorr, *Common Decency: Domestic Policies after Reagan*. New Haven, Conn.: Yale University Press, 1986, Chapter 4.

32. Alternatively, America may face greater regional and temporal ups and downs in its economic fortunes. This pattern may already have begun, for in the mid-1980s international reductions in the price of oil drove up jobless rates in several Sunbelt states that had enjoyed unusually low rates before. During the same period, much of New England, which had previously been considered part of the troubled Frostbelt, was able to attract sufficient high-tech, service, and other firms, to reduce its official jobless rate below the national average. Since people actually work in regional economies or, more accurately, in local labor markets, national figures will probably have less meaning from now on than they had in the past.

33. A thoughtful defense of income grant programs is Fred Block, Richard A. Cloward, Barbara Ehrenreich, and Frances F. Piven, *The Mean Season: The Attack on the Welfare State*. New York: Pantheon Books, 1987.

34. Fred Best, *Worksharing: Issues, Policy Options and Prospects*. Kalamazoo, Mich.: Upjohn Institute for Employment Research, 1981. The most important literature about this policy is now being produced in Europe, however, for several Western European countries began to implement modest worksharing schemes as far back as the 1970s. If machines should someday do much of the work, as utopian writers have proposed for at least a century, everyone may be working part time in the future, i.e., 20 to 24 hours a week.

35. Ideally, computers and other machines which create joblessness should be taxed so that new jobs can be created with the proceeds.

36. I am using the original, purely economic definition of underclass proposed by Gunnar Myrdal, who coined the term. Gunnar Myrdal, *Challenge to Affluence*. New York: Pantheon Books, 1962, p. 14.

37. Bruce B. Williams, *Black Workers in an Industrial Suburb*. New Brunswick, N.J.: Rutgers University Press, 1987.

38. Halle, *America's Working Man*, op. cit., pp. 207–209.

39. William E. Connolly, "The Politics of Reindustrialization." *democracy*, Vol. 1, No. 3, July 1981, pp. 9–10.

40. Michael Lerner, *Surplus Powerlessness*. Oakland, Calif.: Institute for Labor and Mental Health, 1986, pp. 99–102.

41. Most liberals are not very good at such mixing either.

42. Or, as James Scott (and Eric Hobsbawm) put it, "Most subordinate classes are . . . far less interested in changing the larger structures of the state and the law than in what Hobsbawm has appropriately called 'working the system . . . to their minimum disadvantage.' " Quoted in Istvan Rev, "The Advantage of Being Atomized: How Hungarian Peasants Coped with Collectivization." *Dissent*, Vol. 34, No. 3, Summer 1987, p. 344.

Appendix

1. I also used the additional but unpublished tables that the *New York Times* makes available to researchers on request.

2. Strictly speaking, the two terms are synonymous, but polls conducted under academic auspices and those for which the data are analyzed more comprehensively and systematically than those normally conducted by commercial pollsters are often called surveys.

3. The General Social Survey is also useful because it has been asking some questions since 1972, and yet others which were asked by earlier pollsters since 1937.

4. Although the polls themselves cannot tell why attitudes are changing, one reason is the considerable influence of economic conditions on a wide variety of attitudes. However, attitudes are also affected by government action and inaction, the increased sophistication and skepticism on the part of respondents, and perhaps even by people's willingness to answer questions more honestly than in the past.

5. After all, most respondents do not have professional training in data analysis, i.e. the ability to generalize. Questions about behavior must also be treated cautiously because respondents may be reluctant to mention illegal or disapproved behavior.

6. Edward Shils, *Center and Periphery: Essays in Macrosociology*. Chicago: University of Chicago Press, 1975, especially Introduction and Chapter 1.

7. Ibid., p. 39.

8. For example, Shils points to "the periphery's aspiration to protect itself from being known" and to "the megalomanic temptations of centrality." Ibid.,

p. xxxix. He also explains that the center's megalomania helped generate his classic studies of privacy.

9. Ibid., p. xxvi.

10. Other social scientists have used the center-periphery model, often to suggest that they favored whomever they put at the center. However, Marxist and world-systems formulators of "dependency theory" have sided with the periphery, employing the model to analyze and criticize the exploitation of colonial territories and nations by imperialist centers.

Robert K. Merton's earlier distinction between cosmopolitans and locals bears some resemblance to Shils's dichotomy, although Merton is analyzing two types of influential leaders. Also, his analysis does not consider cosmopolitans superior to locals. Robert K. Merton, *Social Theory and Social Structure*. Glencoe, Ill.: Free Press, revised and enlarged edition, 1957, Chapter X.

11. Erving Goffman, *Frame Analysis: An Essay on the Organization of Experience*. Cambridge, Mass.: Harvard University Press, 1974. I am, however, using frame in a simpler way than either Goffman or Bateson.

12. See for example Gaye Tuchman's fine analysis of the use of camera angles in television news, in her *Making News: A Study in the Construction of Reality*. New York: Free Press, 1978, Chapter 6.

13. An informative analysis of the political biases of map making can be found in "Upside Down, Inside Out: How Do You Like Your Maps Served . . . ," *The Economist*, December 22, 1984, pp. 19–24.

14. The discussion of perspectives owes a considerable debt to the work of Karl Mannheim, *Ideology and Utopia: An Introduction to the Sociology of Knowledge*. Translated by Louis Wirth and Edward Shils. New York: Harcourt, Brace, 1936.

15. I owe this distinction and the two terms to Martin Meyerson, and first used them under his supervision, and together with the late Jack Dyckman, in researches on planning theory we conducted at the University of Pennsylvania in the mid-1950s.

16. Peter Saunders, "The Sociology of Consumption: A Research Agenda," unpublished paper, 1986. Saunders and his European colleagues prefer the term consumer, partly because they are concerned with Market-State relations. See also Peter Saunders, *Social Theory and the Urban Question*. New York: Holmes & Meier, 2nd edition, 1986, Chapter 8.

17. Thus, the dichotomy is not meant to replace ideas of class conflict, although user-supplier conflicts may at times replace or complement class conflict.

18. One danger is that the terms are simple enough to lend themselves to unfortunate definitions. For example, in her 1987 election campaign, British Prime Minister Margaret Thatcher campaigned to make government convenient for the "consumers," by whom she actually meant the taxpayers. The "producers" whom she attacked were government officials from the Labor party, whose number and power she has been trying to reduce. Equating consumers with taxpayers neatly ignores poor people who pay no taxes or minimal ones, and is a good example of the resort to loadshedding in privatization.

19. This does not necessarily prevent the researchers from siding with the users they are studying, nor does it prevent those who hire the researchers from ignoring that aspect of the research.

20. The level of abstraction in user-oriented studies has to be lower than in most academic research in order to connect the analysis to specific sets of users. Nonetheless, significant abstractions must not be avoided. For example, studies of Market-State relations, an issue currently topical in all the social sciences and with researchers from nearly every ideological position, must continue, but the user-oriented researcher has to include in the study the actual organizations and suppliers representing both State and Market which users have to confront.

21. I do not mean to suggest that user-oriented social science should or can in any way replace politics. Good research can provide a subtler understanding of how users act, think, and feel than the polling proposed in Chapter 6, and researchers are entitled to offer their own value judgments about their findings. However, even the best research cannot make value judgments for others, and while good data can sometimes aid the political process, they should not be even a partial substitute for that process.

Bibliography

This bibliography includes most of the references cited in the notes as well as other books, and some articles, I found useful in writing this book.

Adams, Walter, and James W. Brock. *The Bigness Complex: Industry, Labor and Government in the American Economy.* New York: Pantheon Books, 1986.

Advisory Commission on Intergovernmental Relations (ACIR). *Changing Public Attitudes on Governments and Taxes 1983.* Washington: The Commission, 1983.

Alexander, Jeffrey C. "The Mass News Media in Systematic, Historical and Comparative Perspective," in Elihu Katz and Tamas Szecsko, eds., *Mass Media and Social Change.* London: Sage, 1981, pp. 17–43.

Altschuler, Bruce E. "Lyndon Johnson and the Polls." *Public Opinion Quarterly,* Vol. 50, No. 3, Fall 1986, pp. 285–299.

Astin, Alexander. *The American Freshman: National Norms for Fall 1986.* Los Angeles: American Council of Education and UCLA, 1986.

Bailyn, Bernard. *The Peopling of North America.* New York: Knopf, 1986.

Banfield, Edward C. *The Democratic Muse: Visual Arts and the Public Interest.* New York: Basic Books, 1984.

Barber, Benjamin R. *Strong Democracy: Participatory Politics for a New Age.* Berkeley: University of California Press, 1984.

Beck, Bernard. "The Politics of Speaking in the Name of Society." *Social Problems,* Vol. 25, No. 4, April 1978, pp. 353–360.

Becker, Howard S. *Outsiders: Studies in the Sociology of Deviance.* New York: Free Press, 1963.

Bellah, Robert N., Richard Madsen, William M. Sullivan, Ann Swidler, and Steven M. Tipton. *Habits of the Heart: Individualism and Commitment in American Life*. Berkeley: University of California Press, 1985.

Bendick, Mark. "Privatizing the Delivery of Social Welfare Service," Working Paper 6 in *Project on the Federal Social Role*. Washington: National Conference on Social Welfare, 1985.

Best, Fred. *Worksharing: Issues, Policy Options and Prospects*. Kalamazoo, Mich.: Upjohn Institute for Employment Research, 1981.

Blau, Peter M., and Otis D. Duncan. *The American Occupational Structure*. New York: Wiley, 1967.

Block, Fred, Richard A. Cloward, Barbara Ehrenreich, and Frances F. Piven. *The Mean Season: The Attack on the Welfare State*. New York: Pantheon Books, 1987.

Bowles, Samuel, and Herbert Gintis. *Democracy and Capitalism*. New York: Basic Books, 1985.

Bluestone, Barry, and Bennett Harrison. *The Deindustrialization of America: Plant Closings, Community Abandonment and the Dismantling of Basic Industry*. New York: Basic Books, 1982.

Boyte, Harry, Heather Booth, and Steve Max. *Citizen Action and the New American Populism*. Philadelphia: Temple University Press, 1986.

Brantlinger, Patrick. *Bread and Circuses: Theories of Mass Culture as Social Decay*. Ithaca N.Y.: Cornell University Press, 1983.

Brodeur, Paul. *Outrageous Misconduct: The Asbestos Industry on Trial*. New York: Pantheon Books, 1985.

Brozen, Yale. *Mergers in Perspective*. Washington: American Enterprise Institute, 1982.

Burawoy, Michael. *Manufacturing Consent*. Chicago: University of Chicago Press, 1979.

Bureau of the Census. *Statistical Abstract of the United States 1987*. Washington D.C.: U.S. Government Printing Office, 1987.

Buss, Terry F., and F. Stevens Redburn. *Shutdown at Youngstown: Public Policy for Mass Unemployment*. Albany: State University of New York Press, 1983.

Byron, Christopher. *The Fanciest Dive: What Happened When the Media Empire of Time-Life Leaped Without Looking into the Age of High-Tech*. New York: Norton, 1986.

Caplow, Theodore D., et al. *Middletown Families: Fifty Years of Change and Continuity*. Minneapolis: University of Minnesota Press, 1982.

Chinoy, Eli. *Automobile Workers and the American Dream*. Boston: Beacon Press, 1955.

Clecak, Peter. *America's Quest for the Ideal Self: Dissent and Fulfillment in the 60s and 70s*. New York: Oxford University Press, 1983.

Cohen, Steven M. *American Modernity and Jewish Identity*. New York: Tavistock, 1983.

Coleman, Richard P., and Lee Rainwater, with Kent A. McClelland. *Social Standing in America: New Dimensions of Class.* New York: Basic Books, 1978.

Coles, Robert. *The Middle Americans: Proud and Uncertain.* Boston: Little, Brown, 1971.

Connolly, William E. "The Politics of Reindustrialization." *democracy*, Vol. 1, No. 3, July 1981, pp. 9–21.

Cook, Constance E. "Participation in Public Interest Groups: Membership Motivations." *American Politics Quarterly*, Vol. 12, No. 4, October 1984, pp. 409–430.

Cooley, Charles H. *Social Organization: A Study of the Larger Mind.* New York: Scribner, 1929.

Crozier, Michael, Samuel P. Huntington, and Joji Watanuki. *The Crisis of Democracy: A Report on the Governability of Democracies to the Trilateral Commission.* New York: New York University Press, 1975.

Currie, Elliott. *Confronting Crime: An American Challenge.* New York: Pantheon Books, 1985.

Davis, James A., and Tom W. Smith. *General Social Surveys, 1972–1986: Cumulative Codebook.* Storrs, Conn.: NORC-Roper Center, 1986.

Delgado, Gary. *Organizing the Movement: The Roots and Growth of ACORN.* Philadelphia: Temple University Press, 1986.

Edsall, Thomas B. *The New Politics of Inequality.* New York: Norton, 1984.

Featherman, David L., and Robert M. Hauser. *Opportunity and Change.* New York: Academic Press, 1978.

Ferguson, Thomas, and Joel Rogers. *Right Turn: The Decline of the Democrats and the Future of American Politics.* New York: Hill and Wang, 1986.

Fisse, Brent, and John Braithwaite. *The Impact of Publicity on Corporate Offenders.* Albany: State University of New York Press, 1983.

FitzGerald, Frances. *Cities on a Hill: A Journey Through Contemporary American Cultures.* New York: Simon & Schuster, 1986.

Form, William. *Divided We Stand: Working-Class Stratification in America.* Urbana: University of Illinois Press, 1985.

Fox, Richard W., and T. J. Jackson, eds., *The Culture of Consumption.* New York: Pantheon Books, 1983.

Freeman, Richard B., and James L. Medoff. *What Do Unions Do?* New York: Basic Books, 1984.

Galbraith, John K. *The Affluent Society.* Boston: Houghton Mifflin, 1958.

Gans, Herbert J. *Deciding What's News: A Study of CBS Evening News, NBC Nightly News, Newsweek and Time.* New York: Pantheon Books, 1978.

Gans, Herbert J. *More Equality.* New York: Pantheon Books, 1973.

Gans, Herbert J. *Popular Culture and High Culture: An Analysis of Taste.* New York: Basic Books, 1974.

Gershuny, Jonathan. *Social Innovation and the Division of Labor.* New York: Oxford University Press, 1983.

Ginsberg, Benjamin. *The Captive Public: How Mass Opinion Promotes State Power*. New York: Basic Books, 1986.

Goffman, Erving. *Frame Analysis: An Essay on the Organization of Experience*. Cambridge, Mass.: Harvard University Press, 1974.

Goldhamer, Herbert, and A. W. Marshall. *Psychosis and Civilization*. Glencoe, Ill.: Free Press, 1953.

Goldscheider, Calvin, and Frances K. Goldscheider. "Moving Out and Marriage: What Do Young Adults Expect?" *American Sociological Review*, Vol. 52, No. 2, April 1987, pp. 278–285.

Goodman, Paul and Percival. *Communitas: Means of Livelihood and Ways of Life*. New York: Random House, 1947.

Goodwyn, Lawrence. *The Populist Moment: A Short History of the Agrarian Revolt In America*. New York: Oxford University Press, 1978.

Granovetter, Mark. "Small Is Bountiful: Labor Markets and Establishment Size." *American Sociological Review*, Vol. 49, No. 3, June 1984, pp. 323–355.

Grossman, Michael B., and Martha J. Kumar. *Portraying the President: The White House and the News Media*. Baltimore: Johns Hopkins University Press, 1981.

Gutman, Herbert G. *Work, Culture and Society in Industrializing America*. New York: Vintage Books, 1977.

Halle, David. *America's Working Man*. Chicago: University of Chicago Press, 1984.

Hamilton, Richard F., and James D. Wright. *The State of the Masses*. New York: Aldine, 1986.

Harrington, Michael. *The Next Left: History of a Future*. New York: Holt, 1986.

Harris, Louis. *Inside America*. New York: Vintage Books, 1987.

Hartz, Louis. *The Liberal Tradition in America*. New York: Harcourt, Brace, 1955.

Herbers, John. *The New Heartland: America's Flight Beyond the Suburbs and How It Is Changing Our Future*. New York: Times Books, 1986.

Herman, Edward S. *Corporate Control Corporate Power*. New York: Cambridge University Press, 1981.

Hirschman, Albert O. *Shifting Involvements: Private Interest and Public Action*. Princeton, N.J.: Princeton University Press, 1982.

Hochschild, Arlie R. *The Managed Heart: Commercialization of Human Feeling*. Berkeley: University of California Press, 1983.

Hoffman, Lily M., and Barbara S. Heisler. " 'Threats to Homes' As a Grievance: Targets and Constituencies," in Louis Kriesberg, ed. *Research in Social Movements, Conflicts and Change*. Greenwich, Conn.: J.A.I. Press, 1988.

Hoffman, Lily M., and Barbara Schmitter. "Community Responses to Unemployment: The Case of Home Mortgage Foreclosures," an unpublished paper presented to the Society for the Study of Social Problems, August 1983.

Hoggart, Richard. *The Uses of Literacy*. London: Chatto & Windus, 1957.

Horowitz, Daniel. *The Morality of Spending: Attitudes Toward the Consumer Society in America, 1875–1940*. Baltimore: Johns Hopkins University Press, 1985.

Howe, Louise K. *Pink Collar Workers: Inside the World of Women's Work*. New York: Putnam, 1977.

Huber, Joan, and William H. Form. *Income and Ideology: An Analysis of the American Political Formula*. New York: Free Press, 1973.

Huntington, Samuel P. *American Politics: The Promise of Disharmony*. Cambridge, Mass.: Harvard University Press, 1981.

Inglehart, Ronald. *The Silent Revolution*. Princeton, N.J.: Princeton University Press, 1978.

Jackman, Mary R., and Robert W. Jackman. *Class Awareness in the United States*. Berkeley: University of California Press, 1983.

Kaplan, H. Roy. *Lottery Winners*. New York: Harper & Row, 1970.

Kasarda, John. "The Implications of Contemporary Redistribution Trends for National Urban Policy." *Social Science Quarterly*, Vol. 61, December 1980, pp. 373–400.

Kietiet, D. Roderick. *Macro-economics & Micro-politics: The Electoral Effects of Economic Issues*. Chicago: University of Chicago Press, 1983.

Kingdon, John W. *Agendas, Alternatives, and Public Policies*. Boston: Little, Brown, 1984.

Kluegel, James R., and Elliot R. Smith. *Beliefs about Inequality: Americans' Views of What Is and What Ought to Be*. New York: Aldine de Gruyter, 1986.

Kraditor, Aileeen S. *The Radical Persuasion: Aspects of the Intellectual History and the Historiography of Three American Radical Organizations*. Baton Rouge: Louisiana State University Press, 1981.

Lane, Robert E. "Market Justice, Political Justice." *American Political Science Review*, Vol. 80, No. 2, June 1986, pp. 383–402.

Lane, Robert E. *Political Life: Why People Get Involved in Politics*. Glencoe, Ill.: Free Press, 1959.

Lasch, Christopher. *The Culture of Narcissism: American Life in an Age of Diminishing Expectations*. New York: Norton, 1979.

Lasch, Christopher. "The Narcissist Society." *New York Review of Books*, September 30, 1976, pp. 5–13.

Lasswell, Harold D. *Psychopathology and Politics*. Chicago: University of Chicago Press, 1930.

Lasswell, Harold D. "The Structure and Function of Communication in Society," in Lyman Bryson, ed., *The Communication of Ideas*. New York: Harper, 1948, pp. 37–51.

Lekachman, Robert. *Visions and Nightmares: America after Reagan*. New York: Macmillan, 1987.

Leontief, Wassily, and Faye Duchin. *The Future Impact of Automation on Workers*. New York: Oxford University Press, 1986.

Lerner, Michael. *Surplus Powerlessness*. Oakland, Calif.: Institute for Labor and Mental Health, 1986.

Levison, Andrew. *The Working Class Majority*. New York: Coward, McCann and Geoghegan, 1974.

Levy, Frank. "The Middle Class: Is It Really Vanishing?" *Brookings Review*, Vol. 5, No. 3, Summer 1987, pp. 17–21.

Lindblom, Charles E. *Politics and Markets: The World's Political-Economic Systems*. New York: Basic Books 1977.

Lingeman, Richard. *Small Town America*. Boston: Houghton Mifflin, 1980.

Lipset, S. M., and William Schneider. "Confidence in Confidence Measures." *Public Opinion*, August-September 1983, pp. 42–44.

Lipset, Seymour M., and William Schneider. *The Confidence Gap: Business, Labor and Government in the Public Mind*. Baltimore: Johns Hopkins University Press, revised edition, 1987.

Lipsky, Michael. *Protest in City Politics*. Chicago: Rand McNally, 1970.

Litwak, Eugene. *Helping the Elderly: The Complementary Roles of Informal Networks and Formal Systems*. New York: Guilford Press, 1985.

Litwak, Eugene, Nancy Hooyman, and Donald Warren. "Ideological Complexity and Middle-American Rationality." *Public Opinion Quarterly*, Vol. 37, No. 3, Fall 1973, pp. 317–322.

Long, Elizabeth. *The American Dream and the Popular Novel*. Boston: Routledge & Kegan Paul, 1985.

Lowi, Theodore J. *The End of Liberalism: Ideology, Policy and the Crisis of Public Authority*. New York: Norton, 1969.

Lukas, J. Anthony. *Common Ground*. New York: Knopf, 1986.

Lukes, Steven. *Individualism*. Oxford: Blackwell, 1983.

Lynd, Robert S. *Knowledge for What? The Place of Social Science in American Culture*. Princeton, N.J.: Princeton University Press, 1939.

Lynd, Robert S., and Helen M. Lynd. *Middletown: A Study in American Culture* and *Middletown in Transition: A Study in Cultural Conflicts*. New York: Harcourt, Brace, 1929 and 1937.

Macdonald, Dwight. "A Theory of Mass Culture," in Bernard Rosenberg and David M. White, eds., *Mass Culture: The Popular Arts in America*. Glencoe, Ill.: Free Press, 1957, pp. 59–73.

Mannheim, Karl. *Ideology and Utopia: An Introduction to the Sociology of Knowledge.* Translated by Louis Wirth and Edward Shils. New York: Harcourt, Brace, 1936.

Marsden, Peter V. "Core Discussion Networks of Americans." *American Sociological Review,* Vol. 52, No. 1, February 1987, pp. 122–131.

Matusow, Barbara. *The Evening Stars: The Making of the Network News Anchor.* Boston: Houghton Mifflin, 1983.

Merton, Robert K. *Social Theory and Social Structure.* Glencoe, Ill.: Free Press, revised and enlarged edition, 1957.

Meyerson, Martin, and Edward C. Banfield. *Politics, Planning and the Public Interest.* Glencoe, Ill.: Free Press, 1955.

Miller, Warren, et al. *American National Election Study, 1984: Pre and Post Election Survey File.* Ann Arbor, Mich.: Inter-university Consortium for Political and Social Research, 1986.

Moynihan, Daniel P. *Family and Nation.* New York: Harcourt Brace Jovanovich, 1986.

Myrdal, Gunnar. *Challenge to Affluence.* New York: Pantheon Books, 1962.

Neuman, W. Russell. *The Paradox of Mass Politics: Knowledge and Opinion in the American Electorate.* Cambridge, Mass.: Harvard University Press, 1986.

Offe, Claus. "Political Legitimation through Majority Rule?" *Social Research,* Vol. 50, No. 4, Winter 1983, pp. 709–756.

Osberg, Lars. *Economic Inequality in the United States.* Armonk, N.Y.: M. E. Sharpe, 1984, p. 34.

Pahl, R. E. *Divisions of Labor.* Oxford: Blackwell, 1984.

Perlin, Leonard, and Carmi Schooler. "The Structure of Coping." *Journal of Health and Social Behavior,* Vol. 19, March 1978, pp. 2–21.

Piore, Michael J., and Charles F. Sabel. *The Second Industrial Divide: Possibilities for Prosperity.* New York: Basic Books, 1983.

Pertschuk, Michael. *Giant Killers.* New York: Norton, 1986.

Piven, Frances F., and Richard A. Cloward. *Democracy Thwarted: Why So Many Americans Don't Vote.* New York: Pantheon Books, 1988.

Rainwater, Lee. "Fear and the House-as-Haven in the Lower Class." *Journal of the American Institute of Planners,* Vol. 32, January 1966, pp. 23–30.

Rainwater, Lee. *What Money Buys: Inequality and the Social Meanings of Income.* New York: Basic Books, 1974.

Reeves, Richard. *American Journey: Traveling with Tocqueville in Search of Democracy in America.* New York: Simon & Schuster, 1982.

Rieder, Jonathan. *Canarsie: The Jews and Italians of Brooklyn Against Liberalism.* Cambridge, Mass.: Harvard University Press, 1985.

Riesman, David. *Individualism Reconsidered.* Glencoe, Ill.: Free Press, 1954.

Riesman, David, Nathan Glazer, and Reuel Denney. *The Lonely Crowd: A Study of the Changing American Character*. New Haven, Conn.: Yale University Press, 1950.

Robinson, John P., and Mark R. Levy, with Dennis K. Davis et al. *The Main Source: Learning from Television News*. Beverly Hills, Calif.: Sage Publications, 1986.

Roy, Donald F. "Quota Restriction and Goldbricking in a Machine Shop." *American Journal of Sociology*, Vol. 57, No. 5, March 1952, pp. 427–442.

Rubin, Lillian B. *Worlds of Pain: Life in the Working Class Family*. New York: Basic Books, 1976.

Saunders, Peter. *Social Theory and the Urban Question*. New York: Holmes & Meier, 2nd edition, 1986.

Saunders, Peter. "The Sociology of Consumption: A Research Agenda," unpublished paper, 1986.

Schell, Jonathan. *History in Sherman Park*. New York: Knopf, 1987.

Schlozman, Kay L., and John T. Tierney. *Organized Interests and American Democracy*. New York: Harper & Row, 1986.

Schlozman, Kay L., and Sidney Verba. *Injury to Insult: Unemployment, Class and Political Response*. Cambridge, Mass.: Harvard University Press, 1979.

Schorr, Alvin. *Common Decency: Domestic Policies after Reagan*. New Haven, Conn.: Yale University Press, 1986.

Schram, Martin. *The Great American Video Game: Presidential Politics in the TV Age*. New York: Morrow, 1987.

Schudson, Michael. *Advertising, the Uneasy Persuasion: Its Dubious Impact on American Society*. New York: Basic Books, 1984.

Sennett, Richard. *The Fall of Public Man*. New York: Knopf, 1977.

Shaiken, Harley. *Work Transformed: Automation and Labor in the Computer Age*. Lexington, Mass.: Lexington Books, 1984.

Shapiro, Robert Y., and Harpreet Mahajan. "Gender Differences in Policy Preferences: A Summary of Trends from the 1960s to the 1980s." *Public Opinion Quarterly*, Vol. 50, No. 1, February 1986, pp. 42–61.

Shils, Edward. *Center and Periphery: Essays in Macrosociology*. Chicago: University of Chicago Press, 1975.

Shils, Edward A., and Morris Janowitz, "Cohesion and Distintegration in the Wehrmacht in World War II." *Public Opinion Quarterly*. Vol. 12, No. 2, 1948, pp. 280–315.

Siegel, Fred. "Notes on the New Right." *Commonweal*, May 8, 1981, pp. 269–272.

Silver, Allan. "Family, Politics and Labor Markets in Modern Society: Preliminary Notes," unpublished paper prepared for the Committee on West Europe of the Social Science Research Council, October 1977.

Smith, James D. "The Distribution of Wealth," unpublished paper invited by the Joint Economic Committee, U.S. Congress, July 1986.

Smith, James D., "Wealth in America." *ISR Newsletter* (Newsletter of the Institute for Social Research, University of Michigan), Winter 1986–1987, pp. 3–5.

Sniderman, Paul M., with Michael G. Hagen. *Race and Inequality: A Study in American Values*. Chatham, N.J.: Chatham, 1985.

Spitz, Elaine. *Majority Rule*. Chatham N.J.: Chatham, 1984.

Srole, Leo, and Anita K. Fischer. "The Midtown Manhattan Longitudinal Study vs. 'The Mental Paradise Lost' Doctrine." *Archives of General Psychiatry*, Vol. 37, February 1980, pp. 209–221.

Sussman, Barry. "The Porcupine Theory: Explaining Contradictory Opinions." *Washington Post Weekly Edition*, August 5, 1985, p. 37.

Toennies, Ferdinand. *Community and Society: Gemeinschaft und Gesellschaft*. New York: Harper & Row, 1963.

de Tocqueville, Alexis. *Democracy in America*. New York: Vintage Books, 2 vols., 1954.

Toffler, Alvin. *The Third Wave*. New York: Morrow, 1970.

Tuchman, Gaye. *Making News: A Study in the Construction of Reality*. New York, Free Press, 1978.

Varenne, Hervé. *Americans Together: Structured Diversity in a Midwestern Town*. New York: Teachers College Press, 1977.

Verba, Sidney, and Norman H. Nie. *Participation in America: Political Democracy and Social Equality*. New York: Harper & Row, 1972.

Verba, Sidney, and Gary R. Orren. *Equality in America: The View from the Top*. Cambridge, Mass.: Harvard University Press, 1985.

Wachtel, Paul L. *The Poverty of Affluence: A Psychological Portrait of the American Way of Life*. New York: Free Press, 1983.

Warren, Donald. *The Radical Center: Middle Americans and the Politics of Alienation*. Notre Dame, Ind.: Notre Dame Press, 1978.

Watts, William. "American Hopes and Fears: The Future Can Fend for Itself." *Psychology Today*, September 1981, pp. 36–52.

Williams, Bruce B. *Black Workers in an Industrial Suburb*. New Brunswick, N.J.: Rutgers University Press, 1987.

Williams, Raymond. *The Year 2000*. New York: Pantheon Books, 1983.

Willmott, Peter. *Social Networks, Informal Care and Public Policy*. London: Policy Studies Institute, Research Report 655, 1986.

Wolfe, Alan. "Is Sociology Dangerous?" *Tikkun*, Vol. 1, No. 1, Summer 1986, pp. 96–101.

Wolfe, Alan. *The Ties That Bind*. Berkeley: University of California Press, forthcoming.

Wolfe, Tom. "The 'Me' Decade and the Third Great Awakening." *New York*, August 23, 1976, pp. 26–40.

Wolff, Kurt, ed., *The Sociology of Georg Simmel*. Glencoe, Ill.: Free Press, 1950.

Wolin, Sheldon. "Editorial." *democracy*, Vol. 3, No. 1, Winter 1983, pp. 2–5.

Zuckerman, Michael. *Peaceable Kingdoms: New England Towns in the Eighteenth Century*. New York: Knopf, 1970.

Zussman, Robert. *Mechanics of the Middle Class: Work and Politics among American Engineers*. Berkeley: University of California Press, 1985.

Index